Attracting Birds to South Florida Gardens

UNIVERSITY PRESS OF FLORIDA

Florida A&M University, Tallahassee
Florida Atlantic University, Boca Raton
Florida Gulf Coast University, Ft. Myers
Florida International University, Miami
Florida State University, Tallahassee
New College of Florida, Sarasota
University of Central Florida, Orlando
University of Florida, Gainesville
University of North Florida, Jacksonville
University of South Florida, Tampa
University of West Florida, Pensacola

Attracting Birds
to South Florida Gardens

JAMES A. KUSHLAN AND KIRSTEN HINES

University Press of Florida

Gainesville · Tallahassee · Tampa · Boca Raton

Pensacola · Orlando · Miami · Jacksonville · Ft. Myers · Sarasota

VIVA FLORIDA 500.
1513-2013
A Florida Quincentennial Book

This book may be available in an electronic edition.

Frontispiece: *Top*, Gray Catbird in American Beautyberry; *middle:* Cape May Warbler in a Strangler Fig; *bottom:* Pileated Woodpecker on a Coconut Palm.

19 18 17 16 15 14   6 5 4 3 2 1

Library of Congress Cataloging-in-Publication Data
Kushlan, James A. (James Anthony), 1947–
Attracting birds to South Florida gardens / James A. Kushlan and Kirsten Hines.
pages cm
Includes bibliographical references and index.
ISBN 978-0-8130-4965-6
1. Gardening to attract birds—Florida. 2. Bird attracting—Florida. 3. Bird watching—Florida. 4. Gardening—Florida. 5. Birds—Florida. I. Hines, Kirsten. II. Title.
QL676.56.F6K87 2014
598.072'34759—dc23
2013047854

The University Press of Florida is the scholarly publishing agency for the State University System of Florida, comprising Florida A&M University, Florida Atlantic University, Florida Gulf Coast University, Florida International University, Florida State University, New College of Florida, University of Central Florida, University of Florida, University of North Florida, University of South Florida, and University of West Florida.

University Press of Florida
15 Northwest 15th Street
Gainesville, FL 32611-2079
http://www.upf.com

Contents

Flock of Cedar Waxwings

Preface

Why yet another book on birds or on gardening? Are not the shelves full of them? Indeed, yes; the vast majority of North American gardeners or birders who wish to share their yard with birds are fortunate to have a wealth of books, articles, and Web sites available to guide them. Such sources tell us about cherry trees, cedars, firs, and maples and their importance to chickadees, goldfinches, and juncos, how to help birds through the cold of winter, and how to encourage them in their short nesting season. Unfortunately, such sources reveal little about how to attract birds to a South Florida garden. Here we care about live oaks, palms, figs, and avocados and their importance to mockingbirds, grackles, and parrots, how to attract migrating birds, and how to encourage them through their long winter stay.

Not only does most of the available guidance not apply to South Florida but trying to follow available bird gardening advice tends to work out rather badly. One deservedly well-respected backyard bird book lists plants to use and birds to expect in a North American bird garden. Of 37 shrubs listed, only 5 are found in South Florida; of 31 trees listed, 7 make it to South Florida; of 102 birds listed, only 18 breed in South Florida and another 14 may be expected to pass through sometime during the year. Obviously that won't do as a guide for a South Florida gardener.

So, that is why we need yet another bird and garden book. This book is about the birds and plants of South Florida. It offers ways to attract birds to a yard by creating a bird-friendly garden, understanding and working within the ecological constraints and gardening opportunities that define South Florida as different from the rest of North America. And, this book suggests that the value of a backyard gardener's engagement in attracting birds does not stop at individual satisfaction, but is of consequential value to bird conservation. As we shall see, in South Florida, every bit of bird-friendly habitat helps.

This book aims to be a guide where South Florida's semitropical environmental conditions prevail, generally south of Lake Okeechobee although along the coasts it has applicability somewhat farther north. As we will repeatedly emphasize in multiple contexts, for gardeners and birders, South Florida is different from the rest of North America and different from the nearby tropics as well, creating unique bird garden options, opportunities, and challenges. As described in more detail in chapter 2, South Florida's climate, fauna, and flora are determined by its position at the end of a long peninsula, attached to the temperate zone, projecting toward the tropics, and surrounded by warm oceans. In brief, this setting is the reason gardens and their bird lists at the end of the Florida peninsula are unlike those of the rest of North America.

This is a book about home gardens, but no garden is an island. It is also a book about the neighbors' gardens, about the neighborhood, the local park, rock pit, canal, and highway margin. This is a book for South Florida's gardeners, for South Florida's birders, for home and condominium owners and apartment renters. But it is also a book for anyone who plants a garden and anyone who cares about participating in the regreening of South Florida. In addition to the home gardener, we hope it will be consulted by residential and commercial builders and developers, landscapers and nurserymen, condominium boards, commercial building owners, park managers, elected and appointed government officials, commercial contractors, parking lot designers, and roadside landscapers; anyone who makes decisions about what plants to plant, where to plant them, and why to plant them. This book is about conserving birds by providing plants.

We hope it is a book that can be helpful not only in attracting birds to these gardens but also in encouraging participation in larger conservation movements on behalf of plants, birds, and the South Florida environment. And, we hope, it is a book that will encourage each resident and family to choose to do their small part to conserve the birds of South Florida—garden by garden, yard by yard, neighborhood by neighborhood.

James A. Kushlan and Kirsten Hines
Key Biscayne, Florida

Note on Names and Informational Codes

The scientific and English common names of most of the birds and plants used in this book are provided in the bird and plant descriptions given in chapters 5 and 6, respectively. The sequence of plants by taxonomic order follows the Angiosperm Phylogeny Group (APG) III system. Common and scientific names of plants found in the wild in Florida are taken from the *Atlas of Florida Vascular Plants* (as accessed in October 2013). Other commonly used names for plants in South Florida are also given in the species accounts.

The sequence of taxonomic families of birds follows that of the American Ornithologists' Union (AOU) *Checklist of North American Birds*, as do the scientific and common names. Names of amphibians and reptiles are from Crother (2012), and those of mammals follow Baker et al. (2003). Names of butterflies follow the North American Butterfly Association's *Checklist of North American Butterflies Occupying North of Mexico*. Following AOU protocol, the English common names of birds are capitalized.

We also provide information on birds and plants succinctly through use of informational codes, or abbreviations. For plants, we list native status, plant type, roles they play in the garden, and their specific value to birds. These abbreviations are self-explanatory. We also give some indication of their availability to gardeners. Some are available widely in nurseries and garden centers (AW); some are available only in specialty nurseries, through plant interest groups or special plant sales, or from private gardeners (AS); and others are rarely available or not at all (AR). Actually a determined gardener can find almost anything. Once source stock is located, most plants can be privately propagated from seed, cuttings, air-layering, or division.

For birds, we list the native status, breeding status, and seasonal status. We have to approach breeding and seasonal status a bit differently from standard practice in other geographic areas, in which summer means nesting and winter means not nesting. In South Florida things are different; breeding status cannot be inferred from seasonal status, so we give season and breeding information independently. The descriptive codes for abundance, season, breeding, and food are used with their ordinary meanings. Seasons are the usual months for the Northern Hemisphere. Resident means that the species occurs in South Florida for extended periods during a particular season whereas migrants pass through, perhaps stopping briefly. Because a bird species may be composed of widespread populations, a single species may include summer residents, winter residents, or migrants, as birds from different populations come and go on their own schedules.

We also sometimes follow a code with a question mark to show uncertainty.

Informational Codes

PLANTS

Native to South Florida	Na	Vegetable/herb garden	Vg
Non-native	Nn	Wildflower garden	Wf
Invasive non-native	X	Nesting sites	Ns
Tree-sized	Tr	Perch sites	Pr
Shrub-sized	Sh	Structure/cover	St
Short-statured plant	Ss	Insects, other invertebrates	In
Vine	Vn	Fruit	Fr
Aquatic plant	Aq	Seed	Sd
Diverse lawn	Ln	Nectar	Nc
Water feature	Wt	Available widely	AW
Epiphyte	Ep	Available from specialty sources	AS
Ground	Gr	Available rarely or not at all	AR
Butterfly/hummingbird garden	Bt		

BIRDS

Native	Na	Migrant	Mg
Non-native	Nn	Summer resident	Su
Invasive non-native	X	Fall resident	Fl
Breeding	Br	Winter resident	Wn
Nonbreeding	Nb	Spring resident	Sp
Year-round	Yr		

Note on Names and Informational Codes

Attracting Birds to South Florida Gardens

1

Introduction

South Florida is a magical place to be a gardener. It is a place where the tropics meet the temperate zone, giving the gardener a nearly unlimited list of plants from which to choose—native North American plants, native West Indian plants, and exotic plants introduced from the world's tropics. Seasonally high rainfall and warm temperatures result in plant growth that at times is nothing less than rampant, creating gardens over a period of months rather than decades. A South Florida garden is also special for its birdlife. A properly designed and maintained garden can create habitat for its year-round resident birds, some of which are found nowhere else in North America, for birds that come from elsewhere to spend the winter, for legions of migrating birds moving from the temperate to the tropics and back again twice a year, as well as for exotic species from around the world's tropics.

Attracting birds to a garden has two interwoven threads, the garden and the birds. Gardening and birding are two of the most popular outdoor activities in America. And while people have long enjoyed watching the birds in their yards, this combination is increasingly gaining mainstream popularity, including through various organized counts and competitions. We suspect that the popularity of watching birds in backyard gardens is because it is such a very human thing to do, bringing together two fundamentally human survival instincts— farming and hunting. In the modern American backyard homestead, we farm our yard and hunt to see its birds. How much more fundamentally human can it be? Satisfying such basic human compulsions is certainly enough to explain and justify spending time gardening and watching birds there.

But of course there is more than immediate fulfillment; in creating habitat that provides conservation benefit for both the plants and the birds in the yard and neighborhood, we have the satisfaction of accomplishing something of wider and greater value. When we garden in ways that attract birds, we are helping compensate for the hundreds of square miles of habitat that have been stripped away by the inexorable march of the human occupancy of South Florida.

The last century of human domination has not been kind to South Florida's native plants and birds. For many species, numbers are tiny, and suitable living space has been hugely contracted. Gardening for birds helps sustain their populations—keeping common birds common, giving rare birds a better chance, and

A well-designed South Florida garden creates habitat for birds, providing food, nesting sites, and structure.

returning bird-friendly plants to the landscape. In South Florida, we help restore ecological health by providing plant cover, enhancing landscape structure, favoring native plants and animals, discouraging environmentally challenging non-native plants and animals, and encouraging natural ecological functioning. To no small degree, these activities add to the quality of life and economic viability of South Florida for its human residents. Connectivity between the natural environment and human welfare in South Florida has not always been well appreciated by its residents and certainly not by most of their elected and appointed leaders. Over the last century, acre after acre and square mile after square mile have been drained of water, denuded of native plant communities, filled or excavated for housing, commerce, agriculture, canals, rock pits, and roadways—all the accoutrements of human settlement. With 6 million-plus people now occupying South Florida's landscape, it is finally dawning on some how much people actually do depend on the environment's ecological functions for water supply, water quality, human health, climate control, air quality, material cycling, parks, natural areas, and outdoor spaces.

Most of South Florida is wetlands, seen by most residents only as they fly over or drive across from one side of the state to the other. The Everglades, Big Cypress, flatwoods, and coastal swamps are mostly still natural, mostly government owned, and standing to benefit from the largest environmental restoration program in the world. With a few exceptions, wetland bird species will profit.

In South Florida, development is generally confined to the periphery, where the high ground is and where higher wetlands were. There, where settlement historically first occurred and has continued unabated for more than a century, the situation is far less encouraging. The natural environment has been scraped off to make way for housing, commerce, and agriculture. There is little left of what South Florida used to be. Remaining natural terrestrial habitats are but slivers of their former selves, existing as isolated patches almost wholly in parks set within a highly modified, privately owned, urban-suburban-agricultural matrix. Unlike restoration of interior wetlands, that of terrestrial habitats, critically important for bird conservation, falls to private property owners, both residents and businesses, on their own patches of land.

For those already committed, we need say little to justify gardening in ways that provide conservation enhancements for plants, birds, and other wildlife. But many dedicated gardeners may not yet have given much thought to how they might enjoy more wildlife or to what their yard could mean to conservation of plants and wild animals more broadly. Or they may understandably be reluctant to alter planting styles, to add plants they do not know, or to sacrifice precious lawn space. For those needing convincing, please consider at the gut level: is it not a joy seeing birds and butterflies outside your back door using plants nurtured in a garden of your own creation? What if by altering gardening style even a bit, you might increase the frequency, intimacy and intensity of such observations? What if this alteration also advanced conservation and helped restore some semblance of a more natural South Florida environment? Might these results make a garden all the more interesting and satisfying? That is what attracting birds is all about—creating a landscape that is pleasing and entertaining to the gardener, is beneficial to plants and animals, and contributes

Many of South Florida's natural habitats, particularly in upland and coastal areas, have been developed into a grid of concrete and lawn, robbing birds and other wildlife of their natural habitat, and humans of their connections to nature.

to conservation. Unfortunately the opposite is far too common in South Florida, with yards consisting primarily of concrete or asphalt.

Bird gardening is not all that complicated. In some ways it is easier than normal gardening because it tends toward informality. Gardening to attract birds follows three overriding principles that set it apart from standard gardening. The most important of these is that a bird garden is naturalistic. It aims to recreate a more natural habitat by providing features in the garden that birds need for their survival: feeding, sheltering, nesting, drinking, and security. The second principle is that gardening for birds is ecological. It makes use of lessons from ecology to inform us what needs to be done in a man-made replication of nature, and why. The third principle is that a garden for birds is diverse. The more diverse in plant species, structure, and landscaping, the better the garden will be for birds.

For developing gardens and other plantings that follow the goals of being naturalistic, ecological, and diverse, South Florida gardeners and others who plant can select from an impressive list of plants that attract a similarly intriguing list of birds. From among these many options, the gardener can choose bird-friendly plants and arrange them in bird-friendly ways. A garden designed to attract birds will have an array of plants that together provide fruit, flowers, insects, and shelter continuously through the year. We discuss options for plants and how to arrange them later in the book, but bird-friendly gardening in South Florida is very flexible, leaving much to the gardener's personal preferences.

What might it mean to be bird friendly? The following chapters aim to answer this question in detail, but at this point it is worthwhile to explore the question in a general way. The garden, above all else, is bird habitat. Habitat is structure that is provided by plants—their form, height, width, branching style, bark, trunk, leaves, and canopy—and the arrangement of plants in a landscape. It is within this habitat structure that birds feed, shelter, drink, bathe, nest, raise young, and escape predators.

Of these uses, food is perhaps the most vital. Birds have high energy requirements relative to their size, and they need quite a lot of food to get through the day or the season. It is exceptionally important for the gardener to appreciate where this food comes from. Bird food comes almost entirely from the plants the garden provides. Whether insects, fruits, seeds, nectar, flowers, spiders, or lizards, it is the garden's plants, directly or indirectly, that provide birds with their food. A seed-filled feeder a gardener might choose to add to the natural food supply will be entirely secondary and in most cases in South Florida, from the birds' point of view, somewhat superfluous. Repeating, the most important fact of gardening to attract birds: bird food is in the garden's plants.

Plants for a bird garden can also be chosen for their own inherent conservation interest. South Florida hosts many plants that in all of the United States occur only here. A few are so specialized for the South Florida environment that they are found nowhere else in the world. These native plants are the ones that have been most disadvantaged by the destruction of the natural plant cover of

Above: The goal of bird-friendly gardening is to create a landscape that is pleasing to the gardener, beneficial to animals and plants, and that contributes to their conservation.

Left: Many homes in South Florida have traded a garden of plants for concrete, not a very bird-friendly situation.

South Florida—but these also, in large part, are plants that fit well into a bird garden.

Birds are a bit different from plants. The gardener selects the plants, but birds select the garden. A well-tended bird garden entices birds to choose it over some other place. If successful, a well-designed garden is among the best places anywhere to observe birds, as they are visible and used to people. In South Florida, a well-planted and well-watched garden can accumulate a "yard bird list" of more than 100 species within a few years. Our house near the coast on Key Biscayne, with 5 percent of an acre of plantable space, accumulated a list of exactly 100 species in just six years. Inland, a well-planted yard in Miami accumulated the same number over 17 years. A house from Naples, tended for 45 years by three generations of naturalists, accrued a list of 130 species. In the larger space of Fairchild Tropical Botanic Garden in Coral Gables, 178 species have been recorded.

Bird garden lists in South Florida are an eclectic mix. Some species of birds are shared with gardens a thousand miles to the north; others are shared with the West Indies and occur in North America only in South Florida. Some are widespread, tolerant, garden-loving native species. Some are found in most gardens, whereas others are restricted geographically, for example, to gardens in the Keys or on the Gulf coast. Some are tightly constrained by habitat, found only in those rare residential gardens meeting their specialized needs. And some species showing up are not native to South Florida. Parakeets from South America, bulbuls from India, sparrows from Europe, and geese from Africa all may contribute to a South Florida garden bird list.

A bird garden's food is in the plants—the fruit produced and the insects housed there. Insects provided by the plants are an especially important food source, the primary food of many birds like this Blue-gray Gnatcatcher.

Attracting Birds to South Florida Gardens

The array of birds using a garden is never static. Some occur year-round; others appear only during their spring or fall migration; still others only spend the winter. Resident breeding birds rely on a garden's supply of fruit, seeds, insects, and nectar year-round but especially during their nesting season. Migrating birds are attracted in numbers to properly prepared gardens because they are motivated by their extremely high food needs. Spring migrants seek gardens with flowers and foliage that provide the abundance of insects they need to prepare for nesting. In winter, flowers provide nectar for hummingbirds, while fruit and insects from throughout the garden and the nearby neighborhood feed other birds.

The bird-attracting potential of a garden is influenced by where it is and what is nearby. Available birds differ between more northerly and more southerly sites, between Atlantic and Gulf coasts, and between inland and coastal habitats. As a bird is seldom confined to the space of a garden, the neighboring landscape, whether rural, suburban, urban, agricultural or natural, affects what birds are around the area. If the neighborhood is bird friendly, a garden's bird-attracting opportunities are enhanced. If a garden is surrounded by an inhospitable neighborhood, full of non-native bird-unfriendly plants or lots of asphalt and concrete, its potential may be lessened. For a bird garden, the neighborhood counts. That is why the lessons of this book need to be applied beyond the garden walls to neighbors' yards, nearby parks, median strips, parking lots, rock pits, and roadsides.

One of the characteristics distinguishing South Florida bird gardening from gardening in the rest of North America is the abundance and diversity of exotic birds, like this White-winged Parakeet, that can be attracted to a garden.

Every bit of bird habitat created adds to the inventory of naturalistic places for plants to grow and birds to thrive. Demonstratively, these Indigo Buntings are feeding on roadside grasses that were allowed to go to seed.

Beyond the neighborhood, a bird garden is a piece of the larger South Florida environment, the health of which in large part determines the health of its bird populations. Fortunately, every bird garden patch has value in re-creating a more bird-friendly South Florida landscape. As more and more bird-friendly gardens are planted, these seemingly insignificant patches become less isolated, creating corridors among larger protected areas. One can dream of the day when a network of bird-friendly habitats stretches from the oceans to the Everglades, effectively regreening South Florida for birds and other wildlife. A gardener creating a bird garden, no matter how small it is, will be contributing to regionwide ecological restoration.

With so much lost, there is so much to regain. The importance of environmental regreening is being increasingly acknowledged, from local municipalities to global initiatives. Nearly every South Florida municipality has programs, guidelines or ordinances that encourage, or even require, landscaping in ecologically sensitive ways, often requiring that a percentage of native plants be used. Of course, some communities still have regulations that tend to inhibit ecologically sensitive planting, but bird-friendly approaches are possible even within such constraints. Birds are attracted to terra cotta containers on porches or condominium balconies, to commercial parking lots, to multi-acre estates, to special plantings, and to native plants volunteering at roadsides. Every bit of bird habitat created adds to the inventory of naturalistic places for plants to grow and birds to thrive.

2

South Florida's Environmental Setting

As we will say repeatedly, a South Florida bird garden is like no other place. The reasons for this are fundamentally geographic and ecological. South Florida is situated at the end of a peninsula projecting southeastward from the North American landmass, linked to the temperate continent but stretching to within a couple of degrees of latitude of the Tropic of Cancer.

It is the resulting interactions of location, physical setting, climate, and biogeography that make gardening in South Florida different from that in either the temperate North American continent to the north or the tropical West Indies to the south. The successful South Florida bird gardener benefits from understanding and respecting the garden's unique environmental setting, which both constrains and empowers its potential. In this chapter, we explore South Florida's geography and environment as a basis for understanding how to garden naturalistically, ecologically, and diversely.

Geographic Location

South Florida may be variably defined depending on context; for this book, it is the peninsula south of Lake Okeechobee through the Florida Keys. It includes the counties of Lee, Hendry, Collier, Monroe, Palm Beach, Broward, and Miami-Dade. Notable localities are Fort Myers, Naples, Immokalee, Everglades City, West Palm Beach, Fort Lauderdale, Miami, Homestead, Key Largo, and Key West.

South Florida covers roughly 12,000 square miles and is delineated mostly by water—Atlantic Ocean on the east, Gulf of Mexico on the west, Florida Bay on the south, and Lake Okeechobee, the Caloosahatchee and St. Lucie Rivers and their associated canals on the north.

Off the Atlantic coast, the Florida Current, or Gulf Stream, passes nearby, bringing warm tropical ocean water northward. A large semi-enclosed lagoon, Biscayne Bay, sits between the southeastern mainland and coastal islands of Miami Beach, Virginia Key, Key Biscayne, and Elliott Key. The south coast of the mainland and the western edges of the Florida Keys abut Florida Bay, and the Gulf Coast is bounded by mangrove-covered islands and estuaries. Water defines South Florida.

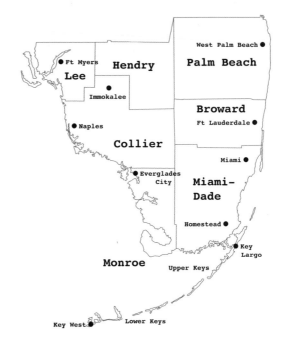

For this book, South Florida is defined as the counties shown on this map—those south of Lake Okeechobee and more or less within the subtropical region of the state. Selected localities are marked on the map for reference.

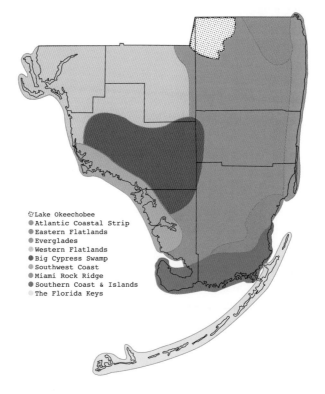

South Florida can be divided into ecologically distinct physiographic regions, as shown on this map. Where a garden is located in South Florida influences its potential. (Map redrawn from J. H. Davis Jr. [1943], *Geological Bulletin* 25, Florida Geological Survey, Tallahassee.)

A

B

C

D

South Florida's physiographic regions divide into quite different habitats. (A) Most of the interior consists of wetlands, shown here as Everglades marsh punctuated with higher elevation tree islands. (B) Much of the coast was historically covered in mangrove swamp. (C) Upland habitats along the coasts were covered in forest, such as pineland. (D) Upland substrate in northern and western South Florida is predominantly sand, but a ridge of limestone called the Miami Rock Ridge provides high ground from the Miami River south and west into the Everglades.

One element of understanding a garden's potential is to appreciate its specific geographic context within South Florida, as that potential differs within the region. South Florida can be divided into several ecologically distinctive physiographic regions. The central core of South Florida is a giant wetland, the Everglades, a huge southward-flowing marshland that once stretched 100 miles south from Lake Okeechobee, occupying much of South Florida. To the southwest is the Big Cypress Swamp, also a seasonally flooded wetland. The Everglades and Big Cypress Swamp flow via short rivers into the mangrove swamps and coastal

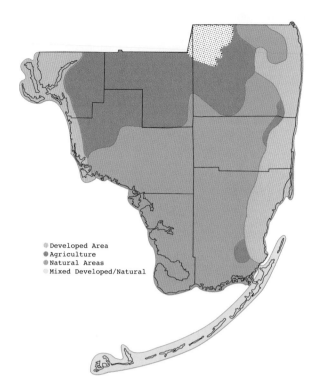

The natural ecology of South Florida has been altered drastically; a rough summary of current land use appears on this map. (Map redrawn from S. Kambly and T. R. Moreland [2009], *Land Cover Trends in the Southern Florida Coastal Plain*, U.S. Geological Survey Scientific Investigations Report 2009-5054, Washington, D.C.)

● Developed Area
● Agriculture
● Natural Areas
  Mixed Developed/Natural

bays of the Southwest Coast and the Southern Coast and Islands. Thus the vast majority of the native landscape of South Florida was once wetland—marsh, swamp, and coastal lagoons. High ground, a very relative term in South Florida, was restricted primarily to the coast. Along the east coast, the Atlantic Coastal Strip is made up of sand. Farther south, the Miami Rock Ridge is made up of limestone. The Eastern Flatlands are lower elevations between the strip and the interior swamps. These historically were quite wet seasonally. Similarly, southwest of Lake Okeechobee are the Western Flatlands, which include the somewhat elevated Immokalee Rise. These flatlands historically were wet for part of the year but are now well drained. The Florida Keys are rocky and relatively dry islands.

Human land use changed things. The central interior core of South Florida remains covered by wetlands, although now occupying less than half their natural range and much altered ecologically. Agriculture consumes the area south of Lake Okeechobee, much of the flatlands, and the now-dry edges of former interior wetlands. Human residency, sensibly, started on the high ground along the coast, but drainage allowed colonization of former wetlands in the interior. Nearly all of South Florida's available land has now been developed, much of it intensively. As bird habitat, much of the built environment is rather sterile, composed primarily of asphalt and concrete of little value to birds.

Geology and Soils

South Florida rests on a block of limestone thousands of feet thick representing millions of years' accumulation of marine carbonates. On a map, Florida looks out of place, as if it had been surgically attached to North America. It has. The basement rock of South Florida started off as part of Africa and was fixed to North America by the Earth's crustal movements.

South Florida's limestone-based geology has implications for gardening. Its limestone and marl derived soils are quite alkaline, having a pH of 7.8–8.1, tempered only where silica sand or peat has been surficially deposited over the limestone, adding some acidity. Plants in South Florida need to be specialized for dealing with the chemical challenges of growing in the alkalinity of limestone. In contact with the limestone, South Florida's water also is alkaline, or "hard." Most of South Florida is not for azaleas.

Despite being uniformly underlain by limestone, South Florida has geological nuances across its width. The limestone was formed differently and at different times and so varies somewhat in its chemistry. The Anastasia Formation along the northern coastlines incorporates significant amounts of silica sand derived from the north and so is less basic than other geologic formations. The Caloosahatchee Formation of the Western Flatlands contains both sand and shell. The Tamiami Formation under the Big Cypress Swamp, the oldest of South Florida's limestones, is composed of sand, silt, and calcium deposits. The Fort Thompson Formation under the northern Everglades is made of shell, marl, clay and sand. The Miami Limestone along the east coast and lower Florida Keys is composed of grains of precipitated carbonate, whereas the Miami Limestone under the Southern Everglades is composed of the remains of bryozoans and other carbonate-making animals and plants. Key Largo Limestone is an exposed coral reef. Soil tends to be shallow in South Florida, so nuances in the underlying geology can affect a garden's drainage and chemistry.

Another salient point of geology is South Florida's youthfulness. It was only about 6,000 years ago that Lake Okeechobee formed and about 5,000 years ago that the Everglades began to accrete as sea level stabilized and the climate became more humid and tropical. It was only then that existing native plant communities began to develop.

Topographically, South Florida is flat. Lake Okeechobee itself occupies a shallow basin in the limestone, historically less than 12 feet deep. The fall from the historic southern berm of Lake Okeechobee to sea level 100 miles away is no more than 18 feet, a declination of less than an inch per mile. Land is a bit lower in the interior than on its margins, natural elevations being 22 feet in Coral Gables, 29 feet at Pine Island Ridge in Broward, 33 feet on the Immokalee Rise southwest of Lake Okeechobee, and 52 feet at Marco Island on the Gulf Coast (an elevation built up by Indians). We can visualize South Florida as a

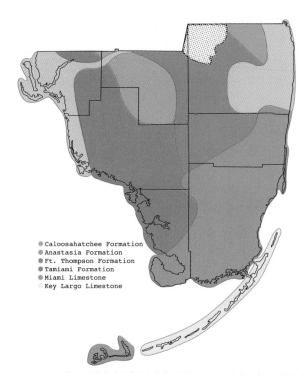

Being entirely underlain by limestone, South Florida's soils are generally alkaline, but growing conditions are influenced by subtle differences among the recognized surficial geologic formations, shown on this map. (Map redrawn from R. O. Vernon and H. S. Puri [1964], Geologic Map of Florida, Florida Bureau of Geology, map series 18, Tallahassee.)

- Caloosahatchee Formation
- Anastasia Formation
- Ft. Thompson Formation
- Tamiami Formation
- Miami Limestone
- Key Largo Limestone

southwestward-tipping saucer from Lake Okeechobee to Florida Bay, slightly more elevated at the top and on the sides.

In South Florida, a few inches of elevation make a huge difference in the duration of seasonal flooding and, therefore, in the kinds of plants that can live in any particular site. The modestly higher grounds of coastal ridges, river banks, barrier islands, and artificial Indian-built mounds were colonized by terrestrial plant communities, mostly derived from the tropics. Over the past century, land once underwater was dried out sufficiently by drainage and filling to provide adequate elevation for development. A garden on a natural elevation, however slight, has different prospects than one on drained land.

South Florida's flatness and wetness are not without consequences to gardeners. Apparently dry ground can revert to wetland with the passage of a tropical storm, a few days of a wet cold front, or a broken water main or drainage pipe. Wetland-derived soils can be slow draining whereas rain on limestone or sand percolates rapidly into the ground. Those gardening in low-lying locations or with poorly draining soils need to manage their runoff and choose plants accordingly. An interesting traditional South Florida approach to poor drainage was to plant trees on piles of rocks.

It is a general rule of gardening that one must know a garden's soil. In South Florida this is fairly complicated. What passes for soil in South Florida is not the rich temperate soil of textbooks with its definable horizons and consistent zonal characteristics, derived from the rock below and plants above. Nor is it the deep, well-leached, sterile soil of the humid tropics. South Florida's natural "soils" consist of geographically differing amounts of sand, limestone bits, marl, and organic matter derived from limestone weathering, atmospheric dust, coastal processes, and organic matter from diverse sources.

Appreciating these differing substrates can reveal something about what can be grown at a site. In South Florida, various sandy soils occur on both sides of Lake Okeechobee, along both coasts, and on barrier islands. These are well draining, even to the point of being xeric, and can be less alkaline than other South Florida soils because of some proportion of silica sand. Wetland-produced peat, technically called Kesson Muck, or just plain "muck," is a black, highly organic substrate found on former Everglades sites. It eventually oxidizes away when exposed to the air. Along former coastal wetlands, as well as in the flatlands, the substrate is fine, poorly draining carbonate marl. On higher limestone sites, the thin surficial layer is a mix derived from weathered limestone, accumulated organic matter, pockets of sand, and atmospheric dust (some of it all the way from the Sahara). Naturally, the soils accumulated mostly in depressions, leaving the bare limestone exposed between. Gardening directly in limestone rock is one of the great adventures of pick-wielding gardeners in southeastern South Florida.

While knowing the native soil can be helpful, in most locations where gardens will be planted, the natural substrate is no longer there. Surficial materials have been altered and moved around, resulting in substrates that have minimal

In most situations South Florida soils no longer reflect their natural condition. Soil in this south Miami-Dade agricultural field consists of a mix of pulverized limestone, sand, and organic material created mechanically by "rock plowing."

resemblance to what was there naturally. Much of the low-lying rocklands of South Florida have been mechanically pulverized for farming, called "rock plowing," turning the matrix of exposed limestone and soil-filled depressions into a uniformly compacted limestone aggregate.

Former Everglades and coastal marshes have been drained and in many cases their peat or marl surface layers stripped off. To make them inhabitable, these and other low-lying sites were elevated using limestone dredgings from rock pits and canals, creating a compacted substrate that is dense and sterile. Muck stripped off the Everglades has been widely distributed as topdressing. For many garden sites in South Florida, information about prior site modifications is more important than knowing the native soil condition.

Given all this, discovering the soil characteristics of any garden site will be complicated, as they depend on an interaction of geographic location, limestone bedrock, naturally occurring soil, fill, surficial additions, elevation, and past history. However, the potential importance of these factors can be teased out in several ways: studying the location and its history; exploring by the shovelful; having soil chemistry analyzed from various parts of the garden; and especially by observing the surrounding landscape to see what actually is growing there.

Climate and Weather

Climate, including annual environmental fluctuations and infrequent weather events, influences bird gardening in South Florida. Those who say that there are no seasons in South Florida are misinformed, or unobservant, or never tried to garden or to watch birds here. South Florida has marked seasons for temperature and for rainfall and in fact has a monsoonal climate, similar to the subtropics elsewhere in the world.

Oddly for its latitude, home to the greatest deserts of the world, South Florida is a seasonally wet place. On average, about 50 inches of rain can be expected yearly—a lot of water. Rainfall does vary across South Florida, though. Coastal cities in Palm Beach, Broward, and Miami-Dade are among those with the highest average rainfall of any cities in North America, with West Palm Beach and Miami being among the very wettest. Rainfall is higher on the east coast than on the west coast, inland, or in the Keys. The differences, on the order of 15–30 percent, are not insignificant. In Key West, a gardener would do best to choose plants with higher drought tolerance than would be necessary in Fort Lauderdale, for example.

As would be expected for a monsoonal climate, rainfall also varies seasonally, a critically important annual cycle for plants and birds. The rainy season is May to October; the dry season, November to April. Unlike unobservant humans, plants and birds take seasonal rainfall variation seriously. South Florida plants and animals must endure both a wet wet season and a dry dry season. Flowering, fruiting, deciduousness, and growth of native plants, and annual nesting

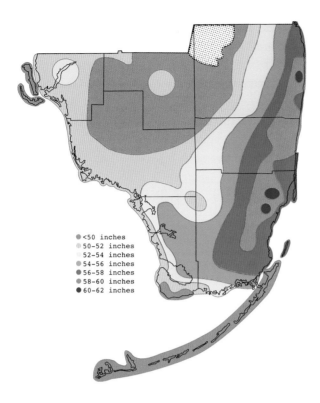

As shown on this map, average annual rainfall in South Florida varies from less than 50 inches in the Keys and northern interior to upward of 62 inches in some areas near the east coast. (Map redrawn from National Oceanic and Atmospheric Administration, South Florida Climate Page, www.srh.noaa.gov/mfl/?n=winteroutlookforsouthflorida.)

cycles of most birds, are decidedly seasonal, in large part responding to rainfall. Non-native plants may not be as attuned to rainfall fluctuations, explaining their sometimes higher maintenance requirements.

While annual rainfall totals and seasonal cycles are of consequence to South Florida's plants and birds, so are infrequent weather events such as droughts and hurricanes. Droughts occur every few years, cutting in half the annual rainfall, creating water deficits, and dropping water tables where not artificially maintained. Tropical storm systems vary in intensity and geographic impact. Most storms hitting South Florida do so between August and October, contributing to the high average rainfall in this period. Named tropical storms and hurricanes range in wind speed from 39 to more than 155 miles per hour, with their wind effects increasing exponentially with speed. Storms of Category 3 (112 mph) can be expected in Miami every 12 years and in the Keys more frequently. While annually unpredictable as to landfall location or effect, they hit South Florida with some frequency.

High rainfall storms can flood broadly and deeply and can even put at risk levees holding back the waters of the Everglades and Lake Okeechobee. Wind and salt spray along the coast can be devastating to plants, which should influence what is planted there in the first place. Hurricane winds tear, twist, and uproot plants; storm surge overwhelms coastal plants and can breach barrier islands; salt spray can affect plants and soil well inland.

South Florida temperatures are generally mild. Annual average temperature is about 78°F in Key West, about 76°F in Miami, and about 74°F in Naples. Miami has recorded a triple-digit temperature only once (100°F in 1942) and the coldest reading was 27°F (in 1917). Like rainfall, temperatures fluctuate in an annual pattern. The cool season is December to February; the warm season, March to November.

The mildness of South Florida's winter is recognized in the traditional USDA climate map, which is based on average annual minimum temperatures. The Hardiness Chart is a familiar feature of any gardening book. South Florida ranges from Zone 9b in the western interior, where lows average 25–30°F, to 11b in the Florida Keys, where lows average 45–50°F. The populated areas along the

South Florida has a monsoonal climate and experiences a marked rainy season from May to October and a dry season from November to April. The graph shows average monthly rainfall for South Florida. Data shown are the means of monthly average rainfall for Miami, West Palm Beach, Key West, and Fort Myers (in inches). (Data from National Oceanic and Atmospheric Administration, National Climate Center, Florida Climate Center, climatecenter.fsu.edu/products-services/data.)

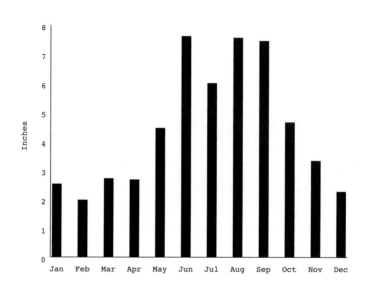

South Florida has a mild climate, with average monthly highs (dark bars) ranging from mid-70s to upper 80s and lows (light bars) averaging upper 50s to mid-70s. The data graphed here are the average of the monthly means from Miami, West Palm Beach, Key West, and Fort Myers. (Data from National Oceanic and Atmospheric Administration, National Climate Center, Florida Climate Center, climatecenter.fsu.edu/products-services/data.)

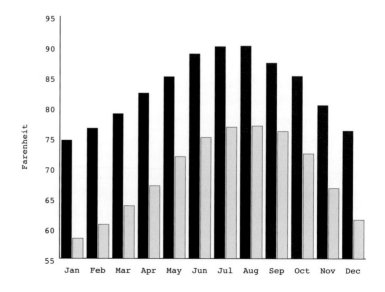

Attracting Birds to South Florida Gardens

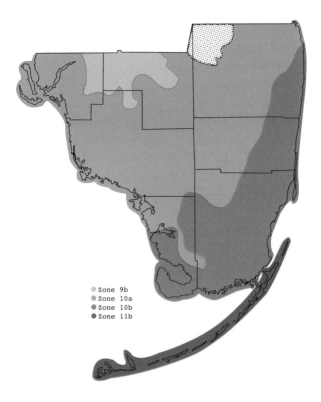

Plant Hardiness Zones for South Florida. These are based on average annual extreme minimum temperatures from 1976 to 2005, demonstrating South Florida's uniqueness within North America. Although most of the continental United States falls within Zones 4–8, South Florida is mostly within Zone 10. (Map redrawn from U.S. Department of Agriculture, Agricultural Research Service [2012], Plant Hardiness Zone Map, Florida, planthardiness.ars .usda.gov/PHZMWeb/.)

Zone 9b
Zone 10a
Zone 10b
Zone 11b

eastern coast are in Zone 10b, with an average minimum of 35–40°F. It does not frost very often there. Gardens in Zone 9b have the highest chance of experiencing below-freezing temperatures, while below-freezing temperatures would be a historic moment in Zone 11b. The climate zone map explains why tropical plants, both native and non-native, can grow in extreme South Florida and why plants needing a winter dormancy period don't do so well in South Florida.

Averages are important in understanding the climate, but as is the case for droughts and hurricanes, infrequent temperature events have disproportionate effects on individual plants and animals and on individual gardens. A night of below-freezing temperatures can in fact occur nearly anywhere sometime. The probability of freezing temperature is an important consideration for selecting garden plants as it suggests the risk a gardener might be taking in selecting sensitive plants. The probability of having freezing temperatures in any year in Miami is only 3 percent, but just a bit farther north in West Palm Beach, Clewiston, and Fort Myers, the probability rises to 20 percent. Freezing temperatures have even been recorded in Key West, although not officially.

Freezes can have big effects on tropical gardens. Periodic freezing temperatures, especially those lasting more than a night, weed out those tropical plants and animals that cannot tolerate that much cold. The Great Florida Freezes of December 1894 and February 1895 were historic. There has not been a cold event of that magnitude for 120 years, but for a plant, it takes only one.

What to do about infrequent freezes is a yearly worry for South Florida gardeners. Postfreeze damage to the gardener's psyche can be nearly as severe as that to the plants themselves. Damage can be avoided or lessened to some extent by planting the right plants for the geographic location in the right places in the garden. Cold-sensitive plants are best placed close to structures, under cover, and in south-facing situations. Tall, hardy, cold-tolerant trees can be used to line northern perimeters, blocking the cold wind, which comes from the north. As a freeze threatens, taking sensitive container plants indoors protects them. Covering sensitive plants left outside helps, as does deep watering before, sprinkling during the event, employing wind-moving fans, or firing up the equivalent of the historic "smudge pot," all to try to keep air temperature at the ground from falling too far below freezing.

Most of South Florida's native tropical plants are able to withstand short frosting temperatures in the low 30s, but not multiple days and not temperatures dropping to high 20s. Non-native tropical plants are often more sensitive than natives. When the worst happens, some plants will die and need to be replaced; others will freeze back to the roots but will resprout; some won't care. Despite the gardener's initial postfreeze trauma, South Florida's rampant plant growth will likely have a garden looking good as new, albeit changed, within a couple of years.

Biogeography

Biogeography refers to the patterns and processes of plant and animal distribution. Thinking biogeographically helps us understand which plants and animals occur naturally in South Florida and which non-natives might survive. Most pertinently it explains: what species are here to populate my garden, and why?

Among native species, a selection of plants, all freshwater animals, nearly all reptiles, most birds, and all nonflying land mammals came to South Florida from temperate North America. Access was easy. They dispersed into South Florida overland bit by bit over thousands of years as environmental conditions there became appropriate for them. No doubt many potential temperate colonists found South Florida too wet, too warm in winter, too pest-laden, too seasonal in rainfall, having too little habitat or too much limestone, and so did not persist. Those plants that did persist invaded gradually overland and were accompanied by entire communities of insects and other invertebrates, nearly all of which provide food for birds.

Lacking a land bridge into the tropics, the tropical component of South Florida's native flora and fauna could arrive only over water. A few reptiles and marine mammals swam or rafted. Tropical birds colonized South Florida by flying over the water barrier, perhaps helped by storms. Many coastal and wetland plants and perhaps some hammock plants arrived via water-borne fruit or seeds. Both plants and invertebrates no doubt came on normal or hurricane winds. It is likely that a vast majority of South Florida's tropical plants were transported from the

Bahamas or Cuba as seeds from fruit eaten and then carried in the guts of birds. The birds could have made the trip (which was much shorter when sea levels were lower) as migrants, as vagrants, assisted by hurricanes, or by serendipity. It is not some cosmic coincidence that so many of South Florida's native tropical plants have small, fleshy, bird-edible fruit.

South Florida's temperate zone plants, like this live oak tree, host a high diversity of insect species that provide food for birds like this migrating Prairie Warbler.

South Florida's native tropical plants are not as good at providing insects for birds as are temperate-derived plants. They arrived mostly as seeds, most probably having passed through the guts of birds, so the insects that liked them did not accompany them. But they do have fruit meant to attract birds, and that is a primary role in a South Florida bird garden.

At the current stage of these ongoing biogeographic processes, about 70 species of native birds nest in South Florida and 360 native bird species are documented to have occurred here. Temperate Maryland (about the same size as South Florida) has 222 nesting species, and tropical Belize (two-thirds the size of South Florida) has 587 bird species. So why is South Florida so avifaunally challenged? There likely are several explanations. The number of nesting temperate birds decreases north to south along the Florida peninsula; this is the pattern for all large peninsulas. Similarly, environmental conditions change markedly from north to south, being far more tropical in the south, influencing what bird species can persist. Despite South Florida's being relatively tropical, it is not filled with West Indian birds in part because all but a few seem not to have the ability or the time to fly over the water gap between Florida and the Caribbean. And finally, both temperate and tropical species encounter an environment in

Most native tropical plants in South Florida produce fruit eaten by birds, and most were likely introduced to South Florida by birds. Here a Cape May Warbler eats fruit from a tropical strangler fig.

South Florida that may not totally suit their needs. Every year stragglers from the Bahamas occur in Florida but have yet to establish breeding populations.

Biogeography also helps explain the third category of South Florida plants and birds, the non-native ones. Many of the traditional non-native plants found in South Florida's gardens are part of an artificial circumtropical flora that can be seen in gardens throughout the tropics. Most established non-native birds are also from the tropics, coming from environmental conditions similar to those of South Florida.

All these biogeographic considerations determine what birds might be expected in a well-stocked South Florida bird garden. A South Florida garden is not like a garden farther north. In South Florida a garden will host Northern Mockingbirds derived from southeastern North America, Gray Kingbirds derived from the West Indies, and parakeets imported from South America.

Some of the birds commonly expected in South Florida's home gardens, parks, and neighborhoods are listed on the facing page in alphabetical order. Of course, expectations will need to differ depending on a garden's location. Chapter 5 provides the scientific names.

American Goldfinch
American Kestrel
American Redstart
American Robin
Antillean Nighthawk
Baltimore Oriole
Barn Owl
Black-and-white Warbler
Black-throated Blue Warbler
Black Vulture
Blue Jay
Blue-and-yellow Macaw
Blue-crowned Parakeet
Blue-gray Gnatcatcher
Blue-headed Vireo
Boat-tailed Grackle
Brown-headed Cowbird
Brown Thrasher
Carolina Wren
Cattle Egret
Cedar Waxwing
Chimney Swift
Chuck-will's-widow
Common Grackle
Common Nighthawk
Common Yellowthroat
Cooper's Hawk
Downy Woodpecker
Eastern Kingbird
Eastern Phoebe
Eastern Screech-Owl
Eurasian Collared-Dove
European Starling
Fish Crow
Gray Catbird
Great Blue Heron
Great Crested Flycatcher
Great Egret
Green Heron
Hill Myna
House Sparrow

House Wren
Indian Peafowl
Indigo Bunting
Loggerhead Shrike
Mitred Parakeet
Monk Parakeet
Mourning Dove
Muscovy Duck
Northern Cardinal
Northern Flicker
Northern Mockingbird
Northern Parula
Northern Waterthrush
Orange-winged Parrot
Orchard Oriole
Osprey
Ovenbird
Painted Bunting
Palm Warbler
Pileated Woodpecker
Pine Warbler
Prairie Warbler
Prothonotary Warbler
Purple Martin
Red-bellied Woodpecker
Red-crowned Parrot
Red-masked Parakeet
Red-whiskered Bulbul
Red-winged Blackbird
Rock Pigeon
Ruby-throated Hummingbird
Scarlet Tanager
Sharp-shinned Hawk
Shiny Cowbird
Short-tailed Hawk
Spot-breasted Oriole
Summer Tanager
Swainson's Thrush
Swallow-tailed Kite
Tree Swallow
Turkey Vulture

continued

White-crowned Pigeon
White-eyed Vireo
White Ibis
White-winged Dove
White-winged Parakeet
Yellow-bellied Sapsucker

Yellow-billed Cuckoo
Yellow-chevroned Parakeet
Yellow-rumped Warbler
Yellow-throated Warbler
Yellow Warbler

Bananaquits are occasional visitors to South Florida from the Bahamas but have not yet established a breeding population here.

3

What Birds Need

The character of a garden, neighborhood, park, or parking lot that will attract birds is rather simple as a generalization: it is some re-creation of aspects of the birds' natural environment. As noted before, birds are attracted to gardens and other areas that provide habitat, which means space, structure, protection, nest sites, feeding sites, food, and all the other things needed by birds for carrying out their lives. Trees, shrubs, vines, short-statured plants, and lawns supply different aspects of a bird's needs. Some birds require special consideration, such as nectar-producing plants. Water features, nest boxes, and feeding stations are artificial elements that mimic resources naturally used by birds. In the following sections, we discuss elements of a South Florida garden that can be used to attract birds.

Trees

Trees are undoubtedly the most important element in attracting birds to a garden, because trees are where most birds will spend most of their time. Traditionally in South Florida, trees are planted as individual well-spaced specimens. Birds will make some use of them, particularly if they are bird-friendly live oaks, slash pines, native figs, or black olives; but in general, isolated trees, especially specimens of non-native trees, function in the garden less like bird habitat and more like statues.

Rather than as single specimens, trees tend to be more beneficial to birds if planted in mixed-species clusters. Clustering allows more species to be planted in available space, increasing the diversity of species, structure, insects, fruit, and timing of food availability. The edges of mixed plantings provide thick, shrubby cover and protection. Mixed-tree plantings are what occur naturally in South Florida's tropical hammocks and pineland understory, and so they are what native birds are used to.

In South Florida, it is exceptionally easy to produce a tree stand that somewhat resembles a native tropical hammock, on even a piece of a small parcel of land. Just plant native hammock trees together and watch them in a few years coalesce into a hammock. The core of a mixed-tree planting for birds in South Florida should be live oaks, native figs, gumbo limbos and one or more large

Trees are essential for attracting birds to a garden but are not very effective as isolated specimens.

Mixed-species tree plantings, especially those emulating the diversity and shrubbiness of native hammock edges, shown here, are best for birds.

palms. If not a native plant purist, a gardener can include non-native trees in these mixed-species stands. Historically, hammocks were used as home sites and camp sites by Indians and early settlers, and as a result most hammocks included non-native trees such as key lime, sour orange, or tamarind as well as Seminole pumpkin, corn, and sugar cane, so some non-native inclusions are not historically incorrect. A planting of hammock trees does best for birds if there are similar tree patches nearby, such as in neighbors' yards, neighborhood parks, and nearby commercial sites. Competition among plants is a way of life in mixed-tree plantings. The gardener can try to manage competition through pruning or, more easily, can allow the mixed-species area to develop as it will. The trees will fill in the spaces themselves. A mixed-species tree stand creates litter that recycles its nutrients, modifies its microclimate, and withstands the stress of hurricane winds better than individual specimen trees.

In South Florida, it's not easy being a tree. Many native trees are on the edge of their natural ranges (either northward for tropical plants or southward for temperate plants), meaning they are pushing the limits of compatible environmental conditions. Non-native trees, too, are mostly outside their optimal range of conditions. South Florida's trees are periodically knocked back by hurricanes and challenged by periodic droughts, and tropical trees additionally suffer infrequently in freezes. Temperate trees requiring some number of days of cool temperatures during the winter do not fruit. South Florida's trees face a paucity of topsoil, unfriendly limestone rock or sand or marl, high water tables, and fast-growing competition. As a result, many species do not do well here.

Trees that do well in most of South Florida need to be adapted to survive in alkaline soils. They also need to thrive through the dry season and the warm wet summer. Many South Florida trees are shallow rooted, a feature quite typical of tropical trees, which have to compete for fast-cycling nutrients at the soil's surface. Few South Florida native trees have the taproots characteristic of temperate trees.

In South Florida, most trees are not very tall, averaging perhaps 30–60 feet. If left without hurricanes, some native trees do have greater potential, perhaps 60–70 or more feet, but such expression is unusual given the frequency of destructive forces. Normal-sized South Florida trees are no more than middle-story size in bona fide temperate or tropical forests. A few native trees and many more non-native trees can breach this height, adding an emergent story to the canopy that provides additional opportunities for large birds that would otherwise pass a garden by. On the other hand, the short height of most of South Florida's trees means that they can be fit into smaller spaces.

That most South Florida trees are rather short also means that the difference between trees and shrubs is not all that great. A plant may function as one or the other or both successively as it grows. This mimics what occurs naturally in tropical hammocks, where a plant might be a long-term seedling, then a shrub, and then a tree, depending on any number of factors such as shading, soil, fire history, water table, disturbance, and time.

Trees most appropriate for any garden will differ depending on its location. In more southerly and coastal gardens, more tropical plants can be used. In more northern or inland gardens, more temperate plants can be used. To see what grows well, it is worthwhile to study the neighborhood and to visit nearby natural areas in parks, public landscaping, and recent highway plantings. And to experiment.

Managing garden trees is very different in South Florida than farther north, with tree pruning being one of these differences. A tree pruned of its branches,

Overly sculpting trees and hedges robs them of much of their wildlife value.

especially dead branches, loses much of its value to birds. The ultimate example is a "hat-racked" tree, its branches cut to stubs, essentially starving both the tree and its birds. A tree sculpted into some desired non-natural shape provides no advantage for birds over a natural tree shape. Why such highly trimmed trees are desirable is not clear, since a concrete statue would be easier to maintain and not require subsidizing workers to keep it trimmed.

Even less extreme pruning, however, can be disadvantageous to birds. Plants and birds need dying and dead branches. This is especially so for palms. Each palm species holds onto its fronds in a characteristic way, dropping them when biologically appropriate. Royal palms self-prune leaves as they die; cabbage palms self-prune at the stem, leaving the bract on the trunk; coconut palms hold onto their leaves for some time. In a bird garden, palms should not be pruned of their dying and dead branches because these provide exceptional habitat for birds as well as for insects, reptiles, and bats. In a South Florida bird-friendly garden, there is little need for massive pruning, removal of dead wood, or painting of wounds.

There are exceptions, of course, to the nonpruning rule. Fruit trees may need a bit of trimming to increase production. Large exposed specimen trees may need trimming to reduce top growth relative to roots. And judicious pruning may be needed for clear and imminent safety concerns, like frail limbs over or touching structures, coconuts over a sidewalk, or limbs low enough and in the wrong place such that visitors might walk into them. When choosing where to plant a tree, avoid situations where it will eventually have to be pruned, such as under utility lines or over roofs. Once a tree is planted in the wrong place or gets in the way of the utility company's business, there will be no recourse when the crews with their big machines arrive.

Whenever possible, for birds, pruning should be avoided and dying and dead branches should be left in place to decay naturally. Even more of a case can be made for dead trunks. In a South Florida garden meant to attract birds, dead trees are as important as live ones. Trees die from disease, old age, lightning, wind, root abuse, or any number of indeterminable causes. South Florida's native tropical trees, being mostly pioneering species, tend to be short-lived in any case. Normal gardening protocol calls for removing failing trees and eliminating dead snags. But not in a South Florida bird garden. Birds need dead trunks. Woodpeckers and other trunk-foraging birds search out insects lurking under dead trunk bark. Cavity-nesting birds use dead trunks for their nesting. Some dead trees hold their dead branches for some time, essentially setting out a buffet of invertebrate bird food.

Dead trees are extremely important in a South Florida yard as many species depend on them for roosting, feeding, and nesting. Here an Eastern Screech-Owl roosts in a dead trunk.

Even in neighborhoods with strict landscaping ordinances, dead trees can often be left standing by the gardener. As indicated by the holes in this dead palm, they will be used by birds, for feeding and also for perching, roosting, and nesting.

Admittedly, sometimes, there are local regulations to deal with; but even in highly controlled neighborhoods, trees can often be left standing, especially if they are within larger plantings and do not pose safety concerns to the wider community. If one is so unfortunate as to lack dead trees, one might consider importing them.

Specific trees that might be chosen for South Florida bird gardens are discussed elsewhere, but the choices are ample, much more so than for any northern bird garden. As noted above, oaks, figs, and palms stand out as being nearly essential to any South Florida bird-attracting garden big enough to accommodate them. Many other native species and topical fruit trees are also highly recommended, including citrus, avocado, mango, and papaya. And there are some trees, both native and non-native, that apart from their bird-friendly rating are so characteristic of South Florida, they demand to be planted in almost any garden.

A list of the ten most important options for trees and tree-sized plants and a list of the birds that might characteristically be seen in trees in the garden are provided below.

PLANTS

Black Olive
Buttonwood
Coconut Palm
False Tamarind
Gumbo Limbo

Live Oak
Native figs
Seagrape
Slash Pine
West Indian Mahogany

BIRDS

Amazon parrots
Blue-gray Gnatcatcher
Blue Jay
Boat-tailed Grackle
Common Grackle
Conures
Cooper's Hawk
Eastern Kingbird
Eastern Phoebe
Eastern Screech-Owl
Eurasian Collared-Dove
Fish Crow
Gray Kingbird
Great Crested Flycatcher

Monk Parakeet
Mourning Dove
Northern Cardinal
Northern Mockingbird
Northern Shrike
Orioles
Red-bellied Woodpecker
Ruby-throated Hummingbird
Swallow-tailed Kite
Thrushes
Warblers
White-crowned Pigeon
White-winged Dove
Vireos

Shrubs

The next element to consider for birds in a garden is the shrub layer. Shrubs play a large role in the overall look and feel of a garden because they are at eye level, and they provide much of the vegetative bulk of the garden used by small to medium-sized birds. If well selected and arranged, they can provide much of the garden's fruit, nectar, insects, nesting sites, perching sites, and sleeping and roosting sites. Shrub plantings are where many foraging and sheltering birds will spend their time. A garden without shrubs under and surrounding the trees will not do well in attracting and holding birds. This principle is particularly important for public gardens and other public spaces to follow, as they are often beset by contrary views and see their shrubs repeatedly hacked away.

The role of shrubs in predator protection in suburban and urban gardens should not be underappreciated; outdoor cats are devastating to backyard birds and are disrupted in their hunt by thick, thorny, and densely branched shrubs. These provide in-garden protection that birds can rely on, especially if placed where birds are most vulnerable, such as near feeders, water features, property edges, and plant zone transitions.

Garden shrubs are best for birds if diverse, thick, and unpruned.

Shrubs can be used in many ways in a bird-friendly garden, including as stand-alone specimens, accents, visual barriers, hedges, backdrops for shorter plantings, butterfly/hummingbird gardens, understory, or edges for tree plantings. Mixed-species plantings are most productive for birds. Birds love hedgerows, and the South Florida equivalent of the northern hedgerow is the nearly impenetrable hammock edge composed of diverse tropical shrub-sized plants. The gardener's goal should be to produce as many linear feet of edge comprising diverse shrubs as might be possible.

There is always the urge to excessively prune, thin, hedge, top, and otherwise manipulate shrubs into predetermined stages of submission. Yard-care workers, park maintenance crews, and most landscapers are deadly to shrub plantings. In South Florida, a garden helper with a cultural fondness for the machete can quickly spell disaster for shrub-dwelling birds. As is the case with trees, pruning and tight hedging are generally of no value to birds, nor are shrub topiaries.

Because plant growth is rampant in South Florida, some judicious trimming may indeed be necessary. Cutting back of shrubs is needed when they outgrow their allotted space, impinge on sites reserved for sun, compete with less hardy plants, or demonstrate an unwanted aspiration to become trees. A garden for birds needs to be composed primarily of shrubs—as many, as dense, and as diverse as possible. Trim shrubs only when safety or the integrity of the garden's design requires it, but for the most part, let shrubs do their thing and fill in their spaces.

There are hundreds of native and non-native shrubs South Florida bird gardeners can consider. Short palms and native tropical shrubs with bird-sized fruit are distinctive options for South Florida bird-attracting gardens. Spiny shrub-sized plants are available for cover and protection. Also in South Florida, as mentioned, the difference between shrubs and trees is not distinct. Many plants may be shrubs or trees depending on the situation or the trimming regime, and many plants are shrubs at one stage but eventually, under the right circumstances, can grow into trees. Various options will be discussed in chapter 6, but a list of important shrub-sized bird plants and typical birds that use them are listed below.

PLANTS

Buttonsage	Palmettos
Cocoplum	Sensitive plants (sennas)
Firebush	Stoppers
Hollies	Wax Myrtle
Marlberry	Wild coffees

BIRDS

Blue Jay	Northern Shrike
Brown Thrasher	Orioles
Common Grackle	Red-winged Blackbird
Common Ground-Dove	Ruby-throated Hummingbird
Eastern Phoebe	Thrushes
Gray Catbird	Vireos
Mourning Dove	Warblers
Northern Cardinal	Wrens
Northern Mockingbird	Yellow-billed Cuckoo

Vines

Vines tend to be overlooked by gardeners, except to cover trellises, but should not be as they provide superior structure for birds where otherwise none would exist. In nature, vines are entangled within the branches of trees and shrubs where they fill voids. Ideally, every tall tree in a South Florida bird garden should have one or two vines assigned to it. The primary function of vines in a South Florida bird-friendly garden is to increase structural complexity by filling in space within and on top of the shrub and tree canopy. Vines in such a situation provide roost and nest sites, and for some species, food.

Vines can also be used as stand-alone features, climbing trellises, fences, or walls. Fences are a way of life in suburban South Florida and can be helpful in a bird garden to deter depredating cats, roaming dogs, and clueless neighbors. Vine-covered fences provide protection, nest sites, and, with proper selection, food for birds.

Vines contribute structure and cover within a bird garden. Here bougainvillea's dense, thorny branches provide ideal protection for this Northern Mockingbird nest.

The vine list for South Florida, native or otherwise, is somewhat slim. Poison ivy is the most important bird vine of South Florida. Although not welcomed in most gardens, it should be, though perhaps toward the back fence. Here is a list of the top ten bird vines to consider and birds that may be expected to use vines.

PLANTS

Bougainvillea	Muscadine
Cape Honeysuckle	Passionflowers
Coral Honeysuckle	Poison Ivy
Golden Trumpet	Virginia Creeper
Greenbriers	White Twinevine

BIRDS

Blue-gray Gnatcatcher	Northern Mockingbird
Brown Thrasher	Orioles
Carolina Wren	Ruby-throated Hummingbird
Gray Catbird	Thrushes
House Sparrow	Vireos
Northern Cardinal	Warblers

Epiphytes

Epiphytes are plants that grow on other plants, although in humid South Florida, fences, walls, roofs, rocks, and utility lines are also fair substrates. Epiphytes, among the more distinctive opportunities for South Florida gardening, add hugely to the structural and species diversity of a garden, as well as being aesthetically pleasing and biologically interesting. A bromeliad attached to three square inches of bark can add hundreds of square inches of surface area of bird habitat to the tree. Many epiphytes hold rainwater and most catch debris, providing water, food, and shelter for insects and other invertebrates eaten by birds.

The long list of epiphyte options includes orchids, bromeliads, cacti, mosses, lichens, ferns, and even a few trees. Under natural conditions, these grow on branches and trunks, often tolerating considerable shading. Because epiphytes gain their nutrients from the air or falling debris, they need little care. Depending on location, some native epiphytes will self-seed into a garden; others may be purchased; sometimes they can be rescued from fallen branches or from the path of a bulldozer. Non-native bromeliads, orchids, and ferns are readily and cheaply available.

Shape, bark morphology, and surface chemistry make some plants more conducive than others to hosting epiphytes. Particularly hospitable trees include oaks, buttonwoods, cypresses, pond apples, pines, and citrus. Epiphytes can also be installed on dead trees, driftwood, rocks, fences, and structures. Epiphytic strangler figs add markedly to bird-friendly diversity, starting as epiphytes and maturing into one of the most important local bird trees. The process has been much maligned by South Florida gardeners, who see the loss of a host tree rather than the gain of a fig tree.

Epiphytes, like the orchids, ferns, and cacti attached to palms in this photo, increase a garden's structural and plant diversity, often translating to larger insect populations for birds to eat.

Below is a list of valuable epiphytes for a South Florida bird garden, and the birds that characteristically poke around epiphytes.

PLANTS	
Air plants	Resurrection Fern
Ballmoss	Spanish Moss
Christmas Cactus	Staghorn Fern
Golden Polypody	Strangler Fig
Mistletoe Cactus	Whisk Fern
Orchids	

BIRDS	
Blue-gray Gnatcatcher	Vireos
Kinglets	Warblers
Phoebes	Wrens

Short-statured Plants

Short-statured plants provide protection for birds feeding on the ground, low in vegetation, or on nearby lawns, and many are nectar supplying, insect producing, or seed bearing. Choices for short-statured plants in South Florida are quite broad, including native species, typical northern bedding plants, and tropical houseplants. The usual nursery bedding plants add color, familiarity, and temporal variety, but this is also the place for native wildflowers. Short-statured native plants can be perennial or reseeding. Herbaceous plants that are perennials elsewhere may be annuals in South Florida as they don't survive the summer.

Short-statured plants, like white crownbeard, provide seeds, nectar, insects, and cover for birds such as the Blackpoll Warbler shown here.

Attracting Birds to South Florida Gardens

Short-statured plants are used as ground cover, along edges of shrubs, under trees, in flowering or herbaceous beds, or in special garden patches such as butterfly/hummingbird or herb/vegetable gardens. From a bird's perspective, short-statured beds and edges are best if the plants include a diversity of species, are relatively tall (1–3 feet), are structurally complex, and as a group produce flowers, small fruit, and seeds over a long period of the year. If non-native bedding plants are used, they should be dispersed in a diverse setting with persistent native plants, rather than installed in a single-species bed, which creates a rather biologically sterile situation.

Here is a list of important short-statured plants and the birds that might be seen using them.

PLANTS

Beggarticks (Spanish Needles)	Milkweeds
Bushy Seaside Oxeye	Porterweeds
Coontie	Rougeplant
Firewheel	Sword Fern
Goldenrods	Tropical Sage

BIRDS

American Redstart	House Sparrow
Black-throated Blue Warbler	Indigo Bunting
Brown Thrasher	Mourning Dove
Common Grackle	Painted Bunting
Common Ground-Dove	Palm Warbler
Cowbirds	Red-winged Blackbird
Gray Catbird	Wrens

Open Ground and Ground Structure

To attract ground-feeding birds, a garden needs open ground. Although the concept of unplanted space may seem odd to a gardener, it is not odd to a bird that finds this feature throughout its native habitat. In South Florida, open ground occurs naturally where trees and shrubs shade incipient plants, such as the interiors of hammocks and swamps. A cover of larger plants over open areas protects foraging birds, allowing them to flee to safety at a moment's notice.

Open ground is used by birds to forage on insects, worms, snails, spiders, other invertebrates, lizards, frogs, seeds, and fallen fruit found there. Birds also seek soil or sand for dust baths, grit for digestion, and snail shells for calcium.

Important garden enhancements for birds are piles of brush, mounds of sticks, stacks of logs, and piles of rocks placed on the open ground under trees and shrubs. These occur naturally in South Florida's hammocks, pinelands, and

Many birds forage on bare ground, like this Black-throated Blue Warbler eating a fallen fig fruit.

swamps. The "brush pile" is an important northern bird-gardening practice providing protection for wintering birds, which of course is not much needed in South Florida. In South Florida such stacks of sticks and piles of rocks provide year-round shelter, structure, low perch sites, and, most importantly, living space for invertebrates and small vertebrates eaten by birds.

What about mulching? Mulching is the antithesis of open ground and sparse litter. As explained in more detail in chapter 4, for birds, it is better to use no mulch at all or to use it very judiciously. The natural equivalent of mulch is the litter from the trees and shrubs themselves, as they shed leaves, fruit, twigs, and branches, much of it during the dry season when many South Florida plants

Ground structures like this pile of limestone rocks provide food and habitat used by many birds, such as this ground-feeding Mourning Dove under a protective canopy of wild coffee plants.

Attracting Birds to South Florida Gardens

are rather deciduous. Natural litter is sparse but well populated by insects, millipedes, centipedes, pill bugs, earthworms, snails, and spiders, as well as by frogs, snakes, and lizards, all of which are bird food. Fallen leaves and twigs in South Florida degrade rapidly, generally within a season or two, to be replaced by new leaf fall, so natively in South Florida, litter is thin, sparse, ephemeral, and full of food for birds.

Birds foraging under the canopy of native South Florida forests find shallow sparse litter, piles of sticks and stones, and open space; this is what a bird gardener would seek to emulate. Nearly all birds will visit open ground at some point, but some habitually feed there. Here are a few of the birds that might be expected to use open ground patches.

BIRDS

American Redstart	Louisiana Waterthrush
Black-throated Blue Warbler	Mourning Dove
Brown Thrasher	Northern Flicker
Common Grackle	Northern Mockingbird
Common Ground-Dove	Northern Waterthrush
Common Myna	Ovenbird
European Starling	Palm Warbler
House Sparrow	Red-winged Blackbird
Indigo Bunting	White Ibis

Diverse Lawn

Lawns are desirable in almost any garden to provide unobstructed vistas, separation of planting areas, dramatic transitions, paths and walks, and open places for backyard activities. Showing a tidy bit of lawn out front, adjacent to the neighbor's tightly manicured lawn, might ensure neighborhood or municipal peace. Lawns are important for birds, too, but what birds do not need are fields of monocultural sod grass. Of all the ways bird gardening differs from other gardening, the diverse lawn may be the hardest to get used to given that so much time, energy, and money are customarily spent tending a typical South Florida sod lawn, and heavy pressure from neighbors and the community is usually at play as well.

What birds *do* need are small patches of diverse lawn. Diverse lawns are composed of many species of short plants, encouraged by infrequent mowing at high wheel settings. These lawns provide a diversity of insects, fruits, and seeds at staggered times. For birds, lawns should not be extensive but rather small patches fitted among other bird-friendly garden elements so as to increase spatial diversity.

While lawns are important features in bird-friendly gardens, large expanses of monoculture sod are not.

The mowed lawn is a temperate-zone invention, totally out of place in the tropics. As a result, the typical South Florida sod lawn, if properly cared for, is an expensive affliction. It has to be mowed using fume-spewing gas-drinking mowers, managed at the cost of the gardener's time or the money to pay someone else to do it, fertilized seasonally, watered regularly, usually using purchased water and a complex irrigation system, treated with pesticides and fungicides, monitored for unwanted weeds, and replaced as it periodically dies off. Why do this? Unlike sod monocultures, diverse lawns are cheap and nearly carefree. They do not require fertilizer, insecticides, fungicides, watering, and certainly not weed control, mainly because diverse lawns are actually composed of "weeds."

For birds, the more diverse the lawn patch, the better. Turkey tangle fogfruit, threeflower ticktrefoil, creeping oxeye, and St. Augustinegrass all contribute to this small but bird-friendly patch of lawn.

The proper bird lawn may (aesthetically or ecologically) be thought of as mimicking a native meadow, prairie, or grassy pineland floor. But frankly, it is better thought of as mimicking a poorly tended ball field or a bush-hogged highway margin. Many plants can be part of a diverse lawn, and no two lawns will be the same. Some lawn plants are readily transplanted from neighboring public spaces and road beds, and most will volunteer once sod management is abandoned. St. Augustinegrass and other sod grass are not banned from diverse lawns; they should be included in the mix as they support many insects, as any keeper of a typical sod lawn knows all too well.

While sod lawns are not overly bird friendly, in South Florida a trend of recent decades has gone even further. Many a South Florida lawn is nothing more than a pad of concrete, divorcing itself from any connectivity to the natural world it replaces, as shown in the figure on page 5. Concreting our lawns replaces everything that is natural, changes microclimate, increases runoff, and has any number of other adverse ecological and social consequences. In the regreening of South Florida, removing the massive coverage of impermeable surface is one of the greatest challenges. Replacing it with bird-friendly plantings and diverse lawns is one of the greatest opportunities.

Gardeners choosing to landscape with small, diverse lawns have lots of company. Reducing sod in favor of hardier, drought-resistant, low-maintenance plants is becoming increasingly popular, as environmental awareness and water-use consciousness increase. Xeriscaping is in.

Bird-friendly lawns consist of small patches of varied grasses and low-lying ground cover plants. A Palm Warbler is nearly hidden in this diverse lawn dominated by turkey tangle fog-fruit and common wireweed.

A diverse lawn need not look like a knee-high, unkempt vacant lot. It needs to be mowed regularly to keep it as lawn, but at a high mower setting. As such, it is no more an affront to neighborhood aesthetics than would be the nearby park. As a diverse lawn develops, it may be worthwhile to let the neighbors know what's going on. There are good justifications besides the birds (argue money) for them to consider adopting your practice. More patches of diverse lawns through the neighborhood will help birds coming to your garden too. Diverse lawns can be kept sufficiently shorn and appropriately green to accommodate most neighborhood demands, and in fact will be green when the neighbors' lawns have browned from winter, dry season, chinch bugs, or fungus. And the birds will appreciate the insects.

Below is a list of plants one might find in a diverse South Florida lawn and birds that may be expected to use such a lawn.

PLANTS

Common Wireweed	Powderpuff
Brown's Blechum	St. Augustinegrass
Mascarene Island Leafflower	Creeping Oxeye
Mendez's Sandmat	Trefoils
Mexican Clover	Turkey Tangle Fogfruit

BIRDS

American Redstart	House Sparrow
Boat-tailed Grackle	Mourning Dove
Brown-headed Cowbird	Northern Mockingbird
Common Grackle	Palm Warbler
Common Ground-Dove	Red-winged Blackbird
European Starling	Rock Pigeon
Eurasian Collared-Dove	White Ibis
Hill Myna	White-winged Dove

Water Features

In Arizona in summer or North Dakota in winter, supplying water for birds can be a matter of life or death—but in South Florida, it would take an incompetent bird to die of thirst. An 80 by 120 foot South Florida lot receives on average 47,000 gallons of rain a year. Birds in most neighborhoods have access to water in canals, rock pits, swimming pools, sprinklers, mud puddles, swales, and dew- and rain-soaked plants. Water gets a bit more dear in the winter dry season and certainly as one moves southward through the Keys, but not fatally so. Nonetheless, whether in the dry season in Key West or wet season in Palm Beach,

gardeners who supply convenient, consistent, permanent, accessible, clean, naturalistic water sources will find that their garden attracts birds that might otherwise have gone elsewhere.

In South Florida, ibis, herons, grackles, blackbirds, jays, cardinals, yellowthroats, redstarts and many other warblers will show up to use water features. Water features increase the garden's food base by diversifying its plants, invertebrates, and small vertebrates. A water feature provides design opportunities, usually elevating itself to a garden's centerpiece. Every South Florida bird garden should have a water feature, or two, or three.

No doubt a gardener's first thoughts turn to traditional birdbaths—a concrete pan on a pillar, perhaps with a cherub spouting water from a selected body orifice. However satisfying it may be to have a cherub on a pillar, traditional birdbaths do not work well in South Florida. They drive the gardener crazy with their incessant demands. In the dry season, they dry immediately; in the wet season, they harbor algae and mosquitoes. Filling, disinfecting, and mosquito killing are near daily activities. And birds don't much like them if given alternatives.

If not the birdbath on a pillar, what? First, the best place for water features is where they occur naturally, on or in the ground. Place any shallow vessel, terra cotta or plastic flowerpot saucer, pie pan, upside-down garbage can lid, plastic basin, or whatever, on the ground, add stones to provide variable water depths, and fill. This can be on the lawn, under the shrubs, or on a patio. While more

Birds like this Gray Catbird prefer ground-level naturalistic water features having shallow areas over traditional basin-on-a-pillar birdbaths.

acceptable to the birds than a pan on a pillar, the pan approach does retain maintenance drawbacks.

A better approach is to make a ground water feature that is more natural, vegetated, and deeper, more like a pond than a traditional birdbath. Guidance for constructing garden ponds is readily available in books, on the Internet, and in garden shops, and materials are easily available. The basic concept and its execution are easy, if kept simple. Decide size and shape; lay out the perimeter; decide location of deep (18 inches or deeper; check local fencing requirements for these depths) and shallow (1–4 inches) portions; dig it out; cover the bottom with thick plastic; and fill the pond with water.

There are nuances to a garden pond for birds, of course. Differing shallow depths allow access by birds of differing leg length, and deep portions protect mosquito-eating fish. Emergent rocks provide alternative entry sites for small birds, homes for invertebrates, and additional protection for fish. It is important that the pond has very shallow areas, provided by rocks or shallowly sloping edges, in order to accommodate small critters. Allowing the pond to overflow creates a marshy area, especially if underlain by a buried retention barrier, such as a sheet of plastic or a kiddy pool. Such damp spots are used as a water source by butterflies, bees and frogs. Water movement attracts birds, so a pump can be added to create water circulation—a waterfall, fountain, streamlet, or just a drip here and there. There even are water-wiggling contraptions one can buy.

Waterfalls are bird magnets. Pumps can be solar powered. Surface runoff and rainfall captured from roofs can be funneled into the pond.

Digging a pond is easy on muck, sand, or fill but difficult to impossible on limestone, in which case the pond can be made above grade, unless digging with a pickax or hiring someone with rock-eating machines is more satisfying. Once the pond is filled, add a bucket of water and soil from a local canal or lake to get the pond's ecology started.

Birds respond best to standard garden-pond designs: wetland trees in the back, shrubs along the edge, submersed or floating-leafed plants in deeper water, and emergent plants in shallow water. Many aquatic plants are available, both native and not, and are described in some detail later.

Some gardens are fortunate enough to be adjacent to existing water features, such as canals, rock pits, stormwater treatment marshes, or semipermanent swales. These can be readily made more bird friendly. Rules differ as to what can be done with these features; but if the opportunity exists, waterscape to emulate a natural pond and its edges.

One of the great benefits of garden ponds is that beyond birds, they attract aquatic life such as dragonflies, butterflies, aquatic insects, turtles, lizards, and frogs. In South Florida, they also attract mosquitoes; so, fish are needed for mosquito control, the best being the native mosquitofish (*Gambusia affinis*). Mosquitofish can be found in any canal or marsh, and its inexpensive domesticated relative the guppy (*Poecilia reticulata*) is also readily available. If the pond is large enough, there is a tendency to want larger and more attractive fish. Non-native fish should be introduced only where they cannot escape. Inexpensive goldfish (*Carassius auratus*), expensive koi (*Cyprinus carpio*), or cichlids (Cichlidae) add beauty and mystery to a pond. However, South Florida does not lack for fish-eating birds, which will be attracted to well-stocked water features. The larger and more obvious the fish, the more likely they will be eaten. For some gardeners, the treat of feeding fish-eating birds is sufficient to justify repeated restocking. For others, seeing a several hundred–dollar koi consumed by a random Great Blue Heron is not much of a treat.

To give fish a chance, whether expensive or not, make the pond sufficiently deep that birds cannot wade (4–5 feet; check local zoning rules on fencing), include structures so fish can hide, and make pond edges unwelcoming to large birds by adding walls, webs of monofilament line, and scary shiny things. Plastic herons are available to scare off competitors, but generally the herons figure out that a pond with a plastic heron is not really already claimed. Monofilament fishing line strung over the pond and unloved DVDs spinning on monofilament lines keep most ponds big-bird free. Rather than hardening the pond against herons, it may be best to divide responsibilities among water features. For spectacular fish, build a pond just for the fish with lots of impediments to herons. For birds, build a pond with easy bird-access points and keep the fish small, gray, and inexpensive.

Here are some water-feature plants and birds associated with water features in South Florida bird gardens.

PLANTS

Bulltongue Arrowhead	Pond Apple
Buttonbush	Swamp Fern
Cattail	Waterhyssops
Lizard's Tail	Water lilies
Pickerelweed	Wax Myrtle

BIRDS

American Redstart	Louisiana Waterthrush
Boat-tailed Grackle	Northern Cardinal
Common Yellowthroat	Northern Mockingbird
Gray Catbird	Northern Waterthrush
Great Blue Heron	Red-winged Blackbird
Great Egret	White Ibis
Green Heron	Yellow Warbler

Nesting Sites

To supply nesting sites for South Florida's birds, the first priority is to provide appropriate plants. Good nesting plants are those offering strong branch support for the nests and good leaf and branch cover to hide them. The very best nesting plants are those that have both thick cover and thorny branches.

Different birds nest at different heights, so structure and cover need to be provided from high in the trees down to the ground. Among the high sites, pines, palms, live oak, mangroves, buttonwood, gumbo limbo, figs, mahogany, citruses, and black olive are among the trees most used by nesting birds in South Florida. At the middle level, many shrubs, such as stoppers, cocoplum, and hibiscus, have strong branches and good leaf cover. Plants that are thick down to the ground, such as saw palmetto and ferns, provide protection for ground-nesting species. Vines provide excellent support and protection within their tangled branches, the more rampant the better. Bougainvillea and trumpet creeper are among the best.

Some birds need trunks in which they can nest. Pines, cypresses, and palms are among those most used by cavity-nesting birds in South Florida. Natural cavities develop as tree limbs break off and leave soft wood exposed, lightning strikes kill parts of trunks, insects and fungi create gaps in trees, and woodpeckers start holes from scratch. Strangler figs especially encourage cavities in the dead and dying trees they engulf. Palm "trunks," bases of palm leaves, and old leaf base material are readily bored into.

Above: Trees like black olive provide high nesting sites that are sufficiently sturdy and concealed to support the likes of this Cooper's Hawk nest. Here a female Cooper's Hawk leaves her nest with the uneaten remains of a freshly killed Eurasian Collared-Dove.

Dead trees provide important nesting habitat. Red-bellied Woodpeckers are the primary cavity excavators in South Florida, making holes in which they and many other species nest. This woodpecker is bringing a caterpillar to its nestlings in a coconut palm.

Woodpeckers are the principal creators of natural cavities in South Florida. Once woodpeckers are finished using their cavity, other cavity-nesting species follow. The importance of retaining dead or dying trees in the garden was noted above, in the section on trees, but can never be mentioned too often.

This is a list of important nesting plants and some of the birds that can be expected to nest in a South Florida garden.

PLANTS

Black Olive	Live Oak
Bougainvillea	Native figs
Buttonwood	Royal Palm
Citruses	Slash Pine
Coconut Palm	Stoppers

BIRDS

Blue Jay	Fish Crow
Boat-tailed Grackle	Hill Myna
Brown Thrasher	House Sparrow
Chimney Swift	Loggerhead Shrike
Common Grackle	Mourning Dove
Downy Woodpecker	Northern Cardinal
Eurasian Collared-Dove	Northern Mockingbird
Gray Kingbird	Red-bellied Woodpecker
Great Crested Flycatcher	Red-winged Blackbird
Eastern Screech-Owl	Spot-breasted Oriole
European Starling	White-winged Dove

Birdhouses

So what about birdhouses? As natural cavity sites become rare, to some extent nest boxes can be substitutes. Owls, woodpeckers, wrens, bluebirds, Purple Martins, and some flycatchers are among South Florida's native cavity nesters. Parrots, starlings, sparrows, and mynas fill out the much longer non-native list.

This list is very different from one compiled farther north, where garden birdhouses attract an array of cavity-nesting, garden-loving, feeder-visiting birds; however, this is not how it is in South Florida. Although the South Florida list is sparser and less garden dependent than one from up north, there are many reasons to set out birdhouses in South Florida. Martins, woodpeckers, and Eastern Screech-Owls, particularly, are attracted to gardens with nest boxes in South Florida. Boxes not used by birds can host bees, ants, frogs, lizards, snakes,

Left: Purple Martins are one of the few native cavity-nesting birds in South Florida. They readily use man-made houses placed in the open and are quite tolerant of proximity to humans.

Below left: Nest boxes in South Florida are used by a range of animals, such as the anole that took up residence in this one. Nest boxes should be considered wildlife boxes and welcome whatever animal shows up.

Below right: Red-bellied Woodpeckers need multiple cavities and may use bird boxes for roosting or nesting.

squirrels, raccoons, and opossums. In fact, they are best considered wildlife boxes, attracting a wide array of species to the garden.

Boxes need to be plain so as to blend into the landscape and be unobtrusive to predators, usually in inconspicuous locations. Decorated bird mansions may be fun for people, but most birds require their nesting efforts to be discreet. Martins and bluebirds are exceptions, preferring their nests in the open. Information on how to make, buy, and position bird boxes is available from many sources. In South Florida particular attention needs to be paid to providing an overhanging roof to protect from rain, as well drain holes, air vents for cooling, predator baffles on the way to the box, and easy access to combat starlings and sparrows.

Other kinds of nesting structures can also be provided. Platforms are used by hawks and owls, old buildings by Barn Owls, and various garden niches by wrens (as well as by House Sparrows). Ospreys are among the more sensational garden birds in South Florida. Along the coast and even inland, nesting platforms can attract Ospreys to nest and any number of species to use Osprey platforms for roosting.

Below: Although people often enjoy the flamboyance of decorative birdhouses, most birds require inconspicuous nest sites.

Right: Artificial nesting platforms in coastal yards and nearby parks may attract Osprey.

Attracting Birds to South Florida Gardens

Houses and structures need to be tended, so they should be situated where they are accessible to the gardener. They should be cleaned out annually, and sometimes bee colonies have to be discouraged. Most importantly, they need to be defended against starlings, which will outcompete martins, woodpeckers, and flycatchers for cavities. Although the number of starlings eagerly awaiting nest boxes is apparently unlimited, they can be managed one pair at a time by removing their nests after eggs have been laid. That pair will move on, giving other species a chance.

Birds most likely to accept artificial nesting sites in South Florida include the following:

BIRDS

Barn Owl	House Sparrow
Carolina Wren	Macaws
Downy Woodpecker	Osprey
Eastern Bluebird	Parakeets
Eastern Screech-Owl	Parrots
European Starling	Purple Martin
Great Crested Flycatcher	Red-bellied Woodpecker

Feeding Sites

A garden's principal value to birds is providing food. To attract birds to a garden, think insects, spiders, fruit, seeds, and nectar. And recall that the place for this food is mostly in the garden's plants. Diverse plantings provide birds with a variety and abundance of these food sources. While the value of plants as fruit sources can be readily appreciated, their value as insect sources may be less so, because insects go unnoticed. Take time to look carefully at the stems and leaves of a plant and all manner of insect bird-food will be seen.

Some plants are better than others at supplying insects. Douglas Tallamy determined that North American oaks support more than 500 species of caterpillars, and pines more than 200. This is certainly why live oaks and slash pines are among the most attractive plants to South Florida birds. More generally, he also found that gardens planted with native plants have more caterpillars and more kinds of caterpillars than do gardens planted with non-native plants. This is because native plants support communities of insects, whereas insects for the most part did not accompany non-native plants from their places of origin. In fact, import rules requiring quarantine and fumigation aim to ensure this to be the case. Dr. Tallamy determined from the literature that the punktree (*Melaleuca*) supports only eight insect species in South Florida, creating a biological desert, but more than 400 back where it evolved in Australia. The punktree arrived in

Gardens with plants providing fruit and insects such as this leaf-footed bug are attractive to birds.

South Florida as seeds in an envelope, devoid of its naturally associated insect fauna.

Fruit and seeds are another important food source provided by plants, particularly in South Florida, where many native plants of tropical origin have fruit that evolved to be dispersed by birds. Migrant birds are quite familiar with South Florida's native fruit supply because they encounter the same fruits in the tropics. Birds migrating through South Florida may pause to feed on gumbo limbo, and then continue on to Central America to find gumbo limbo trees in fruit there as well. Similarly, seeds of grasses, sedges, asters, and other composites are readily familiar to South Florida birds. On the other hand, many non-native plants

Many of South Florida's native tropical plants are bird favorites. In fact, it is likely that most were brought to Florida as seeds carried in the guts of birds. Gumbo limbo, for example, ranges down into South America. A bird on fall migration feeding in South Florida could a day or two later find itself eating gumbo limbo fruit in Guatemala, where this photo was taken.

Attracting Birds to South Florida Gardens

contain unpalatable chemicals, tend to fruit at the wrong time, or have fruits too large or too hard for native birds.

Plants also provide nectar. Hummingbirds are the primary bird consumer of nectar in South Florida, although orioles and some other species also partake. Plants that hummingbirds can use in South Florida are rather few because suitable species must have flowers that particularly accommodate the Ruby-throated Hummingbird's bill size and shape and must be available in winter.

Non-native plants certainly are not unwelcome as food sources in gardens aiming to attract birds. Some provide bird-friendly fruit or seeds, and parrots can handle fruit and seeds that native birds cannot. Interspersing a few well-researched non-native plants can be helpful; birds especially appreciate cultivated fruit trees such as citruses, guava, mango, banana, avocado, Barbados cherry, coconut, and tamarind. Some non-native plants that evolved to attract nectarivorous birds in their native environment can be used by South Florida's hummingbird.

What about bird feeders? Most people's vision of a garden includes store-bought bird feeders. In fact, they are usually the first birdy things added to a garden. Such feeders attract birds that might otherwise pass a garden by and also encourage birds to come out where they can be seen.

But, as in other bird gardening matters, the situation in South Florida differs from that farther north where feeders are frequented by an entertaining community of yard-nesting chickadees, titmice, wrens, finches, nuthatches, creepers, sparrows, and small woodpeckers. This community of backyard seed eaters does not exist in South Florida, so we should do things differently here.

→ Ethics of Bird Feeding

Given that the food a gardener provides to birds is found primarily in the garden's plants, a bird gardener might want to consider, at least in passing, the biology and ethics of artificial bird feeding. Whether to artificially feed birds is a choice for the gardener to make. A gardener might worry that feeding birds is unnatural, adversely affects natural populations, or can make birds overly dependent on supplements. Other concerns might be that food going bad can harm birds, that gathering birds at feeding stations spreads disease, that feeding can change nesting or migration patterns, that it provides inappropriate nutrition, or that feeding wild animals is just wrong. The last is a philosophical point; however, the other concerns are amenable to scientific investigation. The bottom line, based on many many studies, is that feeding neither adversely affects birds nor changes their inherent biology. Issues of health are valid but can be handled with proper feeder hygiene. So if a gardener chooses to feed birds artificially in the garden, there really is no reason not to do so.

A garden is using the space previously occupied by native habitat that supported native birds. Providing enhanced feeding opportunities is a bit of compensation. In South Florida, bird feeders are never native species' primary food sources. Their more preferred food of insects and fruit is not scarce in South Florida, even in winter. Feeding stations do not make birds dependent but do make birds more apparent to the gardener. The primary reasons to feed birds are to bring them into the garden and to be able to observe them once they are there.

As they do in the tropics, South Florida birds will come to fruit, nuts, bread, and other leftovers placed in a tray feeder for their consumption.

So how shall we feed birds in South Florida? Overall, it is best done as in the rest of the tropics, by setting out a variety of foods on trays or on the ground. South Florida's birds can be attracted to trays providing a near endless list of options: water-soaked raisins, grapes, strawberries, pieces of orange, melon, banana, mango, jelly, vegetables, pieces of meat, bread, crackers, cooked pasta, pastries, nuts, sunflower seeds, millet, peanuts, greens, herbs, dog and cat food, mealworms (alive or freeze dried), earthworms, and more or less—whatever. Try some leftovers that were otherwise heading for the compost heap. Peanut butter can be presented in many clever ways. These offerings attract all the garden-feeding birds, but especially Red-bellied and Downy Woodpeckers, sapsuckers, wrens, cardinals, jays, blackbirds, grackles, doves, buntings, and sparrows.

Blue Jays readily find unshelled peanuts, here offered in a tray feeder made from a terra cotta flower pot saucer.

Experimentation is the key; see what works and be patient until the birds get used to the offerings.

So what about bird seed? Commercially available bird seed is not without a place in a South Florida bird garden. Seed feeders attract grackles, blackbirds, cowbirds, Red-bellied and Downy Woodpeckers, Mourning Doves, cardinals, parakeets, and parrots. And seed feeders can be used to attract focal species, such as Painted Buntings in winter. Feeders also attract aggressive crews of House Sparrows, European Starlings, and White-winged and Eurasian Collared-Doves. To avoid encouraging aggressive non-natives, seed feeding in South Florida should be restricted to fall through spring.

Much is written about feeding seeds to birds, most of it at the behest of seed-selling companies and stores. This advice is generally not applicable in South Florida, where seed is neither a winter lifeline nor a breeding season requisite. In South Florida, only two kinds of seeds are needed, black oil sunflower (*Helianthus annuus*) and white proso millet (*Panicum miliaceum*). Other kinds of seeds and mixes are available, in fact, more easily available. Bird seed has become a rather high-end business, and bird seed, especially seed mixes, have become irrationally priced. In South Florida, bird tastes do not run to the gourmet and no native species benefits from seed mixes. Black oil sunflower is available from garden and feed stores in large bags. As the best seed goes into oil production, that sold for bird seed tends to be of lesser quality, so this is a case where "premium" may be better than ordinary. Pure millet is less readily available and we have found it is best purchased online in 8-pound bags.

Black oil sunflower seed is the number one bird seed, period. Except for feeding buntings in winter, you could serve nothing else. Jim's son once did a third-grade science project addressing the well-thought-out hypothesis that birds with smaller bills would prefer smaller seeds. His findings: irrespective of bill size, all

Black oil sunflower seed is the number one bird seed for South Florida gardens, being eaten by more species than any other seed. If a gardener has one feeder and one seed to feed, this is it. This Northern Cardinal is at a tube feeder made of ¼-inch mesh, specifically for sunflower seeds.

Seed feeders are useful for targeting certain species, like Painted Buntings, and luring them to sites where they can be readily observed by the gardener. The cage around this tube feeder keeps large birds and squirrels from getting to the seed intended for small birds like buntings.

feeder birds preferred black oil sunflower seeds. As the name implies, these seeds have high oil content, providing energy, and also quality protein and other nutrients. There are other benefits as well: sunflower seeds do not easily succumb to South Florida's curse of dampness; their hard shell requires some degree of observable processing by most birds; they entertain squirrels; and portion management is easy. Hulled sunflower seed is also available and eaten by a great number of birds, but it is expensive and very rapidly consumed. Its use might best be confined to situations where a mess of empty shells is totally intolerable, such as a very small yard or apartment balcony. Larger striped sunflower seed is also available, but it not only costs more but can be eaten by fewer kinds of birds.

The second bird seed for South Florida is white proso millet, which appeals to smaller-billed birds, although larger birds will eat it too, including quail, doves, towhees, and blackbirds. White proso millet is *the* food for Painted Buntings in winter. Hulled white millet is not to be used in South Florida because it rapidly rots. Red millet is a smaller seed and adds nothing to what white millet can accomplish, other than attracting House Sparrows, which cherish it.

Two other seeds might on occasion be offered. Cracked corn can be used in gardens that are able to cater to quail, peafowl, chickens, or waterfowl, but it may also be eaten by jays, crows, doves, towhees, and sparrows. It can be served alone on the ground or in a ground feeder. Corn does not do well in mixes as it is generally the first thing rejected. In damp South Florida, corn feeding must be done with extreme caution, because when corn gets damp it can become toxic. Corn should be fed only in small amounts that will be eaten right away, preferably cracked; do not use finely ground corn because it will mold quickly.

Peanuts are another specialty food. Crumbled peanuts are readily eaten by a great many birds, especially jays and woodpeckers but also mockingbirds and some warblers, which otherwise seldom come to feeders. They are a great but expensive food in the quantities that will be consumed. Peanuts in the hull will be found by garden jays in a heartbeat, and maybe also by parrots, White Ibis, and certainly by squirrels.

What not to feed? Milo (*Sorghum bicolor*), a common constituent of seed mixes, is seldom eaten by South Florida birds except non-native doves. Rapeseed, small red millet, canary seed, and flax similarly are not much eaten by native species. Niger (Nyjer®, thistle, niger oil seed, *Guizotia abyssinica*), well appreciated by finches up north, is eaten by few birds other than Mourning Doves in South Florida. It is an expensive seed that will sit in an elevated tube feeder or special feeder more or less indefinitely. Safflower is often recommended as cardinal bait, but research shows that cardinals are equally fond of sunflower seeds, so why bother with safflower? Besides, it attracts sparrows and intrusive non-native Eurasian Collared-Doves, which will pass over piles of other seed to get to safflower seed.

Each type of seed should be served in its own dispenser. Seed mixes are a great temptation as they are readily available and attractively marketed, but here are the problems. They are discouragingly expensive, especially in small quantities. A mix will always contain seeds not used by one or more species, as well as poor quality seeds that birds don't eat. Jays toss out millet to get to sunflower seeds; buntings and blackbirds toss out sunflower seeds to get to millet; just about all native birds toss out the milo. When uneaten, seed gets fungus ridden, sprouts, and clogs the feeders. All this is a colossal waste of money and time. There is no value whatsoever in using mixed seed in a feeder.

Suet, rendered animal fat, has high energy content that is very useful to birds up north in winter. But in South Florida, even in winter, suet is often ignored by birds that are off eating insects and fruit. Red-bellied and Downy Woodpeckers,

A few species, like this Gray Catbird, come to suet feeders in South Florida, but these feeders are less popular with birds in South Florida than they are up north. If used, they need to be monitored as suet goes bad quickly.

Blue Jays, bluebirds, grackles, mockingbirds, catbirds, and a few warblers may be attracted to suet, but so are European Starlings. In South Florida even in winter, all but the most specialized suet can go rancid almost immediately. If you must, use only specialty heat-stabilized varieties and feed only in the cool of winter. If a suet block has no takers in a few days, throw it away. Smaller suet kibbles are now available, which may be more amenable to South Florida. Alternatively, peanut butter and peanut butter/cornmeal mix are generally better choices for South Florida's energy-seeking birds.

How about hummingbird or oriole feeders, which are usually expected as bird garden equipment? Sugar-water feeders tend not to work well in South Florida. Except in the extreme north of the area, there are no hummingbirds in summer in South Florida. Wintering and migrating Ruby-throated Hummingbirds have no lack of flowers that they much prefer over feeders. Wintering native orioles similarly tend not to frequent garden feeders while in South Florida, and the non-native resident species does not seem overly fond of them either. A big drawback of sugar-water feeders in South Florida is that they need an inordinate amount of cleaning because fungus, ants, and bees quickly take them over. In some gardens they do work out, and in this situation any small-capacity commercial or homemade design will do. Be sure any feeder is 8 ounces or less and emptied daily. New products are available that may increase the life of sugar water. And if a garden has hummingbirds that like feeders, several spread-out feeders are best. Once you start and have attracted a hummingbird into residence, you have some obligation to continue providing the feeder through the winter. The better approach to attracting hummingbirds is to provide hummingbird flowers. Moreover, hummingbirds do not eat nectar alone but depend as well on insects and spiders to be found among the plants in the rest of the garden; in spring they also eat pollen of live oak.

In South Florida, hummingbirds feed mostly at flowers in a garden. If a gardener is insistent on trying a hummingbird feeder, a small volume feeder that easily disassembles for cleaning is needed. This one is a good example. It holds only 8 ounces, is made of glass, and is designed to discourage bees and wasps. The best way to attract hummingbirds, however, remains the garden itself, with appropriate nectar-producing plants.

The ideal array of feeders in South Florida includes separate tube feeders for white millet and black oil sunflower seeds and tray feeders on the ground or in the air for both seed and other offerings. Feeders are best clumped together into a feeding station near (but not within) shrubs or other protective cover.

Other than hummingbird or suet feeders in some situations, the only two types of feeders needed in South Florida are the tray feeder and the tube feeder.

Tray feeders are simply flat surfaces on which food can be placed. Wood planks, trays, platforms, dishes, or saucers will do. We recommend the one commonly sold in stores having a screen bottom to keep the food from flooding in the rain and sides to keep it on the tray. Tray feeders should not have bird-impeding attached roofs or self-serving bins. Tray feeders can be hung, mounted, and placed on the ground. To accommodate arboreal birds, hang elevated feeders about 5 feet high on a tree, shepherd's hook, post, or wall. Tray feeders on the ground accommodate ground-feeding birds. As noted above, nearly any food can be placed in tray feeders, including seeds.

Tube feeders are cylinders that hold seeds. Sunflower seeds are served in tube feeders with ¼-inch mesh. Millet is served in tubes with openings, usually

Portion management is critical in South Florida. The high humidity and high rainfall cause seed to rot quickly or sprout. Feeders should be filled with no more than a stadium cup's worth of seed.

with perches. Glass or heavy plastic should be used because metal rusts in South Florida and thin plastic can be gnawed through by squirrels. Surrounding a small seed tube feeder with 1½–2-inch wire mesh (making it a "cage feeder") allows small birds to enter while discouraging squirrels and also larger birds. A tube feeder must be sheltered from rain with an intrinsic roof or by hanging under cover, otherwise the seed gets wet and sprouts or rots. In addition, feeders should be chosen that have no impediments to seed movement or cleaning brushes. In South Florida, tube feeders need to be small, holding no more than a day's supply of food, so as to prevent spoilage.

For both tray and tube feeders, portion management is essential in South Florida. Providing only a day's supply of food avoids a long list of issues that otherwise plague South Florida's gardeners, including time management, maintenance effort, seed wastage, expense, disease transmission, feeding rats at night, and non-native bird control. Large tube or hamper feeders are tempting because they offer large storage capacity, less frequent filling, sophisticated design, and clever squirrel baffling innovations. But uneaten seed rots or sprouts, requiring maintenance. Small and simple, no more than about a stadium cupful (four measuring cups) of seed, is best. This is an important point for bird gardeners in South Florida: feed only a day's worth of food.

When to feed? Feeding schedule should be determined by the gardener's schedule; after all, in South Florida bird feeders are primarily for the gardener's entertainment, not the birds' needs. Feeding need not occur every day, as birds are sometimes best left to their own devices. They will accommodate.

→ Birds and Windows

Windows kill birds. Scientifically derived calculations show that more than 300 million birds, and perhaps as many as one billion, are killed per year in the United States by collisions with building glass. More than 300 bird species have been documented among this carnage; few are immune.

Much of the kill is at high-rise buildings and towers kept lighted at night, This is usually unnecessary since principles for operating lights in bird-safe ways are available, as are design options for bird-safe buildings. These can reduce losses while saving energy costs. Those interested in conserving birds should take every opportunity to influence the management of structural lighting.

House windows also kill birds. In a home garden, the first line of defense against window mortality is in the design of the garden. It is crucial to appropriately place feeders, water features, and butterfly gardens so that birds don't die using them. The best places are either very near the house (within 3 feet) so that birds grow accustomed to the walls and windows being there, or very far from it (more than 30 feet) so that birds can leave the feature without encountering them.

In any house, some windows are worse than others, and they may be particularly dangerous at certain times, such as when migrant birds unfamiliar with the garden's configuration are moving around. Look for evidence of impact, such as dead birds or feathered smudges, to determine which windows need attention.

To birds, windows appear to be something to fly through, especially when they reflect nearby vegetation. The solution is to reduce reflections by making the windows more visible. There are several ways to do this. Unfortunately, the commonly used silhouettes of raptors and such applied to windows do not cover enough of the reflecting surface to be effective. Innovative stickers are somewhat transparent to the viewer but visible to the birds. This helps keep a window a window, but unless the glass is well covered, they do not work well. Drawing light-colored curtains and blinds during the day reduces reflection. Taping windows makes them noticeable. Quarter-inch strips of tape can be applied 4 inches apart vertically or 2 inches apart horizontally. Netting, bug screen, or fabric placed several inches outward from the glass is more visible than the window and bounces the birds back before the glass does. Perhaps the most unobtrusive and entertaining approach is to simply hang old CDs and DVDs from monofilament line in front of the window.

Reflections on windows and glass doors can appear to be extensions of the garden, confusing birds who may try to fly through. Precautions should be taken to prevent bird injury or death from such hazards.

Hanging old CDs or DVDs in front of reflecting windows can significantly reduce incidents of bird impact. This particular window was hit by birds five or six times a day after a water feature was installed nearby. After the DVDs were hung, bird strikes stopped.

Where to feed? Feeders should be installed where both birds and the gardener can access them. For the gardener, they should be where they can be conveniently observed and easily serviced. For the birds, they should be away from windows and adjacent to thick shrubs, close enough so birds can come and go safely, but not so close as to allow cats to pounce from the plants. Clumping feeders (other than multiple hummingbird feeders) in one location is preferable to scattering them for ease of observation and management as well as for birds' convenience.

Here is a list of birds attracted to feeders, or, in the case of predatory birds, to the birds at the feeders.

BIRDS

Blue Jay	Northern Cardinal
Boat-tailed Grackle	Painted Bunting
Common Grackle	Red-bellied Woodpecker
Cooper's Hawk	Red-winged Blackbird
Eurasian Collared-Dove	Ruby-throated Hummingbird
European Starling	Sharp-shinned Hawk
House Sparrow	Short-tailed Hawk
Mourning Dove	White-winged Dove

The Predators

In a fully functional garden designed and managed for birds, it will not be long before predation becomes a way of life. Although most bird gardeners should not object to the natural predation of birds on their insects, many do object to natural predation on the birds themselves. Snakes, raccoons, jays, grackles, crows, and hawks are among the natural bird predators attracted to bird gardens. Sharp-shinned, Cooper's, and Short-tailed Hawks, Merlins, and Peregrines are specialized bird eaters. Most come into the garden following the migrations of their prey. A few, such as Cooper's and Short-tailed Hawks, have increased in recent years in suburban South Florida, tracking the increase in non-native doves. Some bird attracting gardeners may feel the need to stop the backyard edition of predators at work—but really, there is no reason to discourage or not to appreciate a native predator operating in your garden; it is a sign of bird gardening success.

Non-native predators are a different matter. Birds have no natural defenses against these predators, which kill native birds in astounding numbers each year. There is, in fact, one non-native predator that cannot be allowed in a garden designed for birds—birds' primary domestic predator, the outdoor cat. Whether feral cats living wild, ownerless cats in cared-for colonies, a neighbor's cat, or the

Successful bird gardens will also attract bird predators. Cooper's Hawks have increased in South Florida because of their taste for non-native doves.

gardener's own cat allowed outdoors, it matters not; cats outdoors kill birds and must be banned from a garden attracting birds.

A recent study shows that free-ranging domestic cats kill 1.4–3.7 billion birds per year in the United States. That's *billion*. Cats are also responsible for killing billions of other garden animals such as lizards, frogs, and small mammals. That too is *billions*. A bird garden's goal is to help birds, not to provide living meals for a cat.

A neighbor's cat killed these two birds, a Rose-breasted Grosbeak and a Northern Waterthrush, birds that we had not even previously recorded in the garden. No cat can ever be allowed unleashed in a bird garden at any time, even for short periods.

It seems unreasonable for someone else's cat to deprive a gardener of the opportunity to use his or her garden to help native birds. Cats kill birds, period; it is what they do. Declawing or neck bells do not stop bird killing. Spaying and vaccinating do not stop bird killing. Being charmed by dead birds presented at the doorstep does not stop bird killing. The only thing that does is keeping all cats indoors or on a leash. So many times one hears the excuse that a cat just insists on being outdoors, and so the owner lets it out; in so doing, he or she inflicts a bird killer on the neighborhood. Although well intentioned, spay/neuter/release programs do nothing more than maintain an army of bird killers in the urban and suburban environments, indefinitely. Such programs are cruel, inhumane, irresponsible, and antienvironmental.

Butterfly/Hummingbird Gardens

Butterfly gardens are patches of plants that provide nectar to adults or leaves to their caterpillars. Some nectar plants also attract wintering Ruby-throated Hummingbirds, especially plants with large tube-shaped red or orange flowers offering nectar at the base of the flower, on plants standing at least 2 feet high and blooming from fall through spring. To have blooms through such an extended period, a gardener must choose nectar-producing plants that bloom successively. Nectar flowers also attract honey bees, bumble bees, ants, flies, and beetles, which in turn attract birds.

Butterfly gardens should also provide larval host plants, which can be selected to attract specific butterflies to lay eggs. Milkweeds attract monarchs; passionflower vines attract zebra longwings; citruses attract swallowtails. Caterpillars attract birds since they are among the most important prey for insectivorous birds, especially those feeding young.

Clustering of plants meant to attract butterflies and hummingbirds is helpful to their being discovered and used. Such patches of butterfly-attracting plants should be thoughtfully designed with small trees or shrubs in the back and tiers of short-statured plants in front, arranged for optimal visibility. Seagrape, orchid trees, Geigertree, pigeon plum, Florida Keys blackbead, firebush, and sensitive plants (senna) are good backdrops. Appropriate mid-tier shrubs are Bahama swampbush, shrimp plant, Chinese hat plant, and hibiscus. Short-statured plants include milkweed, non-native porterweed, pentas, tickseeds, and standingcypress. Plants should be chosen that bloom at different times, so as to provide continuous food supplies for nectar-feeding insects. Some hummingbird plants should also be spread throughout the garden since Ruby-throated Hummingbirds "trapline" their way through the day, moving from plant to plant. As caterpillars may completely defoliate plants, host plants should be placed in back of nectar plants.

Often in gardens other arrangements are made to encourage butterfly visits. Butterflies are attracted to damp mud and very shallow water, which can be

Above: Many butterfly plants are also used by hummingbirds, like the Chinese hat plant in which this Ruby-throated Hummingbird rests.

Left: In addition to supplying nectar plants for adults, butterfly gardens need to include larval host plants to support caterpillars. A zebra longwing is shown here laying eggs on a corkystem passionflower. Already on the plant are tiny yellow eggs and small caterpillars.

Apparently extirpated from South Florida for a time, atala populations have recovered and are one of the treats that might be found in a South Florida butterfly garden.

designed as part of a water feature. Butterflies can be attracted to rotting fruit, although in South Florida it seems few species are.

Butterfly watching is as interesting as bird watching, so not only are these insects well known, but guides also provide identification and clubs look after their welfare. Some native species are highly endangered; a few have been extirpated. Below is a list of butterfly/hummingbird plants that are nearly essential in a South Florida bird garden, and a list of some butterflies that might be expected.

PLANTS

Bahama Swampbush	Hong Kong Orchid Tree
Beggarticks (Spanish Needles)	Milkweeds
Bougainvillea	Necklacepod
Cape Honeysuckle	Passionflowers
Coralbean	Porterweeds
Coral Honeysuckle	Salvia sages
Firebush	Standingcypress
Firecracker Plant	Turk's Cap

BUTTERFLIES AND MOTHS

American Snout (*Libytheana carinenta*)	Carolina Satyr (*Hermeuptychia sosybius*)
Atala (*Eumaeus atala*)	Cassius Blue (*Leptotes cassius*)
Bartram's Scrub-Hairstreak (*Strymon acis*)	Cattail Borer (*Bellura obliqua*)
Black Swallowtail (*Papilio polyxenes*)	Cattail Caterpillar Moth (*Simyra insularis*)
Byssus Skipper (*Problema byssus*)	Ceraunus Blue (*Hemiargus ceraunus*)
Cabbage White (*Pieris rapae*)	Checkered White (*Pontia protodice*)

Clouded Skipper (*Lerema accius*)
Common Buckeye (*Junonia coenia*)
Common Checkered-Skipper (*Pyrgus communis*)
Cutworms (*Agrotis, Nephelodes*)
Dainty Sulphur (*Nathalis iole*)
Dina Yellow (*Eurema dina*)
Dingy Purplewing (*Eunica monima*)
Dorantes Longtail (*Urbanus dorantes*)
Eastern Tiger Swallowtail (*Papilio glaucus*)
Eufala Skipper (*Lerodea eufala*)
Fall Armyworm (*Spodoptera frugiperda*)
Fiery Skipper (*Hylephila phyleus*)
Florida Duskywing (*Ephyriades brunneus*)
Florida Leafwing (*Anaea floridalis*)
Florida White (*Appias drusilla*)
Fulvous Hairstreak (*Electrostrymon angelia*)
Geometer Moth (*Epimecis detexta*)
Giant Swallowtail (*Papilio cresphontes*)
Grass Loopers (*Mocis*)
Gray Hairstreak (*Strymon melinus*)
Great Southern White (*Ascia monuste*)
Gulf Fritillary (*Agraulis vanillae*)
Hackberry Emperor (*Asterocampa celtis*)
Hammock Skipper (*Polygonus leo*)
Henry's Marsh Moth (*Simyra henrici*)
Horace's Duskywing (*Erynnis horatius*)
Hydrangea Sphinx Moth (*Darapsa versicolor*)
Io Moth (*Automeris io*)
Julia Heliconian (*Dryas julia*)
Large Orange Sulphur (*Phoebis agarithe*)
Little Metalmark (*Calephelis virginiensis*)
Lyside Sulphur (*Kricogonia lyside*)
Malachite (*Siproeta stelenes*)
Mallow Scrub-Hairstreak (*Strymon istapa*)
Mangrove Buckeye (*Junonia evarete*)
Mangrove Skipper (*Phocides pigmalion*)
Martial Scrub-Hairstreak (*Strymon martialis*)
Mimosa Yellow (*Eurema nise*)
Monarch (*Danaus plexippus*)
Monk Skipper (*Asbolis capucinus*)

Oak Moths (*Phoberia*)
Obscure Skipper (*Panoquina panoquinoides*)
Painted Lady (*Vanessa cardui*)
Palamedes Swallowtail (*Papilio palamedes*)
Palmetto Skipper (*Euphyes arpa*)
Phaon Crescent (*Phyciodes phaon*)
Pine Webworms (*Tetralopha*)
Pluto Sphinx Moth (*Xylophanes pluto*)
Polyphemus Moth (*Antheraea polyphemus*)
Pyralid Moth (*Dicymolomia julianalis*)
Queen (*Danaus gilippus*)
Red-banded Hairstreak (*Calycopis cecrops*)
Ruddy Daggerwing (*Marpesia petreus*)
Salt Marsh Skipper (*Panoquina panoquin*)
Schaus' Swallowtail (*Papilio aristodemus*)
Seagrape Borer (*Hexeris enhydris*)
Shy Cosmet Moth (*Limnaecia phragmitella*)
Slash Pine Seedworm Moth (*Cydia anaranjada*)
Sleepy Orange (*Eurema nicippe*)
Snout Moths (*Pococera*)
Southern Broken-Dash (*Wallengrenia otho*)
Southern Pine Coneworm (*Dioryctria amatella*)
Spicebush Swallowtail (*Papilio troilus*)
Statira Sulphur (*Phoebis statira*)
Swarthy Skipper (*Nastra lherminier*)
Tantalus Sphinx Moth (*Aellopos tantalus*)
Tawny Emperor (*Asterocampa clyton*)
Tent Caterpillars (*Malacosoma*)
Three-spotted Skipper (*Cymaenes tripunctus*)
Tropical Checkered-Skipper (*Pyrgus oileus*)
Tropical Sod Webworm (*Herpetogramma phaeopteralis*)
White-marked Tussock Moth (*Orgyia leucostigma*)
Twin-spot Skipper (*Oligoria maculata*)
Viceroy (*Limenitis archippus*)
Whirlabout (*Polites vibex*)
White M Hairstreak (*Parrhasius m-album*)
White Peacock (*Anartia jatrophae*)
Zebra Longwing (*Heliconius charithonia*)

Vegetable and Herb Gardens

Like butterfly/hummingbird gardens, vegetable and herb gardens are also excellent bird garden elements. If not poisoned by insecticides, vegetable and herb plants harbor a significant crop of insects that in turn attract birds. The herb and vegetable gardening season in South Florida is the opposite of that up north, late fall to early spring, so vegetable garden insects are most available to birds during their migration and winter seasons. The hot, rainy, and buggy summer is not good for most vegetable or herb gardening in South Florida, although some tropical vegetable plants do last into the summer.

Common insect-supplying herbs that can be grown in South Florida include basil, sage, mint, oregano, sweet fennel, parsley, chives, and cilantro. Bird-friendly vegetable and fruit plants for winter gardening in South Florida include tomatoes, broccoli, green onions, sweet and hot peppers, strawberries, squash, and beans. South Florida gardens also can have tropical plants such as pigeon pea, chayote, malanga, boniato, banana, pineapple, and papaya.

So what about competition with birds? Mostly the birds will be eating insects, but they also do eat the produce. Hot peppers, for example, are especially attractive to birds. The original hot pepper, now called the bird pepper, is adapted to

Vegetable gardens can be a great source of caterpillars, like this tomato hornworm, a favored bird food.

Attracting Birds to South Florida Gardens

be eaten and dispersed by birds and is also apparently native to South Florida. A good bird gardener should be willing to share garden produce. The best strategy is to plant more than is needed and share the fruit and vegetables with the birds. Gardeners can also set out some of these plants just for the birds, to keep them busy. Precious fruit and vegetables can be bagged before ripe. Bird netting, scary shiny things, and motion-detecting sprinklers can be tried. Stringing webs and strings of monofilament fishing line above the garden usually works well for larger birds. But for the most part sharing insects and produce is best.

Needless to remind that garden pesticides are antithetical to birds, including chemical pesticides but also those biological pesticides that are nonspecific, such as Bt (*Bacillus thuringiensis*).

Sometimes an infestation does get to be too much even for the long suffering bird gardener. Generally though, careful monitoring, picking big bugs by hand, spraying leaves with oil, detergent or pepper/nicotine concoctions, planting bug-repelling companion plants, introducing predatory insects, and interspersing and rotating crop species remain the best approaches.

This is a list of bird-friendly plants to consider for vegetable gardens, for either their fruit or their insects.

VEGETABLE AND HERB GARDEN PLANTS

Basil	Sweet Fennel
Beans	Papaya
Bird Pepper and other hot peppers	Parsley
Coriander	Squash
Dill	Tomato

Wildlife Gardens

A good bird garden will also attract animals other than birds, and indeed, the garden should be designed to encourage them. It may be best to think of a bird garden as a wildlife garden.

As insects are the main bird food supplied by plants, attracting these is rather critical to the success of a bird garden. In addition to butterflies and moths, pollinating insects attracted to flowers include bumble bees, carpenter bees, the nonnative honey bees, sweat bees, wasps, beetles, bugs, and flies. Pollinator insects are a conservation issue unto themselves as various populations appear to be in decline. Most insects caught by birds are those feeding on the plants themselves or flying between them.

Water features also attract insects. Dragonflies will find a pond; if it has a detritus layer on the bottom they may breed there, providing birds with their larvae. Darners (*Coryphaeschna*), pennants (*Celithemis, Brachymesia*), and dragonets (*Erythrodiplax*) are the most likely dragonflies to show up. Other aquatic

Pollinating insects are a food source for birds. Here a nectar- and pollen-producing flower of beggarticks, better known locally as Spanish needles, entices a honey bee.

invertebrates readily finding water features include wolf spiders (Lycosidae), water striders (*Gerris*), dark fishing spiders (*Dolomedes tenebrosus*), whirligig beetles (*Dineutus*), predaceous diving beetles (Dytiscidae), giant water bugs (*Lethocerus americanus*), and water stick-insects (*Ranatra*).

Spiders are among the more important garden invertebrates for birds and make up a large portion of the diet of birds. Spiders should be encouraged. Birds eat mostly small spiders and their eggs, but some very sensational web-making gardener-assisting spiders frequent South Florida gardens, including the golden silk orbweaver or banana spider (*Nephila clavipes*), garden spiders (*Argiope argentata* and *Argiope aurantia*), and crab spider (*Gasteracantha cancriformis*). It is quite important to resist the urge to break up webs that are in use. Regal jumping

Above: Nature-emulating water features can attract insects and spiders. This female dark fishing spider guards her nursery web in garden plantings next to a water feature.

Right: The presence of spiders in a yard is a sign that the gardener has achieved a healthy insect population. Golden silk orbweavers (also called banana spiders) are one of the more impressive South Florida spiders, providing a substantial meal for their bird predators. Here a female orbweaver is eating a captured dragonfly.

Green treefrogs are one of the native amphibians that might show up at a water feature in a South Florida bird-friendly yard.

spider (*Phidippus regius*) and other ground spiders also occur. Of the spiders of human safety concern, only widow spiders (*Latrodectus*) range into South Florida, being found mostly under rocks and debris.

Snails and slugs are common garden residents, and important bird food, providing both energy and calcium. Both native and non-native species occur, sometimes abundantly. The most remarkable of South Florida's snails are the native tree snails (*Liguus* and *Orthalicus*), which are becoming ever rarer. They will seldom appear in yards, but if they do, they can do well in dense mixed-tree garden settings with native smooth-barked trees, especially wild tamarind. Two smaller striped tree snails are the lined tree snail (*Drymaeus multilineatus*) and the master treesnail (*Drymaeus dominicus*). Some snails are themselves predaceous, such as the rosy wolf snail (*Euglandina rosea*) and *Haplotrema* species.

Unlike most native snails, many slugs and non-native snails can do considerable damage to gardens by eating plants the gardener would prefer to keep. The non-native Cuban brown snail (*Zachrysia provisoria*), 1–1¼ inches wide, is a significant garden pest, as can be the giant African land snail (*Lissachatina fulica*). Slugs are also damaging. The native Florida leatherleaf (*Leidyula floridana*) and the marsh slug (*Deroceras laeve*) and the non-native Caribbean leatherleaf (*Sarasinula plebeia*) can damage plants. Unwanted snails and slugs are controlled mostly by hand picking and trapping, which can become a continuous process.

Amphibians are much to be desired in a garden. A water feature may attract frogs on its own, or they may be actively reintroduced by the gardener. Desirable frogs include the native green treefrog (*Hyla cinerea*), squirrel treefrog (*Hyla squirella*), southern leopard frog (*Lithobates sphenocephalus*), pig frog (*Lithobates grylio*), oak toad (*Anaxyrus quercicus*), and southern toad (*Anaxyrus terrestris*). The non-native Cuban tree frog (*Osteopilus septentrionalis*) and cane toad (*Rhinella marina*) both eat native frogs and small animals; the cane toad can be dangerous to dogs that bite it. Neither should be welcomed in a South Florida garden. The gardener can attempt to accommodate native frogs in water features and native toads by creating shelter under rocks, lumber, or overturned pots.

The North American racer is a common garden snake in South Florida but well aware of human presence and quick to freeze or flee in order to avoid detection.

Throughout South Florida, native snakes have been suffering population declines for decades and deserve conservation efforts. Red cornsnake (*Pantherophis guttatus*), North American racer (locally called black racer) (*Coluber constrictor*), ring-necked snake (*Diadophis punctatus*), and common garter snake (*Thamnophis sirtalis*) are the snakes most commonly seen in South Florida gardens; all are nonvenomous. Rock and wood piles added to mixed-tree stands provide shelter for snakes.

The green anole (*Anolis carolinensis*) and reef gecko (*Sphaerodactylus notatus*) are small native lizards to be encouraged. The more commonly noticed lizards are non-native anoles, mostly brown anole (*Anolis sagrei*) and in some areas crested anole (*Anolis cristatellus*). The large and sensational knight anole (*Anolis equestris*) is unwelcome in bird gardens as it eats birds as well as frogs and other lizards. The non-native green iguana (*Iguana iguana*) is increasing in South Florida and is destructive in gardens, eating plants and flowers. Spiny-tailed iguanas (*Ctenosaura*) in their native lands eat both plants and animals, including birds and their eggs. Non-native lizards are not protected by law and can be captured and disposed of, humanely of course.

Gopher tortoise (*Gopherus polyphemus*) and Florida box turtle (*Terrapene baurii*) are South Florida's native terrestrial turtles. The first is protected; for a gardener attempting to re-create sand scrub habitat, having one show up is a sign of success. South Florida's distinctive box turtle is increasingly scarce and welcome to a bird garden.

Native water turtles may be added to a water feature, although the two native sliders, Florida red-bellied cooter (*Pseudemys nelsoni*) and Coastal Plain cooter (*Pseudemys cocinna floridana*), will eat aquatic plants. Native striped mud (*Kinosternon baurii*) and eastern musk turtles (*Sternotherus odoratus*) are more pond friendly. A big pond with some fish to sacrifice might support chicken (*Deirochelys reticularia*), Florida softshell (*Apalone ferox*), or snapping turtles

Native green anoles are likely to be present in diversely planted bird gardens.

(*Chelydra serpentina*). The non-native pond slider (*Trachemys scripta*) should not be used because it is an escape artist.

One mammal that will certainly be attracted to a bird garden is the eastern gray squirrel (*Sciurus carolinensis*). For some reason, squirrels seem to annoy most backyard birders (see "The Squirrel Conundrum" for further discussion). The eastern gray squirrel is the most common, although fox squirrels (*Sciurus niger*) might come to rural gardens in western South Florida. The Big Cypress fox squirrel (*Sciurus niger avicennia*) is of great conservation concern.

Virginia opossums (*Didelphis virginiana*) and northern raccoons (*Procyon lotor*) have acclimated well to South Florida suburban life and will likely frequent a bird garden, whether the gardener knows it or not. Both are nocturnal and sleep during the day high in garden trees, in epiphyte patches, or in large bird boxes, which in fact might be put out expressly for them. Black rats (*Rattus rattus*) and

A Florida box turtle would be a welcome visitor to a naturalistic South Florida yard.

→ The Squirrel Conundrum

Foiling squirrels can become an obsession for a bird-feeder devotee. The annoyance comes mainly, it seems, from the anxiety of watching expensive bird food being eaten by a mammal, in great quantity, in broad daylight, and boldly with little deference to the provider's intentions. For decades, creative thinkers have been designing bird feeders to thwart squirrels, mostly to little avail. We have purchased spring-loaded and motorized contraptions, baffles and barriers, posts and hangers—some memorable mostly for entertainment value, none for their effectiveness. Most now feature movable cages designed so that the squirrel's weight cuts off the seed. Some come with guarantees of squirrel-proofing success.

There are only a few serious ways to restrain squirrels. The first thing to try, if space is sufficient, is to place feeders well away from trees or other launching sites and fit poles with moving baffles beneath the feeder. A problem with this is that the feeder's exposure discourages birds. A second effective approach is to place a tube of welded wire mesh around the feeder with a mesh size (1½ inches) sufficient to keep a squirrel from crawling in while making the gap between mesh and feeder too big for a squirrel to reach in. The problem is that such a feeder also obstructs squirrel-sized birds. A third approach is to make the seed unappealing. Peppers evolved to attract birds, since the seeds pass whole through their digestive tract on their way to germination, and to deter mammals that chew the seeds. Make the deterrent by adding crushed, ground hot pepper pods or hot pepper spray to the bird seed. Of course, as do humans, there seems little reason a determined squirrel would not eventually adapt to capsaicin. A fourth approach is to take advantage of the state's hunting season.

But is this really necessary? Why not feed squirrels too? We advocate not only living with squirrels

but also loving them. Feed them somewhere other than near the bird feeder, providing peanuts, corn, and sunflowers seeds on their own tray feeder. Jays and grackles will partake as well. Squirrels are entertainingly territorial, so eventually a normal-sized garden would likely have only a family or two to feed, although if the residents are moved, a dozen or more may be living nearby and ready to move in.

The main squirrel problem for the South Florida gardener shouldn't be the bird seed they steal. It is more likely to be a squirrel's predilection for garden fruits and vegetables. Just before the point of picking, squirrels start gnawing holes in mangos, avocados, bananas, and coconuts, and with some plants they are so inspired that they eat unripe fruit, stripping a tree quickly, or they beat the gardener to fruit after it falls to the ground. Bagging individual fruits on the tree sometimes works, although devoted squirrels can eat through most bags. It may be best for the gardener to pick fruit before the squirrels get to it and to be good enough at growing fruit to produce more than both they and the squirrels can eat.

Eastern gray squirrels seem to enjoy so called squirrel-resistant bird feeders such as this tube feeder of black oil sunflower seeds.

house mice (*Mus musculus*) unfortunately have also accommodated to gardens and homes and are prepared to eat fruit and bird food at night. If a gardener would rather not have their attention, it is important not to put out more bird food than will be eaten in a day.

In the northern and western parts of South Florida, the nine-banded armadillo (*Dasypus novemcinctus*) is common in gardens and can cause distress with its digging. Accommodation is about the only solution. Eastern cottontail (*Sylvilagus floridanus*) and marsh rabbits (*Sylvilagus palustris*) occur in rural areas, and the latter along the coasts. They too might want to share the garden, and some of its foliage. They are discouraged from vegetable gardens by fencing. Eastern spotted skunks (*Spilogale putorius*), common gray foxes (*Urocyon cinereoargenteus*) and coyotes (*Canis latrans*) frequent gardens. Unknown to most residents, coyotes are becoming quite common in residential areas throughout South Florida.

Unlike farther north where they are intensely disliked by gardeners, white-tailed deer (*Odocoileus virginianus*) are seldom garden animals in most of South Florida. Deer do occur in western South Florida, although populations have declined in recent years coincident with increasing numbers of Florida panthers (*Puma concolor coryi*). Where deer occur in gardens, they are likely annoying, and so the usual well-known procedures can be followed, such as deer-unfriendly plants, fencing, yard dogs, scent applications and, in season, venison. Many bird gardeners welcome deer although hardening their garden against them.

One area where deer are persistent backyard animals is in the Lower Florida Keys, especially Big Pine Key and No Name Key. The Key deer (*Odocoileus virginianus clavium*) is an endangered subspecies endemic to the Keys. Once on the verge of extinction, the population has rebounded under protection. Although much of these islands has been set aside in a complex of national wildlife refuges, the government does not own all the land, and new home sites continue to take contiguous habitat away from the deer. Key deer are very comfortable in this home-occupied habitat, munching garden shrubs, herbs, grasses, and handouts, and seeking domestic sources of freshwater. It is unwise (and in fact illegal)

Left: Raccoons are active in the garden at night, spending the day resting high in a garden's trees.

Right: Marsh rabbits may occur in rural yards or those adjacent to parks or other conservation areas, especially near the coast.

Left: Key deer are common yard animals on Big Pine Key and No Name Key where homes are interspersed within their natural pineland habitat.

Right: Gardeners within the Key deer's range need to protect plants that deer are fond of eating.

to provide artificial food or water, since this increases their domestication, encourages high densities in backyards, and exposes them to traffic, their largest source of mortality. Given their protected status, Key deer can be a challenge for a Lower Keys bird gardener since they consider any garden their own produce stand. The Lower Keys bird gardener soon learns what plants deer do not like. Those they do like can be protected with barriers. Bird feeders and water features need to be where deer cannot access them. The more usual deer deterrents, such as fencing, exacerbate landscape fragmentation by keeping deer from their natural habitat and water sources. Fences are regulated by the county and also by guidelines of the Federal Key Deer Habitat Conservation Plan, which need to be followed.

Several species of bats may be attracted to a South Florida bird garden. Species occurring in South Florida, except in the Keys, include the evening bat (*Nycticeius humeralis*), northern yellow bat (*Lasiurus intermedius*), Seminole bat (*Lasiurus seminolus*), and Brazilian free-tailed bat (*Tadarida brasiliensis*). Less common are the Florida bonneted bat (*Eumops floridanus*), big brown bat (*Eptesicus fuscus*), Rafinesque's big-eared bat (*Corynorhinus rafinesquii*) and eastern pipistrelle (*Perimyotis subflavus*) (also known as tricolored bat and *Pipistrellus subflavus*). The velvety free-tailed bat (*Molossus molossus*) is found only in the Keys in Florida and is the only bat native to the Keys. A few other tropical species have been observed rarely. South Florida lacks caves, and its bats roost mostly in dead palm fronds, cavities in dead trees, Spanish moss, or niches in buildings. Seminole bats use pine trees; Brazilian free-tailed bats use breaks in barrel tiles. The way to encourage their presence is to enhance these features, leaving fronds on palm trees and unfilled gaps and niches in buildings. Bat houses too can be tried, but they have not often been successful in South Florida.

4

The Garden for Birds

While almost any garden will attract birds, some are better than others. Gardens successful at attracting birds can stretch for acres or consist of a container plant and bird feeder on the balcony. Most South Florida home yards are modestly sized, and given other needs for the space, the part that can be devoted to plants and birds is even smaller. The more yard there is, the larger, more diverse, and more beneficial it can be, but no space is too small to be useful to birds, and the space available in a normal-sized South Florida yard will do just fine.

Advice on garden design and maintenance is readily available in lots of books and pamphlets, online, and from the neighbors, both in general and for South Florida in particular. There is no need to repeat that information in this book, but there is some value in considering how garden design and management can enhance a garden's attractiveness to birds.

First, it is useful to reset thinking, because in some ways gardening for birds turns normal gardening on its head. Let's pretend that a lucky gardener has just acquired five acres that include a nice patch of native hammock, a block of pinelands with slash pine and palmetto, a solution-hole pond, and an adjacent bit of marsh. Intending to build a home and a garden that will attract birds, would the gardener scrape off the land and then bring in plants? Or might the gardener keep most of the existing plants where they are and fit the living accommodations among them?

This hypothetical scenario illustrates a different way to think about a yard. Normally, the house and living accommodations are situated first, leaving the scraps to be used as a garden. The alternative approach is to consider the yard mostly for birds and other wildlife, with the people-living portions being carefully carved out of what is left. This point of view (even if a little extreme) can inform any home garden setting, even if one is starting with an oversized house on an undersized lot mostly covered with concrete. Figure out how a yard can best be turned into a productive garden and how the human footprint can be reduced to what is really needed.

What Kind of a Garden for Birds?

To attract birds, the more natural the better, so one of the first decisions made by a gardener is, how wild to go? How acceptable to the gardener, spouse, teenage children, neighbors, or the homeowners association is a naturalistic garden made up mostly of native species? The wildness, nativeness, and (to the unconvinced eye) somewhat disheveled look of mixed plantings and nondescript native species might annoy someone comforted by manicured shrubs, endless lawns, and stand-alone specimen trees. The devoted Italianate gardener would have a hard time reconciling with bird gardening, and the birds would have a hard time trying to make a living in such a groomed garden.

Most bird gardeners will land somewhere in the middle between naturalistic and manicured. That's fine; every bird-friendly addition to a garden is of value and not every bit of a yard needs to be dedicated to birds.

It is likely that a bird garden designed to be more naturalistic will look somewhat different from neighboring yards. The neighbors' response may be enthusiasm, curiosity, support, obliviousness, or contempt. A curious neighbor is an opportunity to proselytize bird-attracting gardening. On the contempt end,

The more perfectly manicured a yard, the less bird friendly it is. Gardeners need to decide how naturalistic a garden they can be happy with.

annoyance may elevate to complaints to the homeowners association or even to civic authorities. The law is on the gardener's side, because a Florida state statute (373.185) prohibits homeowner associations and local governments from banning Florida-friendly landscaping, such as that which conserves water, minimizes fertilizer, and consists of noninvasive plants. So proceed in good conscience, but respectfully. It is better to win neighbors and associations over to your way of thinking than to annoy them.

A naturalistic bird gardener needs to decide just how far to go toward emulating natural habitat. For some, converting portions of the yard into hammock holds minimal aesthetic appeal. For others it is the ultimate conservation statement, given how special South Florida's native plant habitats are and how threatened they have become. While full habitat restoration is more or less impossible, the closer a garden or patch of garden comes to emulating natural habitat, the greater the diversity of native plants used, and the more naturalistically the planting areas are configured, the greater will be its attractiveness to birds.

Non-native plants are not inherently unwelcome in a garden built for birds. Non-native plants offer novelty, interest, historical context, intriguing flowers, aesthetic contributions, structure, and perhaps bird-friendly fruit, nectar, and insects. Fruit trees, tropical flowering trees, or the traditional pantropical flora might be desired by a gardener, and some of the more sensational-looking tropical plants certainly are non-natives. South Florida bird gardens tend to end up a mix of native and non-native plants, the balance being a decision for the individual gardener. The best approach for birds is to use native plants as the garden's design core and non-native plants as aesthetic and practical enhancements.

Garden Design Considerations

How to go about attracting birds depends on the space available and the intensity of competition for its use. In any garden, from the multi-acre estate to a collection of containers on the patio, enhancing diversity, structural complexity, and food-bearing plants will benefit birds. Achieving these goals takes forethought.

Sometimes the space is literally a blank slate, a vacant lot prior to construction or a yard scraped clear as part of a rebuilding project. This enviable situation provides maximum flexibility in design and most opportunity for a garden-first approach. More often, buildings, driveways, swimming pools, patios, and other family uses are inalterably in place, and existing plants may need to be incorporated into the new design. Constraints are not necessarily bad, as they provide boundaries to ambition.

Design begins with articulating clearly all the uses a plot needs to deliver to the gardener by identifying what is needed for the garden, lawn, buildings, driveway, and patio. Then examine the present situation, decide what has to stay and what might go, and then lay out the areas for each use.

Within the garden, it is best to decide first where the lawn goes. Bird gardens

Garden design for birds incorporates naturalistic, ecological, and diverse plantings. Naturalistic plantings can be arranged in organized and aesthetically pleasing ways to benefit both human and avian residents. In this example, the driveway has been planted with lawn, surrounded by trees, palms, shrubs, and short-statured plants.

restrict lawn while maximizing other plantings. Determine the minimum lawn needed for family activity areas, walking paths, and desired vistas. For birds, lawn should be gathered into small noncontiguous patches rather than growing in large expanses. Once lawn has been delegated, all space not occupied by lawn or by preexisting artifacts should be considered available for bird-friendly planting.

The type, size, and location of water features are decisions to be made early in the design process as they are rather permanent and can serve as garden focal points. Ideally, water features should be as large as the garden and gardener will allow. Generally they are best placed at the end of a vista and backed by compatible wetland plants. The more diverse and naturalistic the water feature, the better.

Trees create the structure of a bird garden. The designer needs to decide early what trees will be planted where and which of the existing trees will stay. As repeatedly discussed, the ideal for birds is for trees to be gathered into clusters, mini-hammocks or pineland patches designed around a core of mixed native species. The larger the area covered by mixed-species tree plantings, the more arboreal birds can be supported, and the more the garden will contribute to the re-greening of South Florida. Mixed-tree plantings can be arranged and maintained in aesthetically pleasing ways. Trees standing alone in a lawn are not nearly as valuable to birds as trees surrounded by shrubs and short-statured plants and entangled by vines.

Shrub plantings for birds are best if diverse, thick, and thorny, providing lots of cover, small fruit, and insects. Since in South Florida many shrubs have the capacity to grow into the canopy over time, their desired ultimate situation should be calculated and if needed maintained by careful trimming. Some highly desirable shrubs can endure reduced light under trees and should be extensively used, but most shrubs need light and do best forming a dense hedgerow at the edges of tree stands. Interesting plants can be highlighted by positioning. Shrub plantings can be separated functionally. One sector can be for nectar and larval plants as a backdrop for a butterfly/hummingbird garden; another might be made up of wetland plants as a backdrop for a water feature. The shrub line should be irregular or follow pleasant sweeping curves to create long edges.

Short-statured plants can be used as stand-alone beds or as edges between shrubs and lawn. Composites and other flowers, coontie, and native bunch grasses provide superior edge cover. Many ferns thrive in low intensity or dappled light at the edges or even under shrubs and trees. Short-statured patches can be gathered into specialized gardens such as vegetable gardens, herb gardens, butterfly/hummingbird gardens, or flower beds. For birds, plant diversity remains a goal. Design mixed-species beds rather than the large single-species flower beds so common in South Florida commercial landscaping.

If planned early in the landscaping design process, a water feature can be large, naturalistic, and a focal point of the garden, providing aesthetic enjoyment to the gardener and habitat for birds.

Plant diversity is a key to ecological planting and to accommodating birds. A diversity of plants that provide different structure, insects, and fruit at different times of the year all enhance a garden for birds. Because birds need enough food available at any one time to make a garden worthwhile to visit, several specimens need to be planted to provide a critical mass of food.

Most gardeners will take a gradual approach to designing a bird garden. This approach allows iterative experimentation to determine what works and what doesn't. Every yard is different, and the results of any planting are to some extent unpredictable. Experimentation will happen whether planned or not because plants fail, design ideas evolve, new uses need accommodation, and iterative improvements can always be made. Going slow and experimentally in creating a bird garden is just fine.

Garden Management

When it comes to actually managing a garden, gardening for birds is a bit different from normal gardening. The good news is that in nearly every instance, bird-friendly gardens are easier and less expensive to maintain than more standard alternatives. In this section we offer specific advice on maintaining gardens built for birds in South Florida. Of course there is much more to be known about gardening in South Florida, knowledge that is available in many sources noted in chapter 7.

Let's start with the smallest of bird gardens, such as a patio, deck, or balcony. Even a very small space can be designed for birds through selection and installation of bird-friendly plants in containers, creating small water features, and establishing modest feeding stations. Patio gardening lends itself to compression

Bird-attracting gardens can be created in small spaces using containers. Multiple functions can be achieved in one small area. This patio container garden serves as an edible herb garden, a butterfly/hummingbird garden with nectar and host plants, and a place for a few orchids and lilies.

Attracting Birds to South Florida Gardens

of a bird garden's elements into the small space available. This space may simultaneously function as a bird garden, herb garden, butterfly garden, and flower garden. With forethought, planning, good design, and careful maintenance, nearly any patio or balcony can attract birds. Even balconies many floors up in the air can attract birds, although balcony planting does need to take into consideration the increasing harshness of the elements with height, particularly the drying effects of wind.

The larger South Florida bird garden should be developed in harmony with its existing soil, even if the soil presents challenges to plants. Soil additions or amendments seldom have long-term effects. For example, adding high-quality soil to planting holes just delays expression of inevitable incompatibilities between plant and substrate, so in South Florida it is best to simply put the native soil back in the planting hole. Proper South Florida plants are adapted to its alkalinity, and organic supplements that decrease pH are actually detrimental. It is a common experience to remove a dead shrub several years after its planting to find its root ball exactly where it was when planted. Rather than fussing with changing soil qualities, choose plants that are adapted to existing soils in a garden.

Supplemental irrigation is usually not needed over most of a properly designed South Florida garden. For half the year, South Florida's high rainfall is sufficient for any plant (and too much for some). As for the dry season, native plants, being well adapted to South Florida, not only can endure the dry season but thrive on it; many non-native plants from the subtropics also evolved in similar environments. These plants have their deciduous period or flower during the annual dry season. Dry-season watering of these plants is counterproductive. Native plants and diverse lawns are often adversely affected by dry-season watering of adjacent water-needy non-native plants.

There are a few circumstances, of course, when irrigation is needed. South Florida has high evaporation rates year-round, so plants do need additional water when transplanted. Large transplants may need supplemental water for a year. Fast-drying containers, raised beds, non-native epiphytes, and vegetable and herb gardens also need regular watering. In the depths of a drought, some plants may need occasional deep watering, although water use regulations are always in effect at this time, designed to thwart outdoor domestic water use. As is the case universally, timed drip irrigation should be used in place of aerial applications, applying about an inch of water per watering and watering in the early morning since in South Florida afternoon watering encourages fungus. But for the most part, once the plants are established, a South Florida bird garden should not need supplemental water.

There are other reasons to reduce watering. Half of South Florida's potable water is unsustainably used for irrigation. And it is expensive; if taken from municipal water supplies, a twice-weekly drenching of water can cost the gardener hundreds or even thousands of dollars per quarter year.

Water chemistry is an issue with irrigation as well. Ground water is quite alkaline. Municipal water is also alkaline and in addition contains chlorine. Many non-native plants find this high alkalinity stressful. Rainwater is slightly acidic, which tends to be better for container plants, orchids, and vegetable gardens. Catching rainwater in cisterns is a long tradition in South Florida, and one worth reconsidering for sensitive plants, by using modern rain barrels.

South Florida can also have too much water for a garden's comfort. In the rainy season, a downpour is a regular, usually daily event and South Florida also experiences periodic heavy rainfall events. In the summer, tropical systems can flood low-lying areas; in winter, cold fronts can bring with them inches of rain. When 2–6 inches of rain falls on a garden, where is it going to go, and what will it take with it? Managing runoff is essential. Sculpting the garden surface to capture and retain water, especially in natural-looking bird-friendly water features, has benefits beyond the garden. Water management is less important on elevated areas on sand or limestone where the water soon percolates into the soil.

Big hurricanes, prolonged droughts, and freezes are infrequent events in South Florida, and yet they shape the lives of all who live here, including plants, birds, and humans. Gardening in South Florida has a psychological downside, as these events can be feared long before they happen and can be emotionally debilitating for long after they pass. The destructiveness of a rare freeze to tropical plants and the physical and psychological dangers of a powerful hurricane should not be underestimated. A hurricane's destructive power is immense. In a direct hit by a powerful storm, garden plants can be broken, battered, twisted, flattened, and even blown away. Fortunately, native plants are somewhat adapted for lesser events and rapid recovery of many is almost certain if proper post-storm care is given. A few years later, the effects of storms, droughts, and freezes can hardly be seen in a properly restored garden.

Gardening satisfaction is quick in coming in South Florida. Properly chosen plants grow amazingly fast. Up north, it might take 10–20 years for a seedling to reach mature size. Tropical natives, temperate natives, well-adapted non-natives, fruit trees, and lawns all grow fast in South Florida. Our live oak was 3 feet tall when planted, and seven years later is now 30 feet. A gumbo limbo can go from being a stick in the ground to 30 feet tall in that same period. There is a saying in gardening that a tree is planted for the next generation to enjoy; but in South Florida, the one who plants it gets to enjoy the results, as do the garden's birds.

Fertilizing in South Florida generally causes more problems than it solves. It certainly is bad ecologically as excess nutrients run off the garden and make their way to the water table, canals, rivers, rock pits, and coastal bays. It is not so good on the land either, as fertilizing alters root development, adversely affects fruiting, influences competitive relationships among plants, confuses growth patterns, and is expensive. Artificial fertilization for natives and site-appropriate non-natives is not required. Diverse lawns need never be fertilized. Fertilizer should never be applied to transplants.

Despite the contribution of mulch to the aesthetics of a garden, thick layers of commercial mulch create biological deserts for birds by eliminating open ground and the prey that occur there.

Fertilizing is, however, needed for certain plants requiring special assistance. Localized fertilizing might include micronutrients for citruses, manganese for palms near sidewalks, supplements for fast-growing northern vegetables, frequent light fertilizing for non-native orchids, and perhaps a yearly light application to shrubs and trees in situations where dense planting leads to intense competition. Of course, trying to grow acid-loving plants requires constant attention to pH. Studying the requirements of needy plants can suggest how to help them. Planting non-needy plants is an even better tactic.

In a bird garden, additions of organic materials should concentrate on the specific plants known to require a higher organic content than the garden's basic soil provides. In South Florida uplands, organic material naturally oxidizes quickly, leaving little in the soil, so most native South Florida plants do not expect much organic material. The once common practice in South Florida of topdressing lawns and gardens with muck is only a temporary expedient, as the organic material oxidizes away quickly. Bringing in muck or other new soil to create a depth of 3–6 feet, sufficient to support much of the plants' root systems, is the only way to effectively change soil character.

Mulch and compost can add organic matter, temporarily, but the best long-term organic approach is to use the leaves and fallen twigs of the garden plants themselves, reproducing the equivalent of naturally forming litter. It is important for a bird gardener to resist the easy temptation of municipal bulk pickup. Rather, a garden's production of logs, branches, twigs, and leaves should be turned into log piles, natural mulch, and compost. Applied mulch is not the same as natural litter. Thick mulching of gardens, around trees and over the ground, is a relatively new gardening practice in South Florida. Eucalyptus and melaleuca mulches are inherently insecticidal; killing insects and invertebrates is not what bird-attracting gardening is about. Cypress mulch is produced in environmentally unsustainable ways. Commercial mulches often incorporate processed lumber containing contaminants such as arsenic. Mulch increases acidity that is incompatible with many native alkalinity-loving plants. As mulch breaks down,

Small quantities of soil are rather easy to make in South Florida, as composting happens rapidly. Kitchen and small garden waste put in a confined space can produce soil in less than a year.

its bacteria and fungi outcompete the plants for nitrogen. Thick garden mulches kill plants when piled against trunks by enabling pathogens. Thick applications reduce the flow of oxygen to the plant's roots. Mulch, by design, inhibits natural reseeding and seedling growth, which is one of the desired results of naturalistic gardening. One of the benefits touted for mulch is its water-holding capacity, which is not particularly beneficial in the South Florida wet season, when perennially damp mulch ends up mostly feeding fungi.

Mulch, we have to admit, can also have a beneficial side. Mulch does protect roots from aggressive lawn mowers and weed-whackers, keeps out unwanted seedlings, retains more applied fertilizer, and looks nicely tidy. Mulch also does retard evaporation, which can be worthwhile for recent plantings, containers, and vegetable gardens. And it can add organic matter to the limestone, sand, or fill base-soil, although, as we have already argued, in the long run trying to change South Florida's soils by amending them into something they are not is just fighting reality.

Given the negatives and positives, our main complaint about thick and widely spread mulch from the birds' perspective is that mulch destroys the open-ground habitat needed by birds. For birds, it is best to use store-bought mulch only with extreme circumspection—for new plantings and for spots where evaporation needs retarding such as containers and vegetable gardens. If a gardener's aesthetics absolutely call for store-bought mulch, it should be used only along highly visible edges. Store-bought mulch should not be applied under the canopy, where it is essential to leave ground without mulch and available for birds to use.

One thing a South Florida gardener can do is to make small quantities of soil. The rapid oxidation characteristic of South Florida makes composting an almost instantaneous affair. Unlike up north, composting does not take fancy bins, attention to layering, temperature, or moisture, or actually close attention of any sort. Placing kitchen and small garden waste in a confined area, such as made with cement blocks or planks, will generate soil without fuss in less than a year.

Making soil in more space-limited situations such as apartments is understandably a bit more complex and may take worm composting. Compost-generated soil is perfect for containers and vegetable gardens.

In a garden intended to attract birds, pesticides must not be used. Recall that the principal value of a garden to a bird is in the insects it provides. Insecticides, herbicides, and fungicides kill the birds' food, and also the balanced community of prey and predators that keep each other in check, all of which are eaten by birds. A diverse lawn, unlike a sod grass lawn, does not need pesticides. Vegetable and herb gardens are best maintained by encouraging predatory insects, making mixed plantings, planting bug-repelling plants, and practicing rotation. When the bug wars take a bad turn, as they often do for South Florida vegetable gardeners, turn to environmentally benign natural products like soap, oil, and hot pepper concoctions.

The one thing a South Florida bird garden does need is a bit of trimming, because plant growth here is rampant. This sort of trimming is different from manicuring a shrub or pruning away offensive tree branches, as was discussed in chapter 3. This is the trimming that keeps the garden as a whole in shape. For the most part, a garden meant to attract birds should be allowed to evolve as plants

Some trimming may be required to maintain original garden design elements or functionality, as in the case of this otherwise endangered pineland passionflower encroaching on a front walkway.

grow, mature, compete, are outcompeted, and die. But where a need exists to retain the garden's original design and functionality, judicious trimming may be required. Most commonly used native trees, shrubs, and fruit trees take to clipping and some even to hedging. Visual barriers and shrub edges need occasional trimming to increase branch and leaf density, much to the benefit of birds. Limbs can be trimmed when they grow too far over the lawn or vulnerable structures. Trees planted as specimens may need trimming to improve their structure and storm-proofing; however, trees and shrubs planted within a mixed-species hammock-like setting should not be trimmed as the entanglement of branches and roots is their best protection against storms and is friendly to birds. In trimming shrubs and trees, other than fruit trees, exceptional care is usually not required. Most native plants in South Florida are well adapted to having their branches break off in storms and need not be babied.

As already mentioned, dead branches and trees need to be kept. Dead branches, snags, and even entire dead trunks, especially palms and pines, are needed by birds. Pines and coconut palms are prone to dying in suburban settings. Dead palms can stand for years, pines for decades, so let them stand to be used by birds, as long as there is no danger from them. It is also important to let palms keep their dead fronds. These provide exceptional habitat, as well as being good for the palm, which recovers nutrients from them. Each palm loses its fronds in a characteristic timing that should be honored in a bird garden, as long as there is no danger from them.

A South Florida garden is seldom static. Perhaps the most important character traits for a bird gardener are patience and the ability to evolve one's views and expectations as nature takes its own course. Gardening to attract birds is ecological, and these ecological processes will win in the end. Growth, competition, unexpected diseases, severe droughts, excessive rainy seasons, hurricanes, frosts, and freezes all determine the trajectory of any South Florida garden. It is more interesting, and less stressful, to accept that uncontrollable influences are an inevitable part of gardening in South Florida. Because our goal is to provide birds and other wildlife with food and shelter, and because birds prosper in diversity, there is no one garden design and no one choice of plants that is more correct than others. Trial, error, and adaptive management are keys.

What Not to Do

This chapter suggests ways in which a gardener might manage a South Florida garden to attract birds; however, here are short reminders of what not to do.

DON'T ANNOY THE NEIGHBORS, at least more than is required. Different counties, municipalities, homeowner associations, condo boards, and deed covenants all have differing rules when it comes to yards, gardens, patios, and rights-of-way. Planting along canals and rock pits may be prohibited. Sometimes rules such as this restrict the robustness of bird gardening. As noted, by state law, local governments and neighborhood associations are not supposed to restrict conservation gardening, but some do or try to. Changing things is hard. Generally it is better to understand the restrictions and try to garden within them. Usually a lot can be accomplished despite restrictions. Bird gardens can look manicured. Backyards can often be more flexible than front yards. And, frequently, creativity will overcome challenges. At the very local level, such as with associations or even the local municipality, changes in rules or their interpretation can be advocated and your success can be used as an example in an argument for change.

DON'T ALLOW CATS IN THE GARDEN. One cannot have cats in a garden designed to attract birds. Reason and scientific evidence support this notion, but the pro-cat lobby is strong. When local regulation and local advocates are on the side of the outdoor cat, they are not on the side of wild birds. Generally, by law, stray cats trespassing on private property can be captured and returned to owners or, if unidentifiable, transported to animal shelters; however, what can be done is not necessarily what should be done for neighborhood peace and stability. But questioning unecological regulations is certainly in order. Why should the regulations on cats be any less stringent than those on dogs? The question is especially serious since cats are known to carry diseases that can severely affect people. One can only do what can be done, but gardeners should be advocates for keeping cats indoors and insistent that neighborhood cats not be allowed to enter their own gardens.

DON'T PLANT AGGRESSIVE NON-NATIVE PLANTS. South Florida is bedeviled by exotic plants that have taken over large portions of remaining natural habitats, costing governments hundreds of millions of dollars. The state, counties, and municipalities have lists of plants that are discouraged or forbidden. Sources are given in chapter 7. Such official recommendations and restrictions

Some non-native plants, like Brazilian pepper, are a conservation nightmare in South Florida. Invasive non-native plants such as this are regulated and should not be planted despite (or perhaps because of) their popularity with birds such as this Indigo Bunting.

should be carefully considered. Some plants are totally prohibited, but others on the lists are only potential problems in some situations. The risks at any particular garden site need to be understood. A plant that is a danger if placed in one garden may not be a danger in a different location. Ironically, it is often the case that plants are invasive because their fruit is eaten and spread by birds, Brazilian pepper being the casebook example, so a bird gardener has a special responsibility. Below is a list of our interpretation of plants that should not be planted and those that should be used with caution, carefully considering their possible adverse consequences.

DO NOT PLANT

Asian Sword Fern (*Nephrolepis brownii*)
Australian Pine (*Casuarina equisitifolia, Casuarina glauca*)
Australian Umbrella Tree (*Schefflera actinophylla*)
Banyan Fig (*Ficus benghalensis*)
Beach Naupaka (*Scaevola taccada*)
Brazilian Pepper (*Schinus terebinthifolia*)
Burmareed (*Neyraudia reynaudiana*)
China-Shrub (*Ardisia solanacea*)
Common Water-Hyacinth (*Eichhornia crassipes*)
Council Tree (*Ficus altissima*)
Hydrilla (*Hydrilla verticillata*)
Indian Laurel (*Ficus microcarpa*)
India Rubber Plant (*Ficus elastica*)
Japanese Honeysuckle (*Lonicera japonica*)
Javanese Bishopwood (*Bischofia javanica*)
Jio (*Commelina benghalensis*)
Latherleaf (*Colubrina asiatica*)
Life Plant (*Kalanchoe pinnata*)
Orchid Tree (*Bauhinia variegata*)
Oyster-plant (*Tradescantia spathacea*)
Portia Tree (*Thespesia populnea*)
Punktree (*Melaleuca quinquenervia*)
Purple Orchid Tree (*Bauhinia purpurea*)
Scratchthroat (*Ardisia crenata*)
Shoebutton (*Ardisia elliptica*)
Shrub Verbena (*Lantana camara, Lantana strigocamara*)
Small Leaf Climbing Fern (*Lygodium microphyllum*)
Strawberry Guava (*Psidium cattleianum*)
Tuberous Sword Fern (*Nephrolepis cordifolia*)
Weeping Fig (*Ficus benjamina*)
Woman's Tongue (*Albizia lebbeck*)

DON'T USE PESTICIDES. Once a gardener understands that the primary role of a garden is to provide insects for birds, gardening takes on a whole new perspective. A gardener cannot provide insects while killing them. This means no chemical pesticides and also no bacterial pesticides such as Bt, which is about as broadly effective as any chemical. Admittedly there are times when to save a vegetable garden something needs to be done, but there are very green ways to deal with this, which have been noted previously. No garden for birds should ever use any pesticide.

DON'T KEEP YOUR KNOWLEDGE TO YOURSELF. Gardening for birds in South Florida is more or less experimental. No one can say what specifically works for most plants and most birds in most situations, so it is important to share the results derived from garden experiments. This can be done using the outlets noted in chapter 7. The more we all know, the better.

Observing the Garden and Its Birds

Once a bird garden is designed, established, and being maintained, then what? How about sitting back, relaxing, and enjoying all the nature now sharing your space? People battle holiday traffic to spend their free time at beaches and parks because nature is innately de-stressing. A gardener can do this at home, outside the back doorstep. Watch, observe, appreciate. A functioning bird garden provides opportunities to observe nature; why resist the urge?

Once a bird garden is successful, watching the lives of avian neighbors unfold becomes engrossing. One would be hard-pressed to top a baby Eastern Screech-Owl popping its head out of a nest box for the first time.

A gardener should know the garden's plants, and identifying plants can be a challenge, especially if they are rare natives or unusual horticultural varieties. There are many sources of help, as listed in chapter 7. These include books, online sources, and personal communications, the last often being the easiest. Local botanical gardens, commercial garden centers, and specialist plant societies are sources of personal help. Plant society Internet forums and other social media are a good place to start. Monitor Web sites of the local botanical gardens and plant specialty clubs, for their information exchanges, meetings, and plant sales.

Much remains to be learned about these plants in South Florida, their flowering and fruiting, the insects that come to them, and the ways they are used or not used by birds and other wildlife. This is especially so with the many naturally rare and endemic species available for South Florida gardens. It is hoped that personal study of the garden will inform the gardener which plants should be encouraged and which should be replaced; once noted, these lessons can be shared among the bird gardening community so both successes and mistakes can become learning experiences for all.

Those gardeners who take their use of native plants one step further, choosing to emulate native habitat, gain the additional satisfaction of participating in regionwide restoration. Management of a South Florida bird garden might seem a very isolated affair, but in fact, every garden is a link in a regionwide matrix of bird-friendly habitat.

Of course, the gardener will also likely want to be able to identify the birds and other wildlife being hosted in the garden. For native and common non-native vertebrates and common butterflies, this is not all that hard, though it may take some study. Identifying other invertebrates may be more of a challenge, but many valuable references, in print and online, are provided in chapter 7 to help. Usually a scan of one or more of these will produce an answer. A gardener should not hesitate to become part of the birding communication network, where birders are happy to help with identifications. Similarly, the butterfly watching community is always willing to help. For identification of other invertebrates, online sources, county Cooperative Extension offices, and the Florida State Museum can provide guidance.

Once the common birds and other wildlife are known, the gardener can decide which observations are atypical and should be shared. For birds, the Florida Ornithological Society keeps the state list and monitors unusual occurrences. Bird observations in the garden can be recorded directly into an online database, provided in chapter 7. This resource not only provides personal archiving but at the same time makes the data available for science and conservation study. Unexpected observations need to be documented photographically. Images can help solve mysteries, and if the mysteries turn out to be biologically important, images are needed to provide scientifically valid documentation.

At times during the year, special bird counts are made in standardized ways that allow data to be compiled to determine status, trends, and distribution of birds in North America. These counts can happen in the garden. Several to be

Photographs of unusual species or behaviors are important and may become scientific documentation. This photograph of a Lavender Waxbill served as the first record of this African species in the wild in South Florida.

considered are the Audubon Christmas Bird Count, Cornell's Migration Count, Project Feederwatch, NestWatch, Great Backyard Bird Count, and Florida State Breeding Bird Atlas projects. Information on these is provided in chapter 7. By observing birds in your bird garden at the same time and in the same way as thousands of other birders and gardeners, your observations become part of continent-wide analyses. Your garden's data becomes something more than just what is happening outside your back door.

The garden is ultimately for living in. Sharing it with nature is enriching. The plants, animals, and birds serviced by the garden are there not only for relaxed enjoyment but also to be observed, appreciated, and conserved. Gaining intimate familiarity with the details of a single patch of ground, especially a patch for which one has stewardship, can be as fulfilling as a trip to a national park. Establishing and maintaining this patch as a part of South Florida's conservation safety net can be deeply satisfying.

5

South Florida Garden Birds

In this chapter we discuss what birds might be expected to show up in South Florida bird gardens or their neighborhoods. We'll discuss the time of year to expect them, how likely they are, and what garden elements might attract various species. We provide some sense of each species' abundance, seasonality, and breeding status in South Florida.

The following are accounts of birds that might be expected in a South Florida garden given the appropriate location, neighborhood situation, and garden characteristics meeting species-specific needs. Select birds are illustrated by photographs. Species are listed in recognizable ecological and taxonomic groupings. Species can also be found by using the index.

Waterfowl

Egyptian Goose (*Alopochen aegyptiacus*)—Nn, X, Br, Yr

A new breeding resident, these African waterfowl may well come into a large private garden as they are very content in parks, golf courses, and botanical gardens. These are mean birds willing to attack humans, dogs, or other birds getting in their way. This is an invasion that needs to be discouraged. Like other non-native waterfowl, they are not protected by law.

Non-native Egyptian Geese are breeding all too successfully in South Florida.

Informational Codes for Bird Accounts

Native	Na	Migrant	Mg
Non-native	Nn	Summer resident	Su
Invasive non-native	X	Fall resident	Fl
Breeding	Br	Winter resident	Wn
Nonbreeding	Nb	Spring resident	Sp
Year-round	Yr		

Domestic Goose (*Anser anser*)—Nn, Br, Yr

These domesticated geese are found in many pond, lake, canal, and park settings. The species was derived from the wild Graylag goose of Eurasia, but domesticated varieties are not uncommon in ponds, canals, rock pits, and golf courses, so they may be in a neighborhood. They nest in Miami-Dade but are found widely around South Florida.

Muscovy Duck (*Carina moschata*)—Nn, Br, Yr

One of the more unappealing waterfowl, these South American birds have a long history of domestication. They live along canals and rock pits, nesting in nearby yards throughout residential and rural areas of South Florida. They dig in the grass for food but prefer handouts and are readily attracted to feeding stations. They are aggressive and have little to commend them. Like other non-native waterfowl, they are not protected by law.

Muscovy Ducks happily accept food handouts; actually, they usually rudely insist on them.

Wood Duck (*Aix sponsa*)—Na, Br, Yr, Wn

These brilliantly plumaged ducks, assets in any large garden pond, are the most abundant resident wild duck in Florida, with more present in winter. One of the few native nesting ducks, their breeding is concentrated in the Big Cypress Swamp, and they are more likely found in rural than suburban ponds. But they may take up residence in well-vegetated neighborhood ponds elsewhere, although avoiding the Keys, Everglades, and agricultural areas. Natural cavity nesters, they will use predator-resistant nest boxes placed 10–30 feet up in trees. Boxes should be about 10 inches wide by 18 inches deep by 20 tall, with 3–4-inch holes. If unsuccessful in luring this species, boxes may attract Eastern Screech-Owls, raccoons, or opossums.

Mallard (*Anas platyrhynchos*)—Na/Nn, Br, Yr, Wn

Mallards have been domesticated for hundreds of years and developed into many varieties, including Pekin duck—the common big white duck with a yellow bill. More natural-looking Mallards of mixed domestic ancestry form nonmigrating populations. These are the birds typically observed in South Florida. Wild migratory

Mallards are infrequent in winter in South Florida and when present tend to stay in the interior wetlands. A large enough pond, canal, or rock pit may attract domesticated breeds of Mallards, which readily accept feeding stations with corn and bread.

Fowl

Indian Peafowl (*Pavo cristatus*)—Nn, X?, Br, Yr

The Indian Peafowl is quite common in scattered residential localities from Palm Beach to Miami-Dade, Collier, and elsewhere. In some places it is a source of civic pride; Coconut Grove shows off artistically rendered peacock statues and Miami-Dade has an ordinance specifically protecting them. Peacocks (the males) are loud, huge, strong-footed, sharp-toenailed, seed-eating mega-pheasants that can be quite destructive to garden plantings, ground-level bird feeders, and sometimes houses and cars. But their size and the male's striking colors and sensational display make them much beloved by many. They have a broad diet, including seeds, garden vegetables, hibiscus, small fruits, insects, lizards, small snakes, baby squirrels, rats, and mice. If they are in the neighborhood and one wishes to attract them, they can be encouraged with large trees for roosting and large seeds such as sunflower or cracked corn. If one wants to discourage them in the garden, do not provide food, water, or shelter, and try to show them your displeasure, cautiously.

Regal but potentially boisterous neighbors, Indian Peafowl are abundant in some South Florida neighborhoods that have embraced their presence. This is a peacock surveying its garden.

Domestic Chicken (*Gallus gallus*)—Nn, X, Br, Yr

Chickens are derived from Red Jungle Fowl, and some semi-feral individuals look very much like their ancestors. They are cultural necessities in portions of South Florida, with Key West and Coconut Grove topping the list. If they are to be encouraged to a garden, ground tray feeders serving cracked corn or chicken scratch feed are ideal.

Domestic chickens have endeared themselves to some South Florida neighborhoods. Here a Key West rooster explores for food in and around a planted cabbage palm.

Northern Bobwhite (*Colinus virginianus*)—Na, Br, Yr

Quail were once common and widespread in the uplands of South Florida, even in recent decades frequenting gardens in suburban and rural yards, but have become increasingly rare. Quail need cover, food, and an absence of hunting cats. They still occur sparsely in South Florida's pinelands, fields, overgrown pastures, rural gardens, yards, groves, and rural vacant lots. If nearby, they should be encouraged by feeding cracked corn, millet, sunflower seed, bread, or peanuts served in ground tray feeders and ensuring there are no feral cats.

Grebes

Pied-billed Grebe (*Podilymbus podiceps*)—Na, Br, Yr, Wn

These tiny waterbirds are found in suitable aquatic situations throughout South Florida, including open marshes, ponds, lakes, canals, rock pits, and water treatment wetlands. They use emergent vegetation as roosts, as well as a place for their floating nests. They eat fish and invertebrates. They are more common in winter, and it is then that they are more likely in neighborhood ponds or a very large garden water feature.

Pied-billed Grebes occur in ponds, rock pits, and other large water features, more so in winter.

Herons and Ibis

Great Blue Heron (*Ardea herodias*)—Na, Br, Yr, Mg, Wn

Despite their impressive size, these 4-foot-tall wading birds can be garden birds in South Florida. Some individuals are residents year-round, others only in winter; still others pass through on migration. Large aquatic features well stocked with fish have a good chance of attracting foraging herons, especially in winter. As previously explained, the gardener needs to decide whether their presence is to be encouraged or discouraged at such features. Winter residents are especially prone to finding good backyard feeding sites. In the Florida Keys, a special situation exists as the white form

Far left: Great Blue Herons may visit large water features with easily accessible fish. They may be loved or unloved by a gardener, depending on how their predation is viewed.

Left: Great White Herons, a white form of the Great Blue Heron, occur in the lower Keys and are readily attracted to feeding stations offering fish or parts of fish.

of this species, called the Great White Heron, is a typical backyard bird there. These herons are readily attracted to feeding stations providing fish. Research has shown that the Florida Bay environment is so degraded that such artificial food provisioning is needed to maintain the Great White Heron population in northern Florida Bay. If a yard is in a situation to provide nourishment to Great White Herons, doing so will help conserve these distinctive birds

Great Egret (*Ardea alba*)—Na, Br, Yr, Mg, Wn

We think of Great Egrets as waterbirds, but in South Florida they can be seen patrolling yards and edges of highways searching for South Florida's seemingly endless supply of anoles. Although a garden-feeding Great Egret is relatively tame, it is important that it not be overly disturbed by dogs, unaware people, or children as it hunts the shrubs.

Some Great Egrets have become adept at capturing lizards, like this brown anole, from plants in a range of settings, from gardens to roadsides.

Green Herons will frequent yards along vegetated canals or rock pits, particularly if there is an accessible fish-stocked water feature. This one is perched on a backyard fence in front of a docked boat.

Cattle Egret (*Bubulcus ibis*)—Na, Br, Yr, Mg, Wn

Cattle Egrets are attracted to lawns and grasshoppers. They emigrated from Africa 100 years ago and are now the most abundant heron in South Florida. They nest in summer and feed on insects on dry land. They are tame, resourceful, quick, and not at all shy about coming into a garden. They patrol road edges and median strips, where they cleverly avoid traffic, picking the bugs from cars stopped for traffic lights. They check out dumpsters, work car grills in parking lots for squashed insects, and follow lawn mowers for what they scare up. In gardens, they prefer feeding on tall diverse lawns, in adjacent ground cover, and even on top of hedgy shrubs.

Green Heron (*Butorides virescens*)—Na, Br, Yr, Mg, Wn

A vegetated water edge in a garden along a canal or rock pit may attract one or a pair of Green Herons, most likely in winter. Green Herons are adept at catching small fish from garden ponds. In a garden setting, they are attracted to ponds, canals, or rock pit edges planted with shrubs.

White Ibis have adapted well to urban life and often forage in gardens, especially seeking out lawns after a rainstorm.

Attracting Birds to South Florida Gardens

Yellow-crowned Night-Heron (*Nyctanassa violacea*)—Na, Br, Yr, Mg, Wn

These crustacean specialists are attracted to wherever there are crabs or crayfish, but they also eat large insects and lizards. They are not shy of people and will come into a garden, park, dock, or roadside planting. In the Keys and along the coast, they may be seen patrolling coastal gardens. Individuals settle into favorite feeding sites and become daily regulars.

White Ibis (*Eudocimus albus*)—Na, Br, Yr, Mg, Wn

The University of Miami's mascot, the White Ibis is a thoroughly urbanized bird in South Florida. Properly managed gardens with productive lawns are very likely to attract visiting ibis. In suburban and urban settings, they feed on worms, snails, and insects extracted from damp soil and lawns. They can be encouraged in gardens by creating soggy places. They also eat peanuts and other handouts, but this is not encouraged as the nutrition is far from that of their natural diet. White Ibis are among the great treats of South Florida gardens, much better ornaments than plastic flamingos.

Vultures

Black Vulture (*Coragyps atratus*)—Na, Br, Yr, Mg, Wn

Black Vultures are urban birds in South Florida, north of the Keys. Resident birds are augmented seasonally by migrants and wintering birds. They are gaining some notoriety in South Florida for picking window caulking off high-rises and wiper blades off cars. They might not be everyone's choice as a yard bird, but they add a wonderfully surreal character to a garden and can indeed be attracted with dead things set out on the front lawn. More often they are seen overhead, above the garden, in company with Turkey Vultures and other soaring birds.

Most often seen overhead, Black Vultures may roost individually or in groups in a garden, either on the ground or in trees. This vulture is using a dead snag.

Turkey Vulture (*Cathartes aura*)—Na, Br, Yr, Mg, Wn

Well adjusted to urban and suburban settings, Turkey Vultures can be seen over South Florida gardens year-round. They become extremely abundant during migration and in winter. In Miami, they famously inspired political commentary for decades by roosting on the courthouse, at least until taller, grander buildings were added to their collection of urban roost sites. They are attracted to spend the night in stands of trees, usually in parks. They can appear on the ground in suburban and rural settings when there is something to eat.

Hawks

Osprey (*Pandion haliaetus*)—Na, Br, Yr, Mg, Wn

These huge, fish-eating hawks are certainly among the most notable of South Florida's backyard birds. Of course not every backyard can have an Osprey, but yards in the Keys, along the coasts, and near Lake Okeechobee may host one, especially if a natural high perch or an artificial platform is provided. South Florida hosts resident Ospreys, wintering Ospreys, and one of the largest Osprey migrations in North America. Ospreys need tall perches in order to manipulate their fish and use tall trees, stout branches, and various artificial structures. Resident Ospreys naturally nest on mangroves and tall trees, but they also use artificial nest platforms, which a coastal gardener can supply. Ospreys are picky regarding where they nest, and a supply of accessible food needs to be nearby. They seem not to nest in central and northern Biscayne Bay, for example, but do in the immediate south. Osprey platforms should be about 40 inches square, placed securely on top of a utility pole 20–30 feet high. A retaining ledge helps keep the nest intact; attached perches are well used. More information can be obtained from sources given in chapter 7. Osprey nests are large, messy, and smelly, but the rewards are close-up views of a large fish-eating hawk. A garden in the Florida Keys or along the coast having an Osprey nest platform or perch might also attract a Bald Eagle (*Haliaeetus leucocephalus*) or many other birds seeking a high perch.

Swallow-tailed Kite (*Elanoides forficatus*)—Na, Br, Su

These notable, large hawks are surprisingly suburban in South Florida. Returning to South Florida in February and departing by September, they nest typically in pinelands and cypress swamps but also in tall trees in parklike suburban settings. Accomplished aerialists, they feed by grabbing frogs, lizards, and snakes from trees but are usually noticed flying about low above the tree canopy. A well-treed parklike garden may attract their attention for feeding, roosting, or nesting. Although the native pines and cypresses are favorites, they also use Australian pines.

Sharp-shinned Hawk (*Accipiter striatus*)—Na, Nb, Mg, Wn

These modestly sized hawks are often seen in gardens when hunting birds at feeders, especially during migration seasons, although some do stay for the winter. They may stake out a productive bird feeding station for days from their perches in shrubs and trees, mostly taking starlings and sparrows but also Mourning Doves. A Sharp-shinned Hawk monitoring a feeder may be the ultimate confirmation that a garden has created a food chain for its birds.

Cooper's Hawk (*Accipiter cooperii*)—Na, Br, Yr, Mg, Wn

Cooper's Hawks in South Florida are increasingly backyard birds, choosing gardens with a good supply of non-native doves and tall, dense trees for perching and nesting. They perch high on branches, utility poles, or wires, awaiting opportunities to dive on a bird, most typically Eurasian Collared-Doves and White-winged Doves.

Below, left: Waterside yards can attract Osprey. They readily take to artificial platforms for nesting and a diversity of structures for perching. This Osprey is dining while standing on a backyard piling.

Below, right: Red-shouldered Hawks nest in tall trees and palms in well-treed gardens and parks. Immature hawks like this one may linger until the nesting season begins again the next year.

A pile of gray and white dove feathers under a garden tree is a sure sign of a Cooper's Hawk visit. These feathers were formerly a Eurasian Collared-Dove.

The increased numbers nesting in South Florida have been attributed to an increase in these prey species. Blue Jays often sound the alarm at the presence of one of these hawks. Another sign that a Cooper's Hawk has visited a bird garden is a pile of gray dove feathers under a tree branch.

Red-shouldered Hawk (*Buteo lineatus*)—Na, Br, Yr

The most abundant and widespread hawk nesting in South Florida, Red-shoulders breed in large parks and residential areas having diverse tree stands interspersed with lawns, large water features, and preferably snakes. They nest in late winter and spring, building nests in canopies of large trees, especially native figs, or tall palms. Attracting them requires such trees and diversely planted areas where they can feed on a variety of insects, snakes, lizards, and sometimes fish. Once present in a neighborhood, they are quite residential and rather defensive of their nesting territory. Kirsten's attempts to photograph a nest resulted in some talon marks on her head.

Short-tailed Hawk (*Buteo brachyurus*)—Na, Br, Yr, Mg, Wn

These tropical hawks nest in the Everglades in summer, but they increasingly frequent suburban areas in winter, probably in response to the numbers of non-native doves available.

Crested Caracaras are ground-feeding scavengers in rural areas.

Crested Caracara (*Caracara cheriway*)—Na, Br, Yr

These typically central Florida birds are residents in Hendry County, also occurring rarely in western Broward and Palm Beach counties. Attracted to open grassland habitats and improved pasture, they monitor roads for carrion from roadside perches such as residential and rural fences.

Peregrine Falcon (*Falco peregrinus*)—Na, Nb, Mg, Wn

Peregrines occur in South Florida in winter and on migration, tracking migrating birds that they hunt along the way. South Florida, especially the coast and Keys, is a continental hot spot for Peregrine migration, with hundreds passing by on some days. They are most likely to be attracted to a South Florida bird garden during migration, when they may roost or feed there, especially on pigeons and doves.

A Peregrine Falcon is most likely to be seen in a yard while hunting pigeons and doves during their migration.

This American Kestrel is using a dead palm in a backyard as a good vantage point for hunting.

American Kestrel (*Falco sparverius*)—Na, Nb, Mg, Wn

Kestrels historically nested in the once extensive pinelands of South Florida, but no longer because the pinelands no longer exist. These little falcons are around mostly during migration as they work their way through South Florida following the migrations of small birds and large dragonflies. Those that stay for the winter set up territories in rural areas, large gardens, and parklike settings with diverse lawns and suitable perches, such as dead snags, high exposed branches, or utility wires, on which they await the appearance of their prey.

Crane Relatives

Common Gallinule (*Gallinula galeata*)—Na, Br, Yr, Wn

Gallinules are birds of freshwater marshes that also use such cultural features as overgrown canals, rock pits, drainage wetlands and very large, vegetated garden ponds. Garden gallinules spend much of their time walking about the shoreline and on emergent and floating vegetation. Resident birds nest primarily in spring and early summer, although nesting at other seasons is also known. There are few more enjoyable sights and sounds than baby gallinules in a pond, or adults calling to sort out their territories. Wintering birds are more widespread and numerous. They learn to come to feeders and for handouts.

American Coot (*Fulica americana*)—Na, Br/Nb, Yr, Mg, Wn

The most abundant waterbirds wintering in Florida, American Coots are attracted to the same situations as Common Gallinules but are more aquatic, spending their time swimming in deeper water. They feed on submersed vegetation. Some coots do remain into the summer, and a few records exist of nesting in South Florida. They are attracted to canals, rock pits, and large garden and park ponds with sufficient vegetation.

Sandhill Crane (*Grus canadensis*)—Na, Br, Yr

These are serious yard birds when you are looking eye-to-eye past a very large, sharp bill. In South Florida, cranes occur in low-lying rural areas, generally near isolated wetlands especially in parks and golf courses. Cranes very likely will show up in a garden nearby having a damp lawn or marshy swale. They are also attracted to corn or other seed at tray feeders on the ground, and to flower bulbs.

Left: American Coots require large ponds with swimming-depth water.

Right: Large, deep water features with emergent and floating vegetation may attract Common Gallinules.

Sandhill Cranes forage on damp lawns in rural neighborhoods, especially those near shallow wetland preserves.

Shorebirds

Killdeer (*Charadrius vociferus*)—Na, Br, Yr, Mg, Wn

Killdeer are upland shorebirds attracted to feed on expansive, poorly tended lawns, golf courses, airports, and the like. They nest on rocky lots, roadways, and flat gravel roofs. Winter residents use a wider variety of open areas for feeding and can be found in large gardens and parks, provided cats and dogs are not allowed to roam.

Gulls and Terns

Laughing Gull (*Leucophaeus atricilla*)—Na, Br, Yr, Mg, Wn

Laughing Gulls are the most abundant gull and the only gull nesting in South Florida; numbers increase markedly in winter. They are thoroughly adjusted to being around people. Although common along South Florida's coasts, beaches, and bays, they also go inland to parks, large gardens, landfills, highway margins, burger stand dumpsters, farmlands, and other easy food sources. They will hang out in large yards, especially if near the water.

Ring-billed Gull (*Larus delawarensis*)—Na, Nb, Wn

Nesting across the northern United States and much of Canada, the Ring-billed Gull is mostly a winter bird in South Florida. Although often joining Laughing Gulls along the shores, they occur well inland, exploiting landfills, dumpsters, parking lots, and agricultural fields during plowing. They will come to gardens adjacent to rock pits and canals, especially to food sources.

Laughing Gulls frequent water-front properties but may also be found inland near easy food sources.

Attracting Birds to South Florida Gardens

Ring-billed Gulls are winter residents in South Florida. Although they occur along the coast, many venture inland to feed.

Least Tern (*Sternula antillarum*)—Na, Br, Su

Occurring from April through October, these are the only terns nesting on the mainland of South Florida. They nest on open, rocky, disturbed sites and so are attracted to such places, including gravel roofs. They catch small fish by plunging from the air, mostly on the coast but can wander inland to canals and rock pits. If nesting in the neighborhood, they may be seen displaying in flight or flying to and from feeding sites.

Least Terns may be seen flying from coastal feeding sites to their nesting colonies on rocky lots or gravel roofs.

Pigeons

Rock Pigeon (*Columba livia*)—Nn, X, Br, Yr

Familiar as park pigeons, these domesticated varieties of an Old World species have been living with humans for thousands of years and are widely kept as pets. They are found primarily in urban and suburban settings, nesting on buildings and expressway bridges, and feeding on the ground in lawns and parks or along streets. They are attracted by corn or any other seed and bread products provided in tray feeders on the ground. Bird gardeners generally discourage them as they are very messy in numbers. They can be dissuaded from feeders by using large-bird excluders on millet feeders and by managing types, portions, and timing of ground-tray feeding.

White-crowned Pigeon (*Patagioenas leucocephala*)—Na, Br, Yr

In North America, these otherwise West Indian doves nest only in southern South Florida. They are most abundant in the Keys, but nest into the suburban areas of Miami-Dade. Winter numbers vary from year to year as some nesting birds migrate. They feed in trees and on the ground on fruit, flowers, seeds, and invertebrates. They are attracted to gardens with tropical hammock–like plantings that include their favorite trees: blolly, poisonwood, gumbo limbo, native figs, and cocoplum.

White-crowned Pigeons are attracted to southernmost gardens that have their favorite tropical fruit trees, including this strangler fig.

Eurasian Collared-Dove (*Streptopelia decaocto*)—Nn, X, Br, Yr

Eurasian Collared-Doves were introduced into New Providence in the Bahamas in 1974; by the late 1970s they had jumped the Gulf Stream to Florida and now they occur not only over all of developed South Florida but also over much of the United States. They are big doves dominating feeders by their size, numbers, and aggressiveness. They are attracted to seed feeders, consuming pretty much anything a seed

Eurasian Collared-Doves can overwhelm seed feeders. Portion control and leaving feeders empty in the summer are two ways to discourage these potential pests in the garden.

feeder might offer. Although preferring seed on the ground or in tray feeders, they are amazingly agile in getting seed from a tube feeder. They once used these skills to thwart an expensive feeder of ours that had been guaranteed accessible by nothing larger than a cardinal. Because they often appear in pairs or small flocks and cram seed into their crops, huge quantities of seed can be consumed during short feeder visits. They perch obviously in large trees and on utility wires, calling frequently. To discourage them, avoid safflower seed, seed mixes, and millet in tray feeders, employ large-bird screen baffles on tube feeders, stop seed feeding in summer, and encourage the neighborhood Cooper's Hawk.

White-winged Dove (*Zenaida asiatica*)— Na/Nn, X, Br, Yr, Wn

Historically these doves occurred in South Florida as rare wintering visitors, but a resident population was introduced in the 1960s in south Miami-Dade. Originally birds of the southwestern desert, they are most common in rural areas of Miami-Dade and Broward but can be found in neighborhoods and gardens throughout much of South Florida. They feed on small fruit and seeds and are attracted by fruit-bearing trees, seed feeders, and water features. Although some gardeners welcome them, others do not. They can be attracted by seed scattered on the ground or placed in tray feeders on the ground. If management is desired, it is about the same as for Eurasian Collared-Doves. Along with Mourning Doves, White-winged Doves are hunted in Florida.

Rare winter visitors at one time, White-winged Doves are now residents throughout much of South Florida, where they are attracted to seed, especially on the ground or in tray feeders.

Natives of South Florida, Mourning Doves readily accept seed offerings placed in low trays or spread directly on the ground.

Mourning Dove (*Zenaida macroura*)—Na, Br, Yr, Wn

The bona fide garden dove of South Florida, Mourning Doves are abundant in both urban and suburban areas despite having to deal with larger non-native doves and Florida hunters who are allowed to kill up to 15 a day in season. In the lower Keys, the locally nesting Mourning Dove is the Caribbean subspecies. They nest mostly in spring and summer in trees and tall shrubs and perch obviously on wires and in trees. They are attracted to gardens with these. They come to feeders in pairs and small numbers in summer, but form larger flocks in winter. They accept diverse feeder offerings, including black oil sunflower seed, cracked corn, millet, niger (one of the few native South Florida birds to do so), bread, breakfast cereal, and such. They feed most comfortably on seed spread directly on the ground or at ground-level tray feeders; however, they can use elevated tray feeders and acrobatically use sunflower- and millet-sized tube feeders as well. This species' feeder manners are a reason not to serve mixed seeds, because they throw out small seeds to get to the big ones. They also are attracted to water features.

Common Ground-Dove (*Columbina passerina*)—Na, Br, Yr

These tiny doves are residents in agricultural, rural, and some suburban settings, especially on open sandy ground along beachfronts and adjacent parks and gardens. They feed cryptically on seeds, insects, and small fruit on the ground under the cover of shrubs and short-statured plants, especially tall grasses. Although shy, if nearby, they can be attracted to gardens with tray feeders on the ground containing millet or black oil sunflower seed, water features, tall trees for perching, and a lack of cats.

Although shy, Common Ground-Doves can be attracted to seeds at ground level.

Attracting Birds to South Florida Gardens

Parrots

South Florida is blessed or bedeviled, depending on point of view, by parrots, none of which are native. Parrots fly noisily about in pairs or flocks, sometimes of mixed species. All feed on seeds, nuts, and fruits, including fruit that native birds cannot manage, much to the dismay of commercial growers and gardeners. They can be attracted to gardens with fruit trees and bird feeders with sunflower seed, nuts, and peanuts. Most nest in cavities, most frequently in palms in competition with woodpeckers, starlings, and each other for limited cavity opportunities in dead trees. A couple of species use buildings. One constructs huge stick nests.

Parrots in a garden, wanted or not, are exceptional aspects of the South Florida gardening experience. Native fruit trees and palms, non-native palms, and commercial fruit trees are the most important attractors. They can also be encouraged with garden tray feeders containing sunflower seed, nuts including large hard ones, fruit, and peanuts. Feeders hung high in trees are favored. Nest boxes can be provided by the gardener, but these seem less desirable to feral parrots than dead palms.

Beyond the species mentioned below, nearly any parrot in captivity might show up in South Florida, although not all survive long or nest in the wild. Old World parrots (Cockatiels, Budgerigars, lovebirds, African Gray Parrots, Rose-ringed Parakeets) seem less successful at survival than the New World species (Amazons, conures, macaws).

Cockatiel (*Nymphicus hollandicus*)—Nn, Nb

One of the more common cage birds, Cockatiels often escape and show up at feeders, usually in company of other parrots. They do not seem to do well in the wild and can often be readily recaptured.

Budgerigar (*Melopsittacus undulatus*)—Nn, Nb

Recently escaped budgies can show up in gardens anywhere in South Florida. They were the earliest parrot documented to breed in the wild in Florida, on the Gulf coast, but there is currently no evidence of a prospering wild population anywhere in South Florida. They prefer to feed on the ground on seeds, leaves, buds, and flowers, showing up in gardens with diverse lawns, small seed feeders, and water features.

Rosy-faced Lovebird (*Agapornis roseicollis*)—Nn, Nb

Like the Cockatiel, these are common cage birds that often escape and visit backyard feeders. They are not known to reproduce in the wild in South Florida and, depending on the individual bird's personality, can sometimes easily be recaptured.

African Gray Parrot (*Psittacus erithacus*)—Nn, Nb

Once common in captivity, these talented vocalizing parrots sometimes escape, and when they do, they come to feeders. Nesting in the wild in South Florida has been suspected but not proven.

Monk Parakeet (*Myiopsitta monachus*)—Nn, Br, Yr

Also called Quaker Parakeets, these temperate-zone South American species are quite hardy, and introduced populations are found as far north as New York and Washington state. First reported nesting in South Florida in 1969, they are now breeding residents throughout much of Miami-Dade, Broward, Palm Beach, and Lee counties. Their nests, used for communal roosting as well as nesting, are impressively huge mounds of sticks placed high above the ground in coconut, royal, cabbage, and date palms, cypresses, live oak, and punktree, as well as on utility poles, transformers, and other electrical transmission infrastructure. Active management results in nests being destroyed by both electric utilities, which object to the risk to their equipment and electrical delivery, and homeowners, who object to having noisy birds in their specimen palms. Monk Parakeets are agricultural pests elsewhere but not in South Florida. Their diet is quite broad, and they are very attracted to seed feeders. They are also attracted to tall and fruiting plants, including native figs, seagrape, and black olive, and areca (*Dypsis lutescens*), adonidia (*Adonidia merrillii*), and date palms.

White-winged Parakeet (*Brotogeris versicolurus*)—Nn, Br, Yr

These northern South American birds are common breeding residents in Broward and northern Miami-Dade. After their introduction as early as the 1950s, their numbers increased for a couple of decades and then decreased; it is thought this decrease was due to the simultaneous increase in the very similar Yellow-chevroned Parakeet. They are quite comfortable in palms, roosting, feeding, and nesting in fronds, especially Canary Island date palms. White-winged Parakeets travel in noisy flocks, often with Yellow-chevroned Parakeets. They eat fruit, seeds, and flower blossoms and will come to both tube and elevated tray feeders for seed. Tall palms, especially if dead, and seed feeders are the two garden elements that may attract this and the next species.

Yellow-chevroned Parakeet (*Brotogeris chiriri*)—Nn, Br, Yr

Also breeding residents of Miami-Dade and Broward since the 1970s, these are now the more abundant of the two *Brotogeris* parakeets in central Miami-Dade. They form large communal roosts outside the nesting season, traveling in noisy flocks among feeding sites. They feed high in trees on fruits, seeds, and flowers and will come to elevated tube and tray feeders. They roost and nest in palms, especially Canary Island date palms.

Black-hooded Parakeet (*Nandayus nenday*)—Nn, Br, Yr

Also called Nanday Parakeets and Nanday Conures, these pet trade birds are escape artists and are now established in the wild in many places in the world. In South Florida they are known from Palm Beach through the Keys in Monroe County, most abundantly in Palm Beach and Broward. While occurring primarily in residential areas, unlike most non-native parrots, they use natural pinelands as well. If enough are around, they can form very large flocks. They nest in cavities, especially in royal palms and utility poles. Their diet includes palm fruits, acorns, cones of Australian pine, and palm flowers. They also are attracted to seed feeders.

White-winged Parakeets are partial to large palms, particularly Canary Island date palms.

Conures—Nn, Br/Nb, Yr

These parakeets, originally from South and Central America, are common and noisily obvious in urban and suburban gardens from Miami-Dade through Palm Beach. The Blue-crowned, Mitred, and Red-masked Parakeets are the most widespread and most abundant locally. The species are similar looking, some annoyingly so; outside of nesting season, most will join mixed-species flocks. In gardens, tall trees are important to attract most conures. They roost in tall trees, especially Australian pines, cypresses, and figs, and most nest in cavities in palms and trees. Mitred Parakeets are an exception, roosting and nesting in cavities in buildings.

They feed on seeds, fruit (especially palm), berries, flowers, buds, vegetables, and almost everything else they can eat with their relatively small but strong bills. These parrots readily feed at elevated tray feeders with seeds, fruit, bread, and other provisions. Among native fruit, they feed on strangler fig, wild banyan tree, seagrape, royal palm, cabbage palm, and various fruit-bearing hammock trees, and also on crimson bottlebrush, Australian umbrella tree, Brazilian pepper, and punktree—the last three considered ecologically undesirable plants.

Overall, they are attracted to gardens having high tray feeders, tall trees for roosting and perching, fruiting trees and shrubs, and cavities in palms and trees for nesting.

Conures and similar species found in South Florida include the following:

- Mitred Parakeet (*Aratinga mitrata*)—Miami-Dade and Broward; among the most abundant conures, nesting in holes in building soffits and gables.
- Red-masked Parakeet (*Aratinga erythrogenys*)—Palm Beach to Monroe in the Upper Keys; abundant in Broward.
- Blue-crowned Parakeet (*Aratinga acuticaudata*)—Palm Beach to Miami-Dade and Monroe in Upper Keys, most abundant in Broward.
- Dusky-headed Parakeet (*Aratinga weddellii*)—Miami-Dade, especially Miami Springs.

Mitred Parakeets preferentially roost and nest in openings in buildings.

Left: White-eyed Parakeets explore an opening in a Miami-Dade County building.

Above: Red-masked Parakeets, and most of the other conures, use cavities in dead trees and palms for roosting and nesting.

- Orange-fronted Parakeet (*Aratinga canicularis*)—Miami-Dade and Monroe in Marathon.
- Crimson-fronted Parakeet (*Aratinga finschi*)—Broward and Miami-Dade.
- Scarlet-fronted Parakeet (*Aratinga wagleri*)—Miami-Dade.
- Peach-fronted Parakeet (*Aratinga aurea*)—Palm Beach and Miami-Dade.
- White-eyed Parakeet (*Aratinga leucophthalmus*)—Collier, Broward, and Miami-Dade.
- Green Parakeet (*Aratinga holochlora*)—Broward, Miami-Dade, and Monroe in the Keys.
- Maroon-bellied Parakeet (*Pyrrhura frontalis*)—Miami-Dade.
- Green-cheeked Parakeet (*Pyrrhura molinae*)—Miami-Dade.

Rose-ringed Parakeet (*Psittacula krameri*)—Nn, Br, Yr

These Old World parrots are common in captivity and now have been documented to occur on both South Florida coasts for more than 40 years, having nested in all South Florida counties other than Monroe; however, they seem not to persist, and no nesting is presently known on the east coast, and very few remain in Naples. They eat seeds, fruit, flowers, and nectar, especially orchid tree flowers and seagrape fruit. They also will eat seed from tube feeders, and fruit and seed from tray feeders. The similar Red-breasted Parakeet (*Psittacula alexandri*) has been seen in Broward, but nesting has not been documented.

Macaws—Nn, Br/Nb, Yr

Macaws are large South and Central American parrots seen regularly in various urban and suburban locations along South Florida's Atlantic coast northward through Palm Beach. They perhaps are most abundant in and near Coral Gables. Blue-and-yellow, Military, and Chestnut-fronted Macaws are known to nest, but more species likely do and mixed-species pairs occur. Macaws nest in tall palms, royal palms being favored, where they take over woodpecker holes. They have not been found nesting in artificial boxes in the wild, but there seems to be no reason why they would not.

They have powerful bills, which they use to feed on fruit of all sizes, including mangos, royal palms, small coconuts, slash pine cones, live oak acorns, royal poinciana seeds, and West Indian almonds. They also pick flowers. Their depredations on backyard fruit trees are often particularly not well appreciated by South Florida gardeners.

If a gardener desires, they can be attracted to gardens with tall palms and trees and high tray feeders with shelled peanuts, split walnuts, pecans, fresh fruit such as banana, dried fruit, vegetables, commercial parrot food mix, and a caged macaw on the patio.

Possible species include the following:

- Blue-and-yellow Macaw (*Ara ararauna*)—Palm Beach through Miami-Dade and Lee; most widespread macaw and increasing; particularly abundant in Miami-Dade, where it frequently comes to feeders in the south Miami area. It tends not to associate with other macaws.
- Red-and-green Macaw (*Ara chloropterus*)—Broward and Miami-Dade.
- Scarlet Macaw (*Ara macao*)—Broward and Miami-Dade.
- Yellow-collared Macaw (*Ara auricollis*)—Broward.
- Military Macaw (*Ara militaris*)—Miami-Dade.
- Red-shouldered Macaw (*Ara nobilis*)—Miami-Dade.
- Chestnut-fronted Macaw (*Ara severa*)—Palm Beach through Miami-Dade.

Blue-and-yellow Macaws are the most commonly encountered wild macaw in South Florida, occasionally visiting yard feeders.

Orange-winged Amazons are the most abundant Amazon parrot in Miami. They tend to stay in pairs rather than join mixed-species flocks.

Amazons—Nn, Br/Nb, Yr

Amazons are medium-sized New World parrots common in South Florida as pets and also in the wild. During the nonbreeding season most roost communally, with Australian pines, black olives, and figs being among favored roosting trees. Most of South Florida's Amazons travel and feed in mixed-species groups that noisily descend on trees to forage as a flock, where they pretty much disappear into the green foliage. They eat fruits, flowers, seeds, and nuts. They are inherently messy and inefficient feeders, and in their native habitat, other animals follow them around picking up the wastage. They are noisy birds, calling while flying, feeding, and roosting, especially in early morning and late evening. So they are often heard more than they are seen.

Flocks are attracted to gardens having large trees for roosting, native fruit-bearing plants such as figs, oaks, black olive, sabal palm, gumbo limbo, and seagrape, non-native plants such as areca, adonidia, and coconut palm (when coconuts are small), Australian pine (they eat the seed cones), mango and other tropical fruits, orchid trees (flowers and seed), punktree (flowers), and crimson bottlebrush (flowers).

During nesting season they pair off, at times in mixed-species pairs. They use various trees for nesting, favoring woodpecker cavities in palm trees, especially royal and coconut palms.

A number of species of Amazon parrots have been recorded in South Florida, mostly along the Atlantic Coast. These include the following:

- Red-crowned Parrot (*Amazona viridigenalis*)—Historically the most abundant Amazon in South Florida but recently decreasing; still breeding residents in Palm Beach to Miami-Dade and Key West in Monroe.
- Lilac-crowned Parrot (*Amazona finschi*)—Palm Beach to Miami-Dade.
- Orange-winged Parrot (*Amazona amazonica*)—Broward and Miami-Dade. The most abundant Amazon in Miami, where they are long-time breeding residents. Unlike most Amazons, they tend not to join mixed flocks but rather remain paired even when in single species flocks.
- Yellow-crowned Parrot (*Amazona ochrocephala*)—Palm Beach to Miami-Dade; nest in Miami-Dade.

- Turquoise-fronted Parrot (*Amazona aestiva*)—Palm Beach to Miami-Dade; nesting in all three counties.
- Festive Parrot (*Amazona festiva*)—Miami-Dade. Breeding uncertain.
- White-fronted Parrot (*Amazona albifrons*)—Breeding resident in Broward, Miami-Dade, and Monroe. Nesting in Miami-Dade for more than 40 years. Unlike other Amazons, they stay near their home territories, flocking with other species as they pass through.
- Mealy Parrot (*Amazona farinosa*)—Broward and Miami-Dade. Breeding uncertain.
- Yellow-naped Parrot (*Amazona auropalliata*)—Palm Beach to Miami-Dade. Breeding uncertain.
- Yellow-headed Parrot (*Amazona oratrix*)—Palm Beach to Miami-Dade. Breeding uncertain.
- Red-lored Parrot (*Amazona autumnalis*)—Palm Beach to upper Keys in Monroe. Nesting in Miami-Dade.
- Yellow-crowned Parrot (*Amazona ochrocephala*)—Palm Beach to Miami-Dade. Nesting in Miami-Dade.
- Yellow-shouldered Parrot (*Amazona barbadensis*)—Miami-Dade.
- Red-spectacled Parrot (*Amazona pretre*)—Miami-Dade. Breeding uncertain.
- Hispaniolan Parrot (*Amazona ventralis*)—Miami-Dade.

Cuckoos

Yellow-billed Cuckoo (*Coccyzus americanus*)—Na, Br, Mg, Su

In suitable habitat, Yellow-billed Cuckoos breed secretively through much of South Florida, including the Keys, but are more commonly seen in gardens during their prolonged migration. Cuckoos are forest and forest edge birds, requiring densely planted trees and shrubs, in which they lurk. They eat insects and other invertebrates, especially caterpillars, but also small reptiles, bird eggs, and fruit. They are attracted in summer and during migration to gardens with dense native plants having caterpillars and other insects. They are the most likely cuckoo to use a South Florida residential bird garden, especially during migration.

Yellow-billed Cuckoos may visit gardens having naturalistic patches of native plants that yield good populations of caterpillars and other insects.

Mangrove Cuckoo (*Coccyzus minor*)—Na, Br, Yr

These tropical birds nest in the United States only in South Florida, mostly in the Keys, along the Gulf coast, and into Miami-Dade. They occur primarily in and near mangrove swamps and coastal hammocks but will also venture into gardens with dense native trees, especially in the Keys. They nest in mangroves and eat mostly caterpillars but also spiders, other invertebrates, frogs, lizards, and fruits. Foraging in thick shrubs, they are usually seen in glimpses, flying between trees within dense stands. Gardens located near mangroves along the southern coast and in the Keys with thick hammock-like groves of native trees and shrubs are the most likely to attract them.

Owls

Barn Owl (*Tyto alba*)—Na, Br, Yr, Mg, Wn

Although seldom seen, Barn Owls breed throughout South Florida, most records being from Palm Beach to Miami-Dade. Year-round residents are augmented seasonally by wintering birds, which also use man-made structures for roosting. They occur in the Keys only in winter. It is impossible to predict in what neighborhood a Barn Owl might reside or what part of a structure it might claim. Barns, sheds, exposed attics in garages, or rafters in carports are attractive to them. An outbuilding can be enhanced by making a small doorway into a confined interior space or by placing a big nest box, 18 inches wide by 20 deep by 25 tall with a 7-inch hole, under the eaves or high in a nearby tree.

Eastern Screech-Owl (*Megascops asio*)—Na, Br, Yr, Wn

These small owls are found throughout South Florida, except in the Everglades Agricultural Area and Everglades marsh. They are common backyard birds, even if seldom noticed. They nest in late winter and early spring and are quite restricted by the lack of nesting cavities, so nesting boxes established by winter have a good chance of being occupied. Of all South Florida bird boxes, this is the one with the greatest chance of success. Screech-Owls' principal garden requirements are large, densely canopied trees where they spend the day, and nesting cavities—either natural or nest boxes. Live oak trees, because of their size and structure, are excellent for owl houses, but any protected site may be acceptable. Screech-Owl houses are 12 inches wide by 8 deep by 16 high with a 3–4-inch hole, placed 15–20 feet high in a tree. In fact, however, these owls don't seem all that picky as to box or hole size. Boxes need to be accessible for cleaning out competing nests of starlings or honey bees. Eastern Screech-Owls feed in the open on small mammals, birds, and insects, so in addition to trees, a lawn or parkland nearby is desirable. It is possible to attract these garden owls to a feeding station with feeder mice and similar offerings.

Above: Eastern Screech-Owls' nesting efforts can be encouraged by feeding them. They seem quite content with mice.

Left: Eastern Screech-Owls are highly receptive to nesting boxes in suburban settings. Screech-Owls nest annually in our garden, in fact choosing the boxes located near the swimming pool instead of those in the hammock.

Great Horned Owl (*Bubo virginianus*)—Na, Br, Yr

These owls are relatively common in pinelands, cypress swamps, and rural lands of both coasts, although seldom occurring in the interior marshes or in the Keys. Since they use tall trees near open areas, they can be found in large rural gardens and parks. They build nests in oak trees or cabbage palms, or claim existing nests. They will also use artificial platforms, but these need to be secure and placed as high as possible. If these owls are in the neighborhood and sufficiently large trees are available, such nest platforms may attract them.

Barred Owl (*Strix varia*)—Na, Br, Yr

Found mostly in natural, undeveloped forested wetlands, such as cypress swamps, bayheads, wet hammocks, and pinelands, Barred Owls nest throughout South Florida except in the Keys. Rare in urban or developed areas, they may be found in sparsely settled and well-wooded residential areas having diverse lawns near wetlands. They occasionally will nest in boxes mounted 15–30 feet high, hidden within the canopy. Barred Owl boxes are 14 inches wide, 14 deep, and 18 inches high with 8-inch holes.

Nightjars

Lesser Nighthawk (*Chordeiles acutipennis*)—Na, Nb, Mg, Wn

South Florida is the only part of North America where this species winters. They occur mostly in small numbers in Miami-Dade and Broward, being rare migrants on the Gulf coast. They are seen mostly over neighborhoods with agricultural fields, ballparks, large lawns, and ponds. A nighthawk seen in winter is likely this species.

Common Nighthawk (*Chordeiles minor*)—Na, Br, Su

These are common neighborhood birds, and their evening flights can be obvious owing to their characteristic calls and buzzing display flight. They nest on flat-topped buildings and on the ground in open grassy areas. Gravel roofs can be enhanced for nesting by ensuring they are well graveled, without dark tar patches, well drained, with some shade, and with retaining lips. During summer, Common Nighthawks are most likely noticed overhead, making buzzing sounds while diving.

Antillean Nighthawk (*Chordeiles gundlachii*)—Na, Br, Su

These Caribbean birds are summer residents in the Keys and southern Miami-Dade. Identifiable because their calls differ from those of Common Nighthawks, they nest on the ground in rocky and sandy areas, including developed locations, airports, and vacant lots. In the Keys, they use gravel drives, road edges, and lots for nesting and roosting.

Chuck-will's-widow (*Caprimulgus antrostomus*)—Na, Br/Nb, Mg, Su, Wn

Summer nesting residents in the interior of South Florida, they are most abundant during migration periods, when they occur widely in well-wooded parks and gardens.

A few remain as winter residents, especially in the Keys. They nest on the ground in dense tree stands, favoring native hammocks, and roost during the day in dense trees. Dense hammock-like plantings are crucial garden elements to attract them. They are hard to see and usually noticed only as they fly away when disturbed.

Swifts

Chimney Swift (*Chaetura pelagica*)—Na, Br, Mg, Su

Swifts are most often seen in the air while hunting flying insects. They migrate through South Florida seasonally and in recent decades have expanded their nesting range into South Florida along both coasts. In South Florida, they nest exclusively in man-made structures, especially chimneys and air vents. Residential fireplaces are not a South Florida tradition; chimneys that do exist are either fake or seldom used for fires (especially in summer), making them perfect for swifts. To attract swifts, existing chimneys can be enhanced by making the internal masonry rough, leaving a top opening, protecting the opening with a rain shield, and (if the fireplace is real) shutting the flue. A gardener lacking a chimney can try a swift tower as a chimney substitute; it can be 14–36 inches in diameter and 8–10 feet tall, with a metal rain shield above the opening. Seeing increasing numbers of swifts over South Florida neighborhoods is the reward for creating and enhancing swift nesting sites.

Hummingbirds

Ruby-throated Hummingbird (*Archilochus colubris*)—Na, Br/Nb, Mg, Wn

The only hummingbird expected, the Ruby-throat, is the bird on which all South Florida hummingbird-oriented gardening needs to be focused. It does nest in very small numbers in southwest Florida, south to the Big Cypress Swamp, but in most of South Florida it is not expected in gardens in summer. Over most of South Florida, they occur as migrants. South Florida is unique in North America in that some

Ruby-throated Hummingbirds are the only common hummingbird in South Florida. They are migrants and winter residents in most of South Florida and are attracted to gardens by plantings of appropriate nectar plants. This photo shows one of the better nectar-providing hummingbird plants, *Pavonia*.

Ruby-throats remain all winter. During migration and in winter, a long list of native and non-native plants provide these hummingbirds with nectar, tree sap, pollen, and small invertebrates such as scale insects and spiders. To successfully attract hummingbirds, a garden needs appropriate flowers that bloom from fall through spring. Recommended hummingbird plants for South Florida were listed previously, the most important being firebush, Hong Kong orchid tree, porterweeds, yellow necklacepod, bougainvillea, tropical sage, firecracker plant, and Bahama swampbush. A bird gardener might choose to additionally provide sugar-water feeders, but as mentioned previously, these feeders are not often successful in South Florida. Ruby-throats are highly territorial and will defend their feeding areas, so it is good to have hummingbird plants in several places so the bird can move among them. A periodically active water mister can be an extra attractant.

Although nearly every hummingbird seen in South Florida will be a Ruby-throat, other species do occur rarely. Black-chinned Hummingbirds (*Archilochus alexandri*) (Nn, Nb, Wn) are the western equivalents of Ruby-throats. They are rare winter residents, mostly north of South Florida. Rufous Hummingbird (*Selasphorus rufus*) (Na, Nb, Wn) is a western species that is a winter resident in small numbers but in increasing frequency in South Florida. These do use hummingbird feeders. Buff-bellied Hummingbird (*Amazilia yucatanensis*) (Na, Nb, Wn) is a Texas to Central American species. In recent years it has become a rare winter resident or migrant. It eats small insects as well as nectar.

Kingfisher

Belted Kingfisher (*Megaceryle alcyon*)—Na, Nb, Wn

Common winter residents in South Florida, these fish-eating birds are frequently seen along the edges of canals, rivers, rock pits, mangroves, swamps, and lakes. They perch obviously on stakes or on branches and wires overhanging water when not flying from perch to perch calling. They forage by plunging into the water after fish. Many larger water features, including those in residential and urban areas, host kingfishers in winter. Extensive water, fish, and perches are needed to attract kingfishers.

Belted Kingfishers occur in winter in South Florida. They use various perches along shores while watching for fish. Gardens along canals and the coast can attract them.

Woodpeckers

Red-bellied Woodpecker (*Melanerpes carolinus*)—Na, Br, Yr

The most common and familiar woodpecker in South Florida's gardens, the Red-bellied is South Florida's most important cavity-making bird, upon which other species depend. They forage along trunks and branches excavating beetle larvae and other insects from beneath the bark and among leaves. Beyond insects, these woodpeckers are dietary generalists, eating seeds, fruit, nuts, and sap. In winter as much as 80 percent of their diet is fruit and seeds, one reason for their continuing success in garden settings. Woodpeckers roost and nest in cavities, with pairs requiring several cavities for roosting and sequential nesting. There cannot be too many cavities available in and near a garden. Red-bellied Woodpeckers are attracted to gardens with cavities, insect-providing trees, and fruiting plants. For cavity trees, they most frequently use palms, especially royal, coconut, and cabbage palms, and also pines, cypresses, oaks, and sometimes utility poles. To attract nesting woodpeckers, a South Florida garden needs these trees, alive or dead. The woodpeckers will occasionally use nest boxes, mostly for roosting. To meet appropriate specifications boxes must be 10 inches wide and deep, 18 inches tall with a 2-inch hole, and firmly secured 10–30 feet high. A lip of aluminum around the cavity hole keeps it from being overly enlarged. The best insect-providing trees are palms, pines, cypresses, oaks, and native figs. Fruits used by Red-bellieds include American beautyberry, cabbage palm, sweetbay, hollies, wax myrtle, live oak, elderberry, firebush, coconut, mango, loquat, avocado, and citruses. They come to feeders for sunflower seeds, peanuts, fruit, jelly, and sometimes cracked corn. They can be attracted especially by peanut butter, mealworms, or suet (but see previous precautions about suet). These woodpeckers are quite sedentary, so a garden's woodpecker pair becomes part of the family.

Downy Woodpecker (*Picoides pubescens*)—Na, Br/Nb, Yr, Wn

These small woodpeckers occur through most of South Florida except in the Keys, agricultural areas, and the Everglades. Primarily insectivorous, they seek insects along trunks and small branches and also eat small fruits such as poison ivy, Virginia creeper, elderberry, and mulberry. They can also be attracted to feeders with sunflower seeds, cracked corn, peanuts, peanut butter, bread, fruit, and sometimes suet. In South Florida, Downies nest almost exclusively in dead trees, particularly pines.

Red-bellied Woodpeckers are the primary cavity excavators in South Florida, making holes that many species depend on. This woodpecker's cavity is in a cabbage palm.

Each member of a pair excavates its own roost cavity, and new nesting cavities are created annually. They seldom use nest boxes to nest, although they occasionally roost in them. Appropriate boxes are 4 inches wide and deep, 12 inches tall, with a 1¼–1½-inch hole, placed 5–30 feet high in trees. A garden can attract Downies by providing a mix of tall shrubs and trees, especially pines, including dead snags.

Northern Flicker (*Colaptes auratus*)—Na, Br/Nb, Yr, Wn

Although year-round residents, they are most commonly seen in the winter, mostly in urban and suburban habitats north of the lower Keys. Flickers often feed on the ground, primarily on ants and beetles, and also on fruit. They can catch insects in the air. They are attracted to gardens having tall palms and trees, especially oaks and pines, large expanses of diverse lawn, plants with small fruits, and no cats. Flickers may visit tray feeders for sunflower seeds, shelled peanuts, corn, and fruit. They nest in cavities, including in boxes, and roost in trees, birdhouses, and under roof eaves. Appropriate boxes are 7 inches wide and deep and 18 inches high with holes 2½–3 inches, placed 10–20 feet high.

Yellow-bellied Sapsucker (*Sphyrapicus varius*)—Na, Nb, Wn

Sapsuckers are responsible for the rows of holes in palms, pines, and other trees, from which they drink sap and eat insects attracted to the drips. They occur throughout South Florida but are not all that common; the holes have been made by generations of sapsuckers. They are very much at home in suburban and park settings. For the home garden, palms and pines are prime attractants. As sap drinkers, they also occasionally eat sugar water from hummingbird feeders and have a fondness for sweets such as jelly, grapes, apples, and sweet baked goods from elevated tray feeders. They also come to feeders for suet and shelled peanuts.

Generations of Yellow-bellied Sapsuckers drill holes in the same palms, sipping dripping sap and eating insects that are attracted to it.

Pileated Woodpecker (*Dryocopus pileatus*)—Na, Br, Yr

Despite being the largest and most impressive of South Florida's woodpeckers, Pileated Woodpeckers are surprisingly adaptable to residential and rural life. They are widespread, although not overly abundant, south to Key Largo except where large trees are absent such as in the interior wetlands and agricultural areas. They are at-

Among the more impressive yard visitors, Pileated Woodpeckers search for insects in and under the bark of trees and palms.

tracted to gardens having large palms and trees, preferably including pines, oaks, and cypresses, near similarly wooded tracts. A residential pair requires several cavity trees for nesting and roosting over a large territory. Although they will nest in artificial structures such as wooden utility poles, large trunks are key to this species' nesting, especially cypresses and cabbage palms, dead or alive. In addition to excavating insects from beneath bark, they eat fruits, seeds, and nuts, especially acorns. If comfortable in the neighborhood, they may come for large nuts, black sunflower seeds, peanuts, or peanut butter in tray feeders securely attached to a tree trunk, not hanging.

Flycatchers

Eastern Phoebe (*Sayornis phoebe*)—Na, Nb, Mg, Wn

These flycatchers are abundant in winter throughout South Florida, other than the Keys. Perching obviously on shrubs, fences, and utility lines, they sally forth to catch insects, including flies, dragonflies, and wasps, or dip into the canopy or to the ground to pick up ants and other terrestrial insects. In South Florida, they eat small fruit such as hollies, sugarberry, red mulberry, pokeweed, and elderberry. They are also attracted to plants that provide insects such as milkweeds, beggarticks, tickseeds, firewheel, lantanas, goldenrods, coastalplain willow, and of course oaks, pines, and palms. To be attractive to phoebes, gardens should have some of these insect-attracting and small fruit–producing plants. Phoebes also require convenient perches such as exposed tree branches, fences, wires, shepherd's hooks, arbors, trellises, or fence posts, from which they hunt. Perches are best placed near diverse lawns or road rights-of-way.

Above: To attract Eastern Phoebes in winter, a garden should supply small fruit- and insect-producing plants, adding, if necessary, nearby perching opportunities.

Right: Great Crested Flycatchers perch high in trees, like this seagrape. They nest in cavities and may use bird boxes.

Great Crested Flycatcher (*Myiarchus crinitus*)—Na, Br/Nb, Yr, Wn

These conspicuous flycatchers nest sparsely in summer over much of South Florida, although less commonly in the Everglades and Keys. Flycatchers are solitary or in pairs and defend their area vigorously. They range high into the trees, sitting on treetops to swoop down on large insects, especially moths, butterflies, wasps, dragonflies, caterpillars, beetles, grasshoppers, crickets, and katydids. They also eat small fruit like elderberry. They nest in woodpecker cavities and tree hollows, also, unusual for flycatchers, sometimes in nest boxes, mailboxes, and gutters. Boxes need to be deep, so they can be filled with leaf litter by the birds, and placed as high as possible, 15–30 feet. Good dimensions are 6 inches wide and high, 10 inches tall with 2-inch holes located high on the box face.

La Sagra's Flycatcher (*Myiarchus sagrae*)—Na, Nb, Wn

These Caribbean flycatchers are a rare but annual birding treat in South Florida. In recent winters, individuals have established themselves in several locations along the southeastern coast and Keys. Most sightings are in coastal parks near residential areas, so there is no reason they should not show up in a coastal garden.

Gray Kingbirds require high perches, such as this trumpet tree. They also use high wires and buildings. They swoop down to capture large flying insects.

Western Kingbird (*Tyrannus verticalis*)—Na, Nb, Wn

These western U.S. birds are candidates, though uncommon, to show up in a South Florida garden in winter. They perch on trees or power lines, diving for insects in the air or on the ground, or for fruit, which they collect while hovering.

Eastern Kingbird (*Tyrannus tyrannus*)—Na, Br/Nb, Mg, Su, Sp

These flycatchers tend to nest inland toward the Everglades and Big Cypress Swamp but in summer can occur in gardens nearby. They appear more widely during migration, when they come readily to gardens having both trees and lawns. They perch high on trees, shrubs, fences, wires, and utility poles from which they dive to catch bees and wasps. They also eat other insects and fruit, including mulberries and elderberries, which they pluck while flying.

Eastern Wood-Pewees and other small flycatchers are migrants in South Florida.

Gray Kingbird (*Tyrannus dominicensis*)—Na, Br, Su

These summer-nesting tropical flycatchers are amenable to being near people and are readily found in parks and residential gardens along the eastern coast, inland Miami-Dade, and the Keys, where they nest in mangroves, coastal hammocks, parks, gardens, and even parking-lot trees. They perch high, in tall trees, on power lines, or on buildings, from which they swoop down for large flying insects. They also take caterpillars and other insects, worms, lizards, and small fruit from plants or from the ground. They are attracted to parklike open space intermingled with trees.

Other species of flycatchers migrate through or reside in South Florida in winter, mostly in small numbers. Some are hard, almost impossible, to identify in fall but any may be seen in a garden as they pass on migration, including the following:

- Eastern Wood-Pewee (*Contopus virens*)—Na, Nb, Mg. Uncommon migrant.
- Acadian Flycatcher (*Empidonax virescens*)—Na, Nb, Mg. Common fall, uncommon spring.
- Least Flycatcher (*Empidonax minimus*)—Na, Nb, Mg, Wn. Uncommon.
- Ash-throated Flycatcher (*Myiarchus cinerascens*)—Na, Nb, Mg, Wn. Rare migrant and winter resident along the Gulf coast.
- Scissor-tailed Flycatcher (*Tyrannus forficatus*)—Na, Nb, Mg, Wn. Rare in rural areas throughout South Florida; occasionally in developed areas in the Keys and southern Miami-Dade.

Shrike

Loggerhead Shrike (*Lanius ludovicianus*)—Na, Br, Yr

Shrikes breed over much of South Florida, except in the Keys, on the southwest coast, and in the Everglades Agricultural Area. In recent decades they have become increasingly common in suburbs, more so in summer than in winter. They are attracted to open ground near high perches on trees, fences, or utility wires, from which they fly down to catch large insects, anoles, frogs, small mammals, or even small birds, which they take back to a perch to impale on a stick or thorn before eating. They nest in thick, usually isolated, and often thorny shrubs near feeding areas. In developed areas of South Florida, they use shrub thickets in parks, ball fields, cemeteries, golf courses, and parklike gardens. Important garden enhancements are thorny, shrubby thickets and moderately high perches.

Loggerhead Shrikes require moderately high perches in a garden from which to hunt, preferably with sharp sticks or thorns nearby where they can impale their prey.

Vireos

White-eyed Vireo (*Vireo griseus*)—Na, Br/Nb, Yr, Mg, Wn

These small, vocal birds nest over much of South Florida in summer, except along the southeastern coast, with a different subspecies nesting widely in the Keys. In most gardens, they are more likely seen during migration and in winter. These vireos are attracted to gardens having dense shrubs and hammock edges and no cats. Where they occur, they nest low in dense vegetation such as stoppers, darlingplum, saffron plum, and wax myrtle. Because these vireos feed mostly on insects, spiders, and small lizards, insect-producing shrubs and butterfly garden plants are attractive. They less frequently eat small seeds and, as most vireos do, small fruits, especially wax myrtle, elderberry, greenbriers, muscadine, Virginia creeper, and poison ivy.

Black-whiskered Vireo (*Vireo altiloquus*)—Na, Br, Su

These primarily tropical birds nest in North America only in South Florida, along both southern coasts from Miami and Naples south through the Keys, where they are most abundant. They are primarily birds of dense shrub and tree canopy of mangrove forests and coastal hammocks, although found inland in southern Miami-Dade. They nest in tall trees, especially seagrape and Jamaica dogwood. These vireos are also seen on spring migration along the coast. In the Keys or at sites near mangroves, they occur in gardens nearby.

Other species of vireos occur in South Florida, mostly as migrants and sometimes during the winter. Like all vireos, they prefer dense, tall shrubs and tree canopies and might pass through residential gardens if these features are present. Red-eyed Vireos (*Vireo olivaceus*) (Na, Br/Nb, Yr, Mg) are common fall and uncommon spring migrants in South Florida. They are rare year-round breeding residents south to Palm Beach County and more common in and near the Big Cypress Swamp. Blue-headed Vireos (*Vireo solitarius*) (Na, Nb, Mg, Wn) are common migrants throughout Florida, also common winter residents in South Florida, often seen in gardens. Yellow-throated Vireos (*Vireo flavifrons*) (Na, Nb, Wn) are uncommon in South Florida.

White-eyed Vireos are attracted to gardens with dense stands of shrubs and trees, like this buttonwood tree.

Attracting Birds to South Florida Gardens

Red-eyed Vireos are common fall migrants in South Florida, pausing in insect-rich trees like this buttonwood to refuel.

Jays

Blue Jay (*Cyanocitta cristata*)—Na, Br, Yr, Wn

Common year-round with seasonal additions of winter residents, Blue Jays are such expected garden birds that their full beauty and interesting behavior may be overlooked and underappreciated. They are found ubiquitously but never in large numbers along both coasts of South Florida, though absent from the interior agricultural areas, the extreme southwest, or the Keys south of Key Largo. Jays are naturally birds of woodland edges, so to be attractive, gardens should have diverse and densely planted shrubs and trees in a hammock-like setting. Slash pines, live oaks, and native fruit-bearing trees are inducements. They nest cryptically high and so require tall, densely canopied trees. They also relish garden water features. Blue Jays are quite catholic in their food habits, eating fruit, insects (especially butterflies and moths) and other invertebrates, lizards, frogs, small rodents, bird eggs, and chicks. They readily come to tray feeders hanging or on the ground (but not often to tube feeders)

Blue Jays are busy, entertaining, and frequent garden guests. Here a jay pulls Spanish moss for use as nesting material from an epiphytic orchid installed on a coconut palm.

for black oil sunflower seeds and cracked corn, also for mealworms, fruit, dog food, cooked eggs, dry cereal, bread, pastries, and meat. The best way to attract them is with peanuts. Their ability to find peanuts is amazing; put them out and Blue Jays will come. To attract jays, gardens should have hammock-like edges, a water feature, exposed sand or soil for dusting, and a tray stocked with interesting bits of edibles including peanuts.

American Crow (*Corvus brachyrhynchos*)—Na, Br, Yr

Although commonly known for bedeviling farmers across America, in South Florida this species tends to occur in the less developed interior of the state. As a result, American Crows do not occur with any frequency in Palm Beach, Broward, eastern Miami-Dade, or the Keys. Elsewhere, they are year-round breeding residents. American Crows are distinguished from Fish Crows by their size, but mostly by their call. Their bird garden requirements are similar to those of the Fish Crow, discussed below.

Fish Crow (*Corvus ossifragus*)—Na, Br, Yr

While retaining their historic coastal distribution in South Florida, these crows have expanded their range inland in the last fifty years. Now the more common residential crows in much of South Florida, Fish Crows pair off in the summer to nest but form flocks and rookeries numbering in the hundreds to thousands in winter, comprising mostly winter residents. They nest high in shrubs and trees and consume a variety of fruits and insects. They come to elevated or ground tray feeders having sun-

Fish Crows are the common residential crow throughout much of southeast Florida.

flower seeds, peanuts, cracked corn, and nearly anything else from the refrigerator. To attract Fish Crows, a garden should have a hammock/shrub edge of fruiting plants such as seagrape, pigeon plum, and citruses, diverse lawn, water features, and tray feeders.

Attracting Birds to South Florida Gardens

Swallows

Purple Martin (*Progne subis*)—Na, Br/Nb, Mg, Su, Sp

Martins breed southward through Miami-Dade and Collier and also occur as migrants. They feed on the wing on flying insects such as wasps, flying ants, beetles, bugs, emerging aquatic insects, and dragonflies but also take insects from leaves and from the ground. In a garden, they need high perches and open diverse lawns, preferring to be near water. They have been known to come to tray feeders on the ground, especially for mealworms or crushed eggshells during nesting season. To attract them, the most important garden element is a martin house. Martins are almost entirely dependent on humans to provide their lodgings, so houses are readily available commercially, ranging from impressive and expensive to a few dried gourds hanging from a pole. Whatever design, optimal chambers are 8 by 8 by 8 inches with a 1½-inch hole, an opening smaller than might be expected in order to dissuade starlings. Houses should be 10–30 feet high. Martins return to South Florida from their winter range early in the year, so the house needs to be open for them by early February. Martins tend to nest where they hatched or have nested previously. Prospectors periodically venture forth to try out new boxes, so gardeners need to be patient for their boxes to be taken. It took seven years for martins to decide our house was acceptable. Gardeners have to defend houses from starlings by removing their nests. Additional information on martins is available from sources provided in chapter 7.

Houses are critical to attracting Purple Martins to a yard, but it may take several years before they decide to settle into a new location.

Northern Rough-winged Swallow (*Stelgidopteryx serripennis*)—Na, Br/Nb, Mg, Wn

These swallows are seen mostly as migrants but have nested very rarely in Miami-Dade, Lee, Collier, and Hendry and occur rarely in winter. They nest noncolonially in cavities near water, usually in a dirt burrow but occasionally in human structures such as pipes or culverts. They are most likely to be seen over gardens while passing through.

Tree Swallow (*Tachycineta bicolor*)—Na, Nb, Mg, Wn

In South Florida, tree swallows are among the most abundant swallows and the only swallows that commonly winter on mainland North America. The reason they can remain in South Florida for winter is that they eat fruits and seeds as well as insects. In South Florida, they covet wax myrtle, Brazilian pepper, and other small fruits they pick from trees. This is a good reason to plant wax myrtles, elderberry, and other native plants that produce small fruit in winter. Wintering flocks can be impressive in size, activity, and the number of berries they can quickly consume.

Cave Swallow (*Petrochelidon fulva*)—Na, Br/Nb, Mg, Su

These tropical Caribbean birds (*Petrochelidon fulva fulva*) are known to nest in the United States only under bridges in south Miami-Dade, although recently they have been seen as far north as Fort Lauderdale. At gardens and over nearby fields and canals near their bridges, they might be seen flying by. Birds of the Mexican race (*Petrochelidon fulva pelodroma*) occur occasionally in South Florida on migration.

Other swallows can be seen in South Florida, usually flying over the garden during their migration. Barn Swallows (*Hirundo rustica*) (Na, Br, Mg, Su) are common as migrants and rare nesting residents in summer. Bank Swallows (*Riparia riparia*) (Na, Nb, Mg) are common migrants. Cliff Swallows (*Petrochelidon pyrrhonota*) (Na, Nb, Mg) are less common migrants.

Cave Swallows build mud nests under bridges in Miami-Dade. This population comes from Cuba and in North America nests only under these bridges.

Chickadees

Tufted Titmouse (*Baeolophus bicolor*)—Na, Br, Yr

Titmice are great backyard birds farther north but over much of South Florida are rare or absent and not to be counted on as garden birds. They nest locally in Lee, Hendry, Collier, and northwestern Monroe but have become rare as nesting birds in the eastern part of South Florida and are not reported from the Keys. Their natural habitats in South Florida are cypress swamp, pineland, and hammock, and so they prefer gardens with similarly thick shrub and tree cover. Titmice are feeder birds up north, visiting feeders for black sunflower seeds, peanut pieces, suet, safflower, and fruit, although not in most of South Florida. As cavity nesters, they will use nest boxes that are 4 inches wide and deep and 10 inches high with a 1½-inch hole, located 5–15 feet high under cover.

Wrens

Carolina Wren (*Thryothorus ludovicianus*)—Na, Br, Yr

Carolina Wrens nest sparsely throughout much of South Florida, except in agricultural areas and the Keys south of Key Largo. They are also scarce in urbanized areas along the east coast. In the remainder of South Florida, they are prominent garden birds. To attract wrens, a garden needs dense plantings of trees, shrubs, and short-statured plants, ideally including saw palmetto, where the birds shelter while feeding on insects, spiders, and small fruit such as muscadine, cactus, elderberry, and mulberry. Wrens are also attracted by loose brush piles, water features, and tube or tray feeders for millet, sunflower seed fragments, small fruit, mealworms, peanut fragments, small cracked corn, suet, or peanut butter. They nest and roost in sundry sorts of cavities, tree root tangles, palm bases, hanging baskets, abandoned pots, and birdhouses. Carolina Wren boxes, placed low and under cover, ideally are about 8 inches tall and 4 inches wide, with a 1½-inch hole or slit. Most commercially available wren boxes are for House Wrens and too small for Carolina Wrens. Carolina Wren pairs are quite sedentary and use multiple boxes at the same time.

Left: Common feeder birds up north, Tufted Titmice have a limited presence in South Florida gardens.

Right: Carolina Wrens will visit tube or tray feeders for a range of offerings. They are most common in central and western South Florida.

House Wren (*Troglodytes aedon*)—Na, Nb, Wn

These wrens are common in South Florida in winter, although less so toward the south and rare in the Keys. House Wrens sing, even in winter, but prefer to stay deep in thick shrubs and hammock edges where they forage actively for insects and other invertebrates. Very much a garden bird up north, they may be found in rural and suburban gardens in much the same situation as Carolina Wrens. Other species of wrens do occur as nonbreeding residents in winter, but these are rare in gardens.

Bulbul

Red-whiskered Bulbul (*Pycnonotus jocosus*)—Nn, Br, Yr

These originally Indian birds have been breeding in Miami-Dade for 50 years but have not expanded much from the Kendall/Pinecrest area. Bulbuls feed on small, soft fruits, nectar, and insects attracted to flowers, gleaned from branches, or caught in the air. Among the small fruits they eat are Brazilian pepper, orange jessamine, lantanas, and hollies. Among the nectar flowers they visit are bottlebrush, punktree, coconut palm, and Australian umbrella tree. Bulbuls live in family groups in summer, nesting in shrubs and trees, and in fall and winter gather in flocks, roosting in slash pines, Australian pines, figs, and tall grasses. They are attracted to tray feeders offering soft cut fruit, and also sometimes to sugar-water feeders. Softness is important as they cannot get their bills through the skins of many fruits. Planting diverse fruit-bearing plants and providing tray feeders with cut-up soft fruit are the best ways to attract them. Many of the plants they prefer are non-native or invasive, and some are illegal to plant in Miami-Dade, so gardeners should stick to native fruit-bearing options.

Gnatcatcher

Blue-gray Gnatcatcher (*Polioptila caerulea*)—Na, Br/Nb, Yr, Mg, Wn

These tiny birds are common as migrants and wintering residents, tending to form the core of wintering songbird flocks. They nest in pinelands, cypress swamps, mixed hardwood stands, gardens, and parks south to Collier and northern Monroe on the

Blue-gray Gnatcatchers are quite common during migration and in winter, foraging high in trees or in shrubs. They are obvious as they are noisy and often the first bird to respond to any disturbance.

west coast and to Palm Beach on the east. Gnatcatchers feed actively, high in trees and shrubs, gleaning, flycatching, or hovering to take insects and spiders. They are attracted to residential gardens and parks with trees and shrubs of sufficient height and foliage complexity. In winter they flock with warblers, moving among individual gardens.

Thrushes

Eastern Bluebird (*Sialis sialis*)—Na, Br/Nb, Yr, Mg, Wn

These familiar and desirable garden birds nest as far south as Big Cypress Swamp on the west and northern Palm Beach on the east. A few nest in the easternmost pinelands of Everglades National Park. They also rarely are migrants and winter residents. In South Florida, they are birds of open pinelands, prairies, and pastures and are attracted to rural gardens having extensive lawns or pastures with nest boxes. Theirs is the bird house most commonly available commercially, 5 inches wide and deep and 8 inches tall with a 1½-inch hole. Boxes are installed on posts 4–8 feet high near open areas with a snake barrier and need to be monitored for House Sparrow encroachment. Bluebirds eat insects and small fruit, including hollies, elderberry, and mulberry. They are also attracted to tray feeders with live or freeze-dried mealworms, fruit, a peanut butter–cornmeal mix, suet, cooked eggs, cheese, baked goods, blueberries, raspberries, or softened raisins. More information on bluebirds can be obtained from sources listed in chapter 7.

Eastern Bluebirds are not as common in South Florida gardens as they are farther north. Nest boxes are readily available for purchase but are not often successful over most of South Florida.

Hermit Thrush (*Catharus guttatus*)—Na, Nb, Wn

The only thrushes wintering in South Florida, Hermit Thrushes occur irregularly on the mainland and more rarely in the Keys. Not very common and not often seen in small gardens, these thrushes like thick cover in which they feed on insects and small fruit. A hammock-like area with trees, shrubs, and ground litter is the best garden situation for them.

This is also the habitat for other thrush species (Na, Nb, Mg) that occur in South Florida as migrants. Any of these may turn up in the shrubs and small trees of a thickly planted bird garden. Veery (*Catharus fuscescens*) is uncommon and irregular in fall. Gray-cheeked Thrush (*Catharus minimus*) is rare in the spring, most common in the Keys. Swainson's Thrush (*Catharus ustulatus*) is common in fall, less in spring. Wood Thrush (*Hylocichla mustelina*) is a rare migrant.

Swainson's Thrushes are common South Florida migrants. Like all thrushes, they prefer thick vegetation, like this fig tree.

American Robin (*Turdus migratorius*)—Na, Nb, Wn

The presence, number, and distribution of wintering robins in South Florida vary greatly and unpredictably from one year to the next. Wintering robins feed in flocks in shrubs and on the ground in native pinelands, hammocks, and mangroves, and in rural areas, suburbs, parks, grassy lawns, median strips, and gardens. Although famous as invertebrate eaters, in South Florida robins eat berries, so they frequent gardens having a good supply of small fruits, especially holly and Brazilian pepper. They are attracted to water features and more rarely to tray feeders for fruit, bread, raisins, and dog food. The ideal garden setting for robins is a stand of dense native shrubs having small fruit in late winter, adjacent to a diverse lawn with a water feature on the ground.

During their South Florida winter residency, American Robins primarily eat small fruits, like those of the cabbage palm pictured here.

Mimids

Gray Catbird (*Dumetella carolinensis*)—Na, Nb, Wn

Catbirds are common winter residents in South Florida gardens, both males and females calling obviously through the season. They are readily attracted to South Florida gardens having a dense, tangled, hedge-like shrub layer under a thick hammock-like overstory. They typically feed within and under the shrubs on insects and spiders, but in South Florida also on fruit including wax myrtle, elderberry, mulberry, hollies, American beautyberry, rougeplant, and American pokeberry. They use water features if under or near cover. They are not common at feeders, as they are quite shy about revealing themselves but can be attracted to secluded feeders with bits of peanuts, peanut butter, mealworms, suet, raisins, jelly, berries, and small grapes. Cats are a significant threat to these birds.

Gray Catbirds are winter residents in South Florida gardens, hiding in the shrubs while calling their presence.

Northern Mockingbird (*Mimus polyglottos*)—Na, Br, Yr

Mockingbirds are South Florida's most characteristic and well-known garden birds. Their singing is the background music of any South Florida bird garden, nearly any month of the year. Well adjusted to humans, mockingbirds divide neighborhoods into a succession of territories whose boundaries and nest sites are conspicuously defended from other fruit-picking birds, the dog, or even the gardener. Mockingbirds sing from tall perches in trees and on utility poles, sometimes well into the night. They eat ground insects and other invertebrates such as worms, spiders, and snails, and also small fruit including wax myrtle, dahoon, stoppers, elderberry, muscadine, Virginia creeper, poisonwood, and poison ivy. They seldom come to feeders but can sometimes be enticed with mealworms, peanut butter, and fresh and dried fruit served on or near the ground; they do use water features, however. They nest in dense vines, shrubs and short trees, 6–10 feet high, with small live oaks and black olives being favorites. To attract Northern Mockingbirds, a garden should have tall trees with exposed perches, dense tall shrubs for nesting, a diverse lawn, fruit-bearing shrubs and trees, and a water feature.

Bahama Mockingbird (*Mimus gundlachii*)—Na, Nb, Wn

These Bahamian birds are rare but appearing with increasing regularity in the extreme southeastern coast of South Florida and the Keys. They tend to stay near the coast and be sedentary for some weeks. Compared with Northern Mockingbirds, the species uses scrubbier habitat, is less amenable to developed areas, and is shier, but it can show up in a garden or park along the southeastern coast.

Left: Bahama Mockingbirds are rare but somewhat regular Bahamian visitors to South Florida's southeastern coast and the Keys. This one is perched in a wild dilly tree.

Above: The Florida state bird, Northern Mockingbird, is a characteristic garden bird throughout South Florida. Mockingbird song fills a South Florida garden both day and night for much of the year.

Brown Thrasher (*Toxostoma rufum*)—Na, Br/Nb, Yr, Wn

Although seldom noticed by those not looking, these relatively large ground-feeding birds are quite content to use appropriate gardens. They nest throughout South Florida north of the Keys, except in the interior wetlands. Additional birds occur in winter. Thrashers are birds of thick, dense shrubs and usually stay deep inside the shrub cover, although in summer they sing from high perches in trees and on utility poles. They feed on the ground by rummaging in leaf litter, digging and scattering it with their bills, catching beetles, grasshoppers, and caterpillars, and collecting small fruit, acorns, and seeds. Some individuals learn to visit tray feeders on the ground for peanuts, cracked corn, bread, sunflower seeds, oranges, grapes, raisins, or leftovers, and some may use water features. They nest on or near the ground in dense cover, especially among palm stems. To attract thrashers, gardens should have tall trees with exposed branches, dense and thorny shrubs, including saw palmetto (especially) and other palms, native fruiting shrubs, short-statured plants, a sparse layer of litter, a feeder tray on the ground, water feature, and no outdoor cats.

Starlings

European Starling (*Sturnus vulgaris*)—Nn, X, Br/Nb, Yr, Wn

Occurring throughout South Florida's developed areas including the Keys, these overly abundant, originally Eurasian birds are the bane of South Florida bird gardeners. Other than occasional mimic vocalizations, there is little to commend them as they displace native cavity-nesting birds such as woodpeckers, Great Crested Flycatchers, and Purple Martins. Birds pair off to nest in late winter to spring but form flocks by midsummer that last through the winter, augmented by incoming winter residents. Starlings have very catholic tastes, eating insects, fruit, seeds, suet, and assorted human food. Although they forage naturally on the ground by probing in the

European Starlings are aggressive non-native birds that compete with native birds for cavity nest sites and food.

grass with open bills, they will feed at any height where food is available. Starlings are skilled feeder birds and harass other species. To thwart them, avoid feeding milo, mixed seed, or suet, and set out only small daily portions of food for other birds. Feeders that dangle and swing discomfort starlings, and they can be excluded from seed meant for buntings with cage tube feeders. Their nesting also needs to be managed since they aggressively evict other cavity nesters. They tend to nest early, in late winter and early spring. The best approach is to let them lay eggs and then remove the nest; this discourages that pair. As other pairs are in the waiting, this may have to be done several times. Unlike most native birds, European Starlings are not legally protected and so can be live trapped, entangled in rat glue traps, or otherwise disposed of. Although none of this will make a dent in the population, it may bring some local relief and satisfaction. The best approach is to feed birds in a garden in ways that do not attract starlings and to protect birdhouses through nest-by-nest control.

Common Myna (*Acridotheres tristis*)—Nn, Br, Yr

These originally Asian birds occur across the eastern portion of South Florida from Palm Beach through Miami-Dade to Homestead and in Collier near Everglades City. They are highly urbanized, nesting in various sorts of cavities including building niches, broken street lights, signs, and birdhouses. They feed on the ground on fruit, nuts, seeds, or tasty human litter, foraging in small flocks. Parking lots, especially of restaurants, are favorites. They will come to parks and to large gardens with open areas and sufficient food.

Hill Myna (*Gracula religiosa*)—Nn, Br, Yr

The South Florida population of these originally Asian birds is centered in Miami, but as numbers rise they are increasingly found elsewhere, even as far inland as parking lots in the Everglades. Hill Mynas are naturally birds of forests and in South Florida are found in suburbs having abundant fruiting trees and shrubs. They feed in the canopy, mostly on fruits, but also on seeds and insects. They perch obviously on trees, poles, and wires and nest in cavities and within clusters of palm stems.

Originally from Asia, Common Mynas have adapted well to urban life in South Florida and may occur in gardens with large open areas.

Waxwing

Cedar Waxwing (*Bombycilla cedorum*)—Na, Nb, Mg, Wn

Waxwings inconsistently come to South Florida in late winter and, when they do, can be found anywhere on the mainland, although rarely in the Keys. In South Florida they appear in flocks that descend on gardens and parks having good fruit supplies. Although they eat insects elsewhere, in South Florida they seek primarily fruit, especially wax myrtle and Brazilian pepper, as well as elderberry, mulberry, dahoon, and many more. They are attracted to gardens having many large trees and shrubs that bear small fruit in late winter.

Although unpredictable in their occurance, in late winter Cedar Waxwings may flock to fruit-rich South Florida gardens.

Breeding Warblers

Northern Parula (*Setophaga americana*)—Na, Br/Nb, Mg, Wn

Parulas nest in Central Florida, extending barely into South Florida in Glades, Hendry, and Collier. In the remainder of South Florida, they are migrants, with a few remaining as winter residents in extreme South Florida and the Keys. These birds actively forage along tree branches for insects and spiders. In South Florida, they are mostly birds of cypress swamps, hardwood swamps, and oak hammocks. During migration and winter, they are attracted to gardens having diverse stands of tall trees, especially oaks, native figs, cypresses, and pines.

Northern Parulas act as natural insecticide in the garden as they scour branches and leaves for whitefly, scale insects, caterpillars, and other invertebrates.

Yellow Warbler (*Setophaga petechia*)—Na, Br/Nb, Yr, Mg, Wn

South Florida has a residential population of the West Indian race (*Dendroica petechia gundlachii*), which nests along the shores of southern Biscayne Bay, the Keys, Florida Bay, and southern Collier. The nesting population is unlikely to appear in gardens, but migrants and wintering residents do occur. Yellow Warblers tend to be rather tame, feeding in shrubs and trees, gleaning spiders, flycatching insects, or taking small fruit. During migration, they are attracted to native hammocks and to gardens with diverse shrub and tree stands providing ample cover, fruit, and insects.

Pine Warbler (*Setophaga pinus*)—Na, Br/Nb, Yr, Mg, Wn

Forest birds during the nesting season, Pine Warblers nest in some remnant pine stands from northern Palm Beach to the pinelands of western Miami-Dade, as well as in the western portions of South Florida. They are more abundant during migration and in winter when they are found in a diversity of habitats. They feed by gleaning and flycatching insects and spiders from bark, leaves, and pine needles. In winter in South Florida, they also eat small fruits and seeds, expanding their feeding area from high in trees to all levels, including on the ground. They are attracted to gardens having diverse trees, shrubs, and lawn. Pine Warblers are among the few warblers that will come to feeders for sunflower pieces, peanut butter, finely cracked corn, and suet.

Pine Warblers are typical of pine forests. In summer, they nest in pines like this slash pine but diversify in the winter, being found in many habitats including gardens.

Prairie Warbler (*Setophaga discolor*)—Na, Br/Nb, Yr, Mg, Wn

South Florida has an endemic breeding race (*Dendroica discolor paludicola*) that nests along the coasts into the Keys in mangroves and less frequently in dense shrubs near the coast. Although birds of this subspecies seldom make it into gardens, northern-breeding birds occur in South Florida as migrants and less frequently as winter residents. They forage actively in shrubs and lower branches of trees for insects and spiders. These birds prefer dense hammock, pinelands, and other wooded areas, especially with live oaks, and so are attracted to gardens with insect-producing patches of dense shrubs and tree canopy.

Prothonotary Warbler (*Protonotaria citria*)—Na, Br/Nb, Yr, Mg, Wn

The Prothonotary Warbler is a swamp-nesting species, and its breeding range in South Florida is limited to Collier and northern Monroe counties. It appears in other places as a migrant and more rarely as a winter resident. It feeds by gleaning insects and spiders off tree trunks, branches, floating logs, and the ground. It nests in tree cavities and sometimes uses various nest boxes. This warbler will be seen in South Florida gardens mostly during migration.

Migrant Prairie Warblers are quite commonly attracted to insect-rich gardens across South Florida. This one is sitting in poor-man's patch (*Mentzelia floridana*).

Common Yellowthroat (*Geothlypis trichas*)—Na, Br/Nb, Yr, Mg, Wn

Birds of dense, low-lying vegetation near water, Common Yellowthroats breed in much of South Florida, although rarely along either of the developed coasts, in mangrove swamps, or in the Keys. Other populations are migrants and winter residents. Yellowthroats hop around in the shrubs near the ground, eating insects and spiders. By preference, they are shrubby-wetland birds but occur in gardens having dense shrubs, especially those with a water feature.

Migrant and Wintering Warblers

South Florida is on the migratory pathway of many species of warblers and similar small insect-eating birds that spend their summers nesting north of South Florida and winter in the tropics. Some of these remain in South Florida as winter residents; others pass through on their way farther south. Warblers migrate at night and spend the day feeding and resting, which is when they are seen in gardens. If a frontal system delays them on migration, they may linger in a garden for a day or longer; a garden may come alive with birds during such a "fallout."

Migrating warblers can be seen with some predictability by gardeners who know the species' schedules and study unfolding weather patterns. Each species is on its own schedule, but many overlap. During the fall, migration tends to be a prolonged process, with individuals leisurely working their way south, feeding as much as they can while awaiting good passage weather for their overwater journey southward. In contrast, spring migration is compressed, with birds rushing back to their nesting areas, often passing over or around South Florida unless stopped by weather.

Although insectivorous while nesting, these birds also eat fruit during migration, gaining the energy used to fuel their migratory flight. Migration is a time when many

Common Yellowthroats are adept at finding invertebrates, like the one captured here, on and near the ground. They are especially attracted to gardens having water features.

Warblers like these Northern Parulas are attracted to garden water features. Well-vegetated features provide feeding, drinking, and bathing opportunities. Warblers usually feed by working shrub and tree branches and leaves but also catch insects in the air.

South Florida native plants have ripe small fruit, no doubt to accommodate migrating birds that disperse their seeds. This is also the time when a few species of warblers may come to feeders for seeds, fruits, or peanut butter. When migrating songbirds land in South Florida, they need places to roost, to feed, and to drink. They are attracted to dense hammocks and their garden equivalents, especially those with water features.

Some warblers and other northern-nesting songbirds are winter residents in South Florida, in some cases the only portion of North America where they remain for the season. More than twenty species of warblers and other small songbirds may winter in South Florida. Although each species is different, generally they winter in areas having relatively short, shrubby habitat mixed with open areas. Gardens and parks match these requirements well. The birds search branches and leaves of shrubs, trees, and lawns for insects, fruit, and seeds. Native plants with small fruit, butterfly plants, and native insect-producing trees and shrubs form the core of their South Florida habitat; most important are oaks, palms, and native figs. Wintering warblers may come to gardens in mixed-species flocks, moving through any one garden relatively rapidly; however, some individuals may work a garden all winter.

Yellow-rumped Warbler (*Setophaga coronata*)—Na, Nb, Mg, Wn

These are among the more common warblers seen in South Florida gardens, at least in some years. They use dense shrubs and tree canopy, sometimes in loose flocks, to feed on insects and spiders (and their egg cases) found by gleaning trees, shrubs, or eaves of houses. They also eat small fruit, especially wax myrtle (eastern birds used to be called Myrtle Warblers). Some visit feeders for energy-rich foods such as orange pieces, jelly, sugar water, or suet. They are attracted to residential gardens having dense shrubs, particularly wax myrtle, and dense tree canopies, particularly live oaks.

Yellow-rumped Warblers specialize in eating spiders and their egg cases.

Palm Warbler (*Setophaga palmarum*)—Na, Nb, Mg, Wn

These are among the most commonly seen warblers in South Florida, not only because they are abundant but because they are obvious, flicking their tails while foraging in the open. They are found throughout South Florida in winter and also as migrants. They feed on insects and other invertebrates, also eating small fruit and seeds. Unlike most warblers, Palm Warblers use open, diverse lawns. They are generally found in small flocks feeding on the ground or in low shrubs in fields, beaches, lawns, parks, and gardens.

Palm Warblers are the most noticeable warblers through the winter in South Florida. They forage obviously in the open and are frequent in gardens. This individual is just beginning to gain its summer plumage of rufous and yellow feathers around its face.

The following are some, though not all, of the warblers and similar birds to be seen in South Florida gardens in winter or on migration.

- Ruby-crowned Kinglet (*Regulus calendula*)—Na, Nb, Wn. Not a warbler; kinglets are rare in winter, eruptively more common in some years than others.
- Blue-winged Warbler (*Vermivora cyanoptera*)—Na, Nb, Mg. Regular in fall throughout South Florida; in spring, especially in the Keys and west coast.
- Tennessee Warbler (*Oreothlypis peregrina*)—Na, Nb, Mg. Common in fall; rare in spring.
- Chestnut-sided Warbler (*Setophaga pennsylvanica*)—Na, Nb, Mg. Uncommon in fall; very rare in spring.
- Blackburnian Warbler (*Setophaga fusca*)—Na, Nb, Mg. Common in fall; uncommon in spring.
- Bay-breasted Warbler (*Setophaga castanea*)—Na, Nb, Mg. Uncommon in fall; rare in spring.
- Blackpoll Warbler (*Setophaga striata*)—Na, Nb, Mg. Unusual in fall as their migration route takes them offshore unless easterly weather pushes the ocean-migrating birds inland; more common in spring.
- Kentucky Warbler (*Geothlypis formosa*)—Na, Nb, Mg. Uncommon.
- Hooded Warbler (*Setophaga citrina*)—Na, Nb, Mg. Uncommon.
- Orange-crowned Warbler (*Oreothlypis celata*)—Na, Nb, Mg, Wn. Uncommon.
- Magnolia Warbler (*Setophaga magnolia*)—Na, Nb, Mg, Wn. Uncommon migrants; rare wintering in southern South Florida including the Keys.
- Cape May Warbler (*Setophaga tigrina*)—Na, Nb, Mg, Wn. Uncommon migrant, fewer in fall than spring, principally along the east coast; rare in winter in extreme southern portions of the mainland and Keys.
- Black-throated Blue Warbler (*Setophaga caerulescens*)—Na, Nb, Mg, Wn. Among the more common fall and spring migrants; rare in winter but occurs in extreme southern portions of the mainland and Keys.
- Black-throated Green Warbler (*Setophaga virens*)—Na, Nb, Mg, Wn. Fairly common in fall; uncommon in spring; uncommon in winter in Keys and less so in the rest of South Florida.

A Cape May Warbler in spring breeding plumage eyes a meal of whiteflies on a seagrape leaf.

Black-throated Blue Warblers are one of South Florida's most common migrant visitors. They forage anywhere from high in trees to the ground.

Black-and-White Warblers are generally seen moving up and down tree trunks, searching for tasty morsels like this caterpillar.

- Yellow-throated Warbler (*Setophaga dominica*)—Na, Nb, Mg, Wn. Common migrants and winter residents, preferring pinelands and hammocks.
- Black-and-white Warbler (*Mniotilta varia*)—Na, Nb, Mg, Wn. Common winter residents in South Florida including the Keys; more numerous during migration peaks in fall and spring. Generally seen hunting, hopping from place to place on trunks and branches.
- American Redstart (*Setophaga ruticilla*)—Na, Nb, Mg, Wn. Uncommon in winter; common and easily noticed during migration; more numerous in fall. Redstarts are one of the great joys of bird migration in a South Florida bird garden as they flit from the canopy to the ground, flashing their tail colors and enjoying water features.
- Worm-eating Warbler (*Helmitheros vermivorum*)—Na, Nb, Mg, Wn. Uncommon in winter in the southern mainland and Keys; uncommon migrants in both seasons; found particularly along the coast.
- Swainson's Warbler (*Limnothlypis swainsonii*)—Na, Nb, Mg. Rare migrants, found particularly along the coast.
- Ovenbird (*Seiurus aurocapilla*)—Na, Nb, Wn, Mg. Uncommon winter residents in South Florida, including the Keys; common migrants in both seasons, sometimes visiting gardens in numbers, spending the day foraging for invertebrates in the leaf litter beneath the tree and shrub canopy.
- Northern Waterthrush (*Parkesia noveboracensis*)—Na, Nb, Mg, Wn. Uncommon winter residents in South Florida, including the Keys, more common in the southern Everglades; common migrants in both seasons; feed on the ground in a garden's leaf litter.
- Louisiana Waterthrush (*Parkesia motacilla*)—Na, Nb, Mg, Wn. Rare winter residents in South Florida and the Keys; uncommon migrants in both seasons; feed on the ground in a garden's leaf litter.
- Yellow-breasted Chat (*Icteria virens*)—Na, Nb, Mg, Wn. Uncommon migrants and winter residents throughout South Florida and the Keys.

Yellow-throated Warblers may be seen throughout the winter in gardens with pineland or hammock-like plantings.

American Redstarts like this female are most easily spotted as a twirl of color as they hunt insects midair, tail flared to expose yellow (female) or red (male) patches.

Secretive Ovenbirds sort through leaf litter for insects, sheltering under thick shrubs as much as possible.

Sparrows

Eastern Towhee (*Pipilo erythrophthalmus*)—Na, Br, Yr, Wn

Towhees are ground-dwelling birds that scratch about the leaf litter under dense, hedgy shrubs and thick tree patches, feeding on seeds, fruits, insects, spiders, millipedes, snails, and other ground invertebrates. They roost in shrubs and nest close to the ground in dense vegetation, especially saw palmetto. Towhees are now quite unusual in gardens along the developed east coast but may come to gardens in more rural areas having dense thickets of shrubs, leaf litter, and scattered trees; loose brush piles inside tree zones are a further asset. Where they occur, towhees may be attracted to ground feeders or to forage under elevated feeders for cracked corn, nuts, sunflower seeds, peanut bits, berries, and mealworms. In winter they eat more seed, and loose flocks may forage under elevated feeders. They are extremely vulnerable to cat predation and so benefit from thorny shrubs.

Few sparrows may be expected in gardens in South Florida; some possibilities are the following:

- Chipping Sparrow (*Spizella passerina*)—Na, Nb, Wn. Uncommon on mainland South Florida, rare in the Keys; will flock with warblers and may come to feeders.
- Lark Sparrow (*Chondestes grammacus*)—Na, Nb, Mg, Wn. Uncommon in winter and during migration.
- Savannah Sparrow (*Passerculus sandwichensis*)—Na, Nb, Wn. Very common, sometimes appearing in gardens.
- Grasshopper Sparrow (*Ammodramus savannarum*)—Na, Nb, Wn. Wintering birds are rather common, not to be confused with the highly endangered Central Florida population.
- Swamp Sparrow (*Melospiza georgiana*)—Na, Nb, Mg, Wn. Uncommon in winter on mainland; uncommon migrant in the Keys.
- White-crowned Sparrow (*Zonotrichia leucophrys*)—Na, Nb, Wn. Uncommon winter resident; migrants may rarely pass by the Keys.

Grasshopper Sparrows are one of the more common wintering sparrows in South Florida. The highly endangered Central Florida race is very rare and seldom seen.

White-crowned Sparrows, such as the immature one pictured here, are uncommon in winter in South Florida. As is typical for them, this sparrow is eating seeds.

Tanagers

Summer Tanager (*Piranga rubra*)—Na, Br/Nb, Yr, Mg, Wn

Likely once a breeding species in the pinelands of Miami-Dade and Monroe, these tanagers still breed in southern Hendry County. They are more common as migrants and rarely, but increasingly, as wintering residents. They forage in trees and shrubs for insects, especially bees, wasps, caterpillars, and beetles, and for small fruit. They may be attracted to gardens having diverse plantings of insect-producing and fruit-bearing trees.

Scarlet Tanager (*Piranga olivacea*)—Na, Nb, Mg

Less common migrants than Summer Tanagers, they are found in similar situations.

Scarlet Tanagers, like this female, may be attracted during migration to yards with insect- and fruit-producing trees such as this gumbo limbo.

Northern Cardinal (*Cardinalis cardinalis*)—Na, Br, Yr

Cardinals are one of the more sensational-looking birds of South Florida's gardens, the male having bright scarlet plumage. They are naturally birds of thick shrubs and hammock edges, feeding in trees and shrubs and on the ground underneath. They nest low, 4–8 feet, in dense tangles of shrubs, short trees, and vines. Although keeping under cover, cardinals are common garden birds in South Florida. They are attracted to gardens having dense patches of shrubs and trees, especially stoppers, wild coffees, hollies, and firebush. During nesting, both members of the pair announce their claim with an array of songs; they are more gregarious in nonbreeding seasons. They feed on seeds and fruits, but during nesting eat insects and other invertebrates. Tending to stay under cover, cardinals will come to sheltered tray feeders on the ground for sunflower seeds and sometimes for cracked corn, peanut butter, and watermelon seeds. They also are quite attracted to water features.

Two rarely seen Bahamian tanager-like species are birds to look out for. Western Spindalis (*Spindalis zena*) (Na, Nb, Wn) is a rare visitor to South Florida from the Bahamas. It was previously called the Stripe-headed Tanager. The Bananaquit (*Coereba flaveola*) (Na, Nb, Wn) is the ultimate West Indian garden bird. It is a rare winter resident in South Florida, more frequent in the Keys than on the mainland.

Despite their striking red color, male Northern Cardinals can seemingly disappear into thick vegetation. Gardens with dense plantings are almost guaranteed to attract a nesting pair of cardinals.

Seed Eaters

Indigo Bunting (*Passerina cyanea*)—Na, Nb, Mg, Wn

Although nesting in North Florida, in South Florida these buntings are migrants and winter residents. They are most obvious in spring when males have taken on their remarkable blue plumage. Indigo Buntings feed in shrubs and on the ground on insects, spiders, small fruits and seeds, preferring shrubby sites and hammock edges, especially near agricultural fields. Indigo Buntings do come to tube feeders and to tray feeders near the ground for millet, canary seed, peanut bits, or crushed cornflakes, and they are attracted to gardens having thick stands of shrubs, beds of seed-bearing composites, tall grasses, and feeders.

Painted Bunting (*Passerina ciris*)—Na, Nb, Mg, Wn

Attracting this beautiful little bird is usually a goal for South Florida bird gardeners. Painted Buntings are fairly common migrants and uncommon to locally common as winter residents. Normally they feed on or near the ground on grass and other seeds, the fruit of low-growing herbaceous plants, and small ground-dwelling insects. But they readily come to feeders for millet, especially white proso millet served in tube feeders having small perches, and this is what many a South Florida bird gardener is hoping for. They also eat canary seed, sunflower seed bits, bread crumbs, small cracked corn, and red proso millet. A good practice, if concentrating on feeding buntings, is to use cage tube feeders with 1½-inch wire mesh, which buntings can go through but many other birds and squirrels cannot. Although attracted to millet, given the option, they prefer natural grass seeds and small fruit. So to increase the chances of attracting Painted Buntings, a South Florida bird garden should have plantings of winter-seeding grasses and small-fruiting short-statured plants, preferably near cover. It should also have a shallow water feature as well as the tube feeders

Coveted South Florida feeder birds, Painted Buntings can be attracted by white proso millet in tube feeders, particularly in gardens having other winter-seeding grasses and small-fruiting plants.

serving white millet. Buntings are traditional in their wintering sites, so it may take some time, perhaps years, for buntings to find a garden and its feeder. If the garden supports a small flock, additional feeders can be added.

Other seed-eating birds are less common, but some do occur in South Florida gardens. Rose-breasted Grosbeaks (*Pheucticus ludovicianus*) (Na, Nb, Mg, Wn) are rare in winter and uncommon migrants. They flock in winter when they may frequent garden seed feeders. Blue Grosbeaks (*Passerina caerulea*) (Na, Nb, Mg, Wn) are uncommon migrants and rare winter residents in South Florida, despite nesting in southern Central Florida. Dickcissels (*Spiza americana*) (Na, Nb, Mg, Wn) are uncommon winter residents and uncommon migrants whose presence in South Florida is unpredictable. When they show up, they may frequent seed feeders.

Blackbirds

Red-winged Blackbird (*Agelaius phoeniceus*)—Na, Br/Nb, Yr, Wn

Red-wings are beautiful birds, which is clear when a pair adopts a feeding station, but not as easily appreciated when they occur in large flocks. They are quite common in many situations throughout South Florida. In spring and summer, during nesting, residents occur in family groups and will come to seed feeders then. From late summer through winter they form flocks, some of significant size. Red-wings are found in many habitats, including freshwater marshes, ponds, lake edges, canal edges, coastal forests of mangrove and buttonwood, agricultural areas, and suburbs. They nest, sometimes in loose colonies, in cattails, sawgrass, mangroves, and small shrubs. Nests are low, below 10 feet, and often, although not necessarily, near or over water. Red-wings readily come to gardens to feed on lawns, under shrubs, and especially

Red-winged Blackbirds are fond of garden water features and bird feeders.

Attracting Birds to South Florida Gardens

at feeders stocked with millet, sunflower seeds, cracked corn, wheat, peanuts, and bread. They also use garden water features, the larger and more vegetated the better. Red-wings are attracted to gardens with diverse lawns, shrubs, beds of short-statured fruiting plants, tube and tray feeders, and a water feature. In winter at some locations, flocks may overwhelm a garden; if this becomes a problem, it is best to stop filling feeders until they move on.

Common Grackle (*Quiscalus quiscula*)—Na, Br/Nb, Yr, Mg, Wn

Found throughout South Florida, except in the Keys and perhaps mangrove swamps, Common Grackles use a wide variety of natural and artificial habitats, including cypress swamps, marshes, pinelands, agricultural areas, parks, groves, and suburbs. In spring and summer, they occur in family groups but in fall and winter accumulate in large flocks enhanced by winter residents. Grackles nest in pairs or small colonies in dense shrubs, short trees, and marsh vegetation. Grackles forage by walking, feeding mostly on seeds and small fruit but also on insects, snails, lizards, and even small birds, as well as human food. At feeders they eat black oil sunflower seeds, cracked corn, peanuts, wheat, leftovers, dog or cat food. Winter flocks, often involving other blackbirds, scavenge in urban and suburban areas, especially in parks and parking lots. They are attracted to gardens having diverse lawns, water features, feeding stations of either tray feeders or feed scattered on the ground, stands of shrubs, and native and commercial fruit trees, especially citrus, which they use as anti-parasitic coating.

Common Grackles nest in dense vegetation, such as this black olive tree. Here a nestling is being fed an anole, one of the many things the omnivorous grackle will eat.

Fundamentally water birds, Boat-tailed Grackles are particularly attracted to garden water features.

Boat-tailed Grackle (*Quiscalus major*)—Na, Br, Yr

Common throughout much of South Florida other than the Keys, this large black-bird is a common sight in residential and urban neighborhoods, especially near water, including beaches, coastal and inland marshes, ponds, rock pits, canals, water treatment areas, and roadside drainage features. They preferentially cluster their nests in cattails and shrubs over or near water, but do nest in other situations as well. Boat-tails forage mostly by walking on the ground collecting insects and seeds but will feed almost anywhere and eat almost anything. Their diet includes fruit, worms, snails, fish, frogs, lizards, small birds, bird eggs, human refuse, and dead stuff. They come to garden tray feeders for black oil sunflower seeds, cracked corn, peanuts, table scraps, bread, and fruit. Grackles are attracted to gardens with lawns, shrubs, trees, tray feeders, and large water features. As fundamentally aquatic birds, the latter feature is especially important to them.

Shiny Cowbird (*Molothrus bonariensis*)—Na, Br, Yr, Mg

A common bird throughout South America, this blackbird began colonizing South Florida in 1985. It is known primarily from coastal areas of the Keys to central Miami-Dade but increasingly farther north to Palm Beach. Cowbirds breed by placing their eggs in other birds' nests (called nest parasitism) and so are of conservation concern as they may affect native South Florida birds that have no inherent defense against them. Shiny Cowbirds feed by walking on the ground, distinctively scratching with one foot, and also in trees and shrubs. They favor grassy areas with scattered trees and shrubs such as lawns, parks, roadsides, and gardens. They are attracted to bird feeders for seeds and bread. Solitary in the nesting season, they form flocks and communal roosts with other blackbirds during the nonbreeding season when they are most likely to be noticed.

Brown-headed Cowbird (*Molothrus ater*)—Na, Nb, Mg, Wn

These North American blackbirds are primarily nonbreeding winter residents in South Florida, where they join mixed blackbird flocks. In the last half century, they have extended their breeding range down the Peninsula and since the early 1990s have been known to breed in South Florida, although verifiable records are few. Like Shiny Cowbirds, they are nest parasites, and their possible impact on endemic South Florida populations of Black-whiskered Vireos, Yellow and Prairie Warblers, and Seaside Sparrows is a matter of conservation concern. They prefer grassy habitat with trees and are often seen in neighborhoods, parks, and landscaped parking lots. They feed by walking on the ground searching for insects and seeds and can be attracted to seed scattered on the ground or in tray feeders on the ground. Cowbirds will come to millet feeders, especially if near the ground. Brown-headed Cowbirds are attracted to gardens having interspersed lawn and trees, a feeding station providing seed on or near the ground, and if possible a cow.

Bronzed Cowbird (*Molothrus aeneus*)—Na, Nb, Wn

These primarily Central American blackbirds have become locally common in South Florida, especially in south and central Miami-Dade and Naples. Like other cowbirds, they are nest parasites and feed on the ground on insects, seeds, and small fruit, often in flocks with other cowbirds. They regularly occur in gardens, sometimes in large numbers in winter, being attracted to seed feeders on the ground.

Bronzed Cowbirds are one of three cowbird species, all nest parasites, in the process of colonizing South Florida. This is an issue of conservation concern as several of Florida's rare or endangered birds subject to their parasitism have no history of nest parasitism and so have limited defense mechanisms.

Orioles

Spot-breasted Oriole (*Icterus pectoralis*)—Nn, Br, Yr

Originally from Mexico and Central America, this oriole has been breeding in South Florida for more than 60 years, although the population seems to be gradually decreasing. They occur from Palm Beach through Miami-Dade, especially in mid Miami-Dade. In South Florida, they are birds of residential areas, feeding in trees and shrubs, gleaning insects from leaves, drinking nectar from flowers, and picking small, sweet fruit such as mulberry, muscadine, citruses, and loquats. Spot-breasted Orioles build nests that hang from tree branches and sing from perches high in trees or on utility wires. Like most orioles, they are attracted to tray feeders offering sweet food such as fruit, especially open oranges, and jelly. A standard garden accoutrement farther north is the oriole sugar-water feeder, which is like a hummingbird feeder but usually larger, orange-colored, and with perches. In South Florida, these are even less successful than hummingbird feeders.

Orchard Oriole (*Icterus spurius*)—Na, Nb, Mg, Wn

Orchard Orioles are rather common migrants in fall and spring, when they appear in gardens while passing through South Florida. They are more common in the lower Keys than on the mainland. They are also very rare winter residents. Like other orioles, Orchard Orioles forage and roost in shrubs and trees. In South Florida, they tend to stay hidden in thick cover but can be found in gardens with stands of dense shrubs and trees.

Baltimore Oriole (*Icterus galbula*)—Na, Nb, Mg, Wn

Like the Orchard Oriole, the Baltimore Oriole is also a regular migrant and sometimes a winter resident. Wintering numbers vary from year to year. Garden preferences are similar to those of the other species of orioles.

Finches and Similar Birds

House Finch (*Haemorhous mexicanus*)—Nn, Br/Nb, Yr, Wn

Introduced from western North America, the House Finch is found through much of the eastern United States and is in the process of colonizing South Florida. Primarily winter residents in South Florida, a few are known to have nested in Fort Lauderdale and mid Miami-Dade. Where it occurs, this species is a common backyard bird, a habit that has fueled its range expansion. They readily adopt artificial feeders where they eat, especially black oil sunflower seeds but also niger, white proso millet, canary seed, hulled peanuts, fruit, suet, miscellaneous leftovers, and sugar water. They nest in various niches, including birdhouses, mailboxes, air vents, light fixtures, ledges, garden trees, and hanging plants. Artificial nest sites are 4 by 4 inch wooden platforms placed under cover, or a typical birdhouse 6 inches on each side with a 2-inch hole, placed about 10 feet high. Water sources are another attractant. No doubt this species will expand its range and will increasingly be seen in South Florida gardens.

American Goldfinch (*Spinus tristis*)—Na, Nb, Wn

Although common garden-nesting feeder birds in the north, goldfinches are only winter residents in South Florida, more common some winters than others and usually remaining into late spring. They eat seeds of asters, thistles, milkweeds, grasses, and similar plants and have acclimated to feeding opportunities presented by roadways, farms, suburban gardens and, during eruptive years, seed feeders. In South Florida, goldfinches form flocks that are attracted to gardens that have tall trees for perching, thick shrubs for roosting, or plants bearing small fruit in late winter and spring. Tube and tray feeders with sunflower seeds are also visited.

Yellow-fronted Canary (*Serinus mozambicus*)—Nn, Nb, Yr

These originally African birds have been seen regularly in Miami-Dade for many years. Males may occasionally sing from tall trees, although nesting has not been proven. As popular cage birds, they should not be unexpected visitors at South Florida garden feeders.

Island Canary (*Serinus canaria*)—Nn, Nb, Yr

Even more widely kept as cage birds in South Florida, canaries often escape and appear in gardens and at seed feeders. Highly domesticated, they seldom survive long in the wild.

Nutmeg Mannikin (*Lonchura punctulata*)—Nn, Br, Yr

Also known as Spice Finches, Ricebirds, and Scaly-breasted Munia, these birds from Southeast Asia through Australia are well represented as cage birds and nest in Miami-Dade. Highly social, they feed on seeds and small fruit. They have become locally common in southeastern Miami-Dade and come to seed feeders there.

House Sparrow (*Passer domesticus*)—Nn, X, Br, Yr

These originally European weaver finches are widespread in developed areas in South Florida, absent only from the interior wetlands but even there present around human sites. They are perhaps the most abundant bird in suburban and urban areas, where they feed on the ground in lawns, parks, road edges, and parking lots, picking up seeds, insects, fruits, and other small bits of matter. Although paired during a prolonged spring and summer nesting season, they flock from late summer through winter. They frequent seed feeders, either on the ground or hanging, especially for millet, but will eat other small seeds as well as bread and other scraps. They are niche nesters and will attempt to take over bird boxes and nearly any other niche, including signs and street lights. Not putting out seed feeders in summer is a way to discourage them in a garden.

House Sparrows are abundant wherever people occur in South Florida. They take advantage of garden seed feeders for food and use building niches for nesting.

6

South Florida Bird Plants

The array of plants available to South Florida bird gardeners is nothing short of immense. An enviable problem facing South Florida's bird gardeners is dealing with the long list of options. Options make things interesting but also require more study than merely heading to the local big box garden store, grabbing a pot from the rack, and popping the contents into the ground. Following that approach in South Florida more often than not results in disappointment.

There is no single list of plants right for every South Florida yard. Choices can be made based on any number of criteria, including importantly the gardener's personal preferences: the formal and personal aesthetics of garden design, practicalities of available space, existing plantings to be complemented, personal uses the yard accommodates, bird species available in the neighborhood, bird species targeted for attraction, personal affinity to certain plants, start-up and maintenance costs, and more. Fortunately, the many options that exist give South Florida bird gardeners opportunities to please both the birds and themselves, but this does require some study.

In this section, we discuss some plants to be considered for attracting birds to a South Florida garden. We give local and scientific names, describe the flowers, fruits, insects, and structure that determine their value to birds, and sometimes add bits about their biology that suggest their biological or cultivation potentials. We don't go into the details of plant descriptions or horticulture, as this information is extensive and readily available from other sources, which we provide in chapter 7. Select plants are illustrated by photographs. This list of plants, although very long, certainly does not cover all the choices; personal innovation is welcome. More kinds of plants become available to gardeners all the time, and hopefully our knowledge of their value to birds will be perfected.

Plants included are some of those with known bird-friendly properties that work in a garden in South Florida and are more or less available. A plant can be found by wandering down the list or by using the book's index.

Informational Codes for Plant Accounts

Native to South Florida	Na	Vegetable/herb garden	Vg
Non-native	Nn	Wildflower garden	Wf
Invasive non-native	X	Nesting sites	Ns
Tree-sized	Tr	Perch sites	Pr
Shrub-sized	Sh	Structure/cover	St
Short-statured plant	Ss	Insects, other invertebrates	In
Vine	Vn	Fruit	Fr
Aquatic plant	Aq	Seed	Sd
Diverse lawn	Ln	Nectar	Nc
Water feature	Wt	Available widely	AW
Epiphyte	Ep	Available from specialty sources	AS
Ground	Gr	Available rarely or not at all	AR
Butterfly/hummingbird garden	Bt		

Ferns

Giant Leather Fern (*Acrostichum danaeifolium*)—Na, Ss/Sh, St, Wt, AS

True to its name, this is the largest native South Florida fern, up to 15 feet tall and 5 feet wide. Growing from suckers and forming large clumps, it provides exceptional cover for birds. It is best in large, semishaded, damp locations such as on the edges of a garden water feature, borrow pit, or canal. Long appreciated for its primeval appearance, the Giant leather fern can be an exuberant addition to South Florida water gardens.

Swamp Fern (*Blechnum serrulatum*)—Na, Ss/Sh, Aq, Wt, St, AS

Also called the toothed midsorus fern, this is one of the more abundant ferns in South Florida wetlands. The 2–4-foot-tall plants do best in damp soils and so provide excellent cover next to garden water features.

Sword Fern (*Nephrolepis exaltata*)—Na, Ss, St, AW

Growing 3–6 feet tall, these shade-tolerant native ferns, also called wild Boston ferns, provide ground cover for birds either under or edging the shrub canopy. They similarly hide a diverse community of invertebrates including Florida fern caterpillars (*Callopistria floridensis*), thrips, spider mites, mealybugs, whiteflies, snails, and slugs as well as frogs and lizards. Native not only to Florida but also to much of the world's tropics, they can be terrestrial, container plants, or epiphytic as they can be found naturally on cabbage palms, oaks, and dead logs. This is the plant from which the common houseplant was derived more than a hundred years ago, from Florida specimens. Many cultivars do well in a bird garden. Similar-looking non-native ferns, called the

Named for their suede-looking spores, giant leather ferns are excellent water feature plants—attractive while providing ample cover for birds and the insects they eat.

tuberous sword fern (*Nephrolepis cordifolia*) and Asian sword fern (*Nephrolepis brownii* or *multiflora*) need to be avoided as they are among the most aggressive species in South Florida, and in fact are now shunned even in the nursery trade.

Staghorn ferns are sensational epiphytic ferns that can grow to several feet wide, providing ample habitat for insects and birds.

Giant Sword Fern (*Nephrolepis biserrata*)—Na, Ss/Sh, Wt, St, In, AS

These ferns natively grow in damp shaded areas of hammocks. Like the Boston fern, Florida plants were taken into cultivation more than a century ago and are well appreciated house and garden plants. A well-known and very attractive variety, the fish-tail fern, has bifurcated frond tips. Growing 4–6 feet tall or even taller, it is best placed in the background of low plantings, in the shrub zone, or as an accent. It provides substantial cover for birds, including nesting cover, as well as housing a community of invertebrate and vertebrate bird food similar to that of the sword fern.

Royal Fern (*Osmunda regalis*), Cinnamon Fern (*Osmunda cinnamomea*)—Na, Ss/Sh, Wt, St, AS

These large, refined, beautifully fronded ferns are natives of South Florida marshes and do well in wet or well-watered garden situations. At 3–5 feet tall, they provide excellent low cover for birds on the ground, such as Eastern Towhees, warblers, and sparrows. Both ferns are considered overexploited and cannot be removed from the wild but are available commercially.

Staghorn Fern (*Platycerium bifurcatum*)—Nn, Ep, St, In, AW

Also called elkhorn ferns, these are among the most sensational ferns in South Florida gardens. Their epiphytic colonies grow to 3 feet or more wide. In South Florida, staghorns are installed outdoors in the shade, attached to trunks, hung in pots, or affixed to pieces of wood. Not only are they exceptional garden elements on their own, but they also support a microcosm of invertebrates around their debris-trapping bases, rhizomes, and fronds. Small insectivorous birds, especially in winter, continuously work through the plants.

Golden Polypody (*Phlebodium aureum*)—Na, Ep, St, In, AS

Most commonly found as epiphytes in moist hammocks, often with shoestring ferns (*Vittaria lineata*). They grow most commonly in the detritus-filled boots of cabbage palms. Fronds reach 2–3 feet long. They are difficult to transplant and should not be collected from the wild, but are available commercially in several cultivars and will volunteer on their own if a source is nearby.

Resurrection Fern (*Pleopeltis polypodioides*)—Na, Ep, St, AR

These ferns, growing most commonly on live oaks, are fascinating in their ability to dry out during the dry season, returning to green lushness when the rains return. Like other epiphytes, they create their own little ecosystem of invertebrates on which birds forage.

After spending the dry season shriveled up, resurrection ferns burst to life with the first rains. These epiphytic ferns, here on a live oak branch, provide for a community of insects and other invertebrates. Birds forage among the fronds.

Cycads

Coontie (*Zamia pumila*)—Na, Ss, Bt, St, In, Sd, AW

Historically harvested for their starchy roots, South Florida's native cycads bring historical context to a garden. Growing 1–5 feet tall depending on genetics and site, they provide considerable structure either individually or in mass as an herbaceous border. Their fleshy red seeds attract jays and mockingbirds. Coontie hosts beetles (*Pharaxonotha zamiae* and *Rhopalotria slossoni*) and the once near-extinct atala caterpillars, but these appear to be distasteful to birds. Non-native *Zamia* are available that are hard to distinguish. These will serve the same function for birds as the native species but do not provide the native species' historic context. Coontie should be an essential part of a South Florida garden.

An essential component of a South Florida butterfly garden, coontie is the larval host for atala caterpillars, seen here next to hatched eggs (upper right). Coontie provides low structure and cover for birds.

Conifers

Slash Pine (*Pinus elliottii*)—Na, Tr, Ns, Pr, St, In, Sd, AS

South Florida's principal native pine, this tree was once found over most of the uplands and a good part of the lower lands of South Florida. Unlike most pines, it can survive with wet roots for extended periods. Seeds, released in fall, are eaten by turkey, bobwhite, jays, thrashers, cardinals, doves, goldfinches, meadowlarks, towhees, Red-bellied Woodpeckers, crows, Chestnut-fronted Macaws, and also gray and fox squirrels. Slash pines support an exceptional community of insects under rough bark, within clusters of 5–10-inch needles, in cavities, and in cones. Insects include beetles (*Isa, Dendroctonus, Pissodes,* and *Hylobius*), southern pine coneworm caterpillars, slash pine seedworm caterpillars, honey bees (*Apis mellifera*), wasps, snout moths, pine webworms, sawflies (*Neodiprion merkeli*), scale insects (*Oracella*), and many more. Not surprisingly, spiders are abundant as well. These invertebrates provide food for many insect-eating birds including woodpeckers, flickers, mockingbirds, tanagers, gnatcatchers, chickadees, titmice, Yellow-rumped Warblers, Pine Warblers, other wintering and migrant warblers, and Brown-headed Nuthatches, as well as frogs, lizards, and snakes. They are important feeding trees for sapsuckers.

At 40–80 feet high, pines are among the tallest native trees in South Florida and their open branches serve as high perches for hawks, mockingbirds, Swallow-tailed Kites, owls, vultures, macaws, Mourning Doves, flycatchers, crows, and bulbuls. Great Horned Owls, Mourning Doves, and crows will nest within the crown. Dead trunks are critically important as food sources and cavity sites for woodpeckers. Woodpecker cavities are later used by Eastern Screech-Owls, Great Crested Flycatchers, conures, starlings, and honey bees.

Being among the tallest native trees, slash pines provide nesting sites and roosting perches for birds such as this Mourning Dove. In addition to structure, slash pine provides exceptional crops of insects and spiders. Small birds will often be seen foraging along its branches.

As argued in previous chapters, dead pine trunks are important garden assets. Pre-existing living pine trees in gardens require care as they are usually at risk from mowing, overwatering, and soil compaction. They also fare badly in hurricanes, so replacement trees need to be planted periodically. Pines are best planted as small seedlings within a setting of shrubs or other trees, preferably on natural soil rather than fill. Any existing slash pines should be preserved and protected, and it is most worthwhile to try establishing more.

Sand Pine (*Pinus clausa*)—Na, Tr, Ns, Pr, St, In, Sd, AR

These are the pines of Florida sand scrub, an elevated xeric habitat that now occurs primarily north of Lake Okeechobee. Most of South Florida's limited sand pine habitat was destroyed by development, so few sand pines remain. A garden on deep sandy soil would be enhanced by attempting to reestablish them. The typical bird of the sand pine is the Florida Scrub-Jay, but because of habitat destruction it is now seldom found in South Florida, but many other species occur, including woodpeckers, doves, bobwhites, and wintering songbirds. Sand pine seeds from 2–4-inch cones are eaten by Scrub-Jays, Mourning Doves, turkeys, bobwhites, and squirrels, although cones open infrequently, usually in response to fire. The 2–4-inch needles and rough trunk support clusters of insects and spiders; as with slash pine, the branches of sand pine serve as perches. As bird habitat, sand pines are best landscaped surrounded by their natural associates of oaks, palmettos, and typical scrub species such as rusty staggerbush (*Lyonia ferruginea*), Florida rosemary (*Ceratiola ericoides*), shiny blueberry (*Vaccinium myrsinites*), and gopher apple (*Licania michauxii*).

Bald-Cypress (*Taxodium distichum*), Pond-Cypress (*Taxodium ascendens*)—
Na, Tr, Aq, Wt, Ns, Pr, St, In, Sd, AS

At 30–100 feet high, bald-cypress is among the tallest of South Florida's native trees. Pond-cypress is somewhat smaller having sparse foliage. Together they dominate the swamps of southwestern South Florida and persist naturally in some locations on the eastern coast as well. Although swamp trees, they can survive well in garden settings. Remnant trees should certainly be protected in gardens and replacements planted as well. Their seeds, in 1-inch cones, can be used by strong-billed birds such as grosbeaks and parrots, as well as by squirrels. Once on the ground, the seeds are eaten by more species such as cranes, ducks, and various mammals. Short and soft leaves, scaly bark, and abundant detritus-trapping epiphytes support wasps, honey bees, ants, fall webworms (*Hyphantria cunea*), cypress leaf beetles (*Systena marginalis*), coneworms (*Dioryctria amatella* and *Dioryctria pygmaeella*), and flies such as bald-cypress seed midge (*Taxodiomyia cupress*) and cypress twig gall midge (*Taxodiomyia cupressiananassa*), also spiders, millipedes, and centipedes. As a result, insectivorous birds continuously work the canopy and bark, including gnatcatchers, kinglets, vireos, and warblers, especially Northern Parulas and Yellow-throated Warblers.

Bald-cypress provides exceptional structure, especially for perching and roosting. The leaves of pond-cypress grow upward, more needlelike than those of bald-cypress and offering a bit less cover for birds. Red-bellied and Pileated Woodpeckers make and use holes in the soft wood of living and dead trunks, which are then used by other cavity-nesting birds and by wildlife. Cypresses are prime nesting and roosting trees for herons, ibis, storks, owls, Red-shouldered Hawks, Swallow-tailed Kites, and, in developed areas, Monk Parakeets. Cypresses can be planted in most garden settings and are especially appropriate in larger yards by a water feature.

Bald-cypress attracts numerous birds, like this Palm Warbler, for roosting, nesting, and insects.

Water Lilies

Water lilies are always a temptation for any aquatic feature—and why not? In addition to adding visual interest, they support insects, insect larvae, snails, and other aquatic invertebrates, which birds can access by walking on the floating leaves. Gallinules have long toes that serve them well when walking on lily leaves. Warblers such as Common Yellowthroats as well as Red-winged Blackbirds and grackles also feed from the leaves. Native lilies are well adapted for South Florida and provide the best insect value for birds. Native water lilies (Na, Aq, Wt, St, In, AS) include spatterdock (*Nuphar advena*), American white waterlily (*Nymphaea odorata*), tropical royalblue waterlily (*Nymphaea elegans*), yellow waterlily (*Nymphaea mexicana*), little floatingheart (*Nymphoides cordata*), and big floatingheart (*Nymphoides aquatica*). The horticultural options for non-native water lilies (Nn, X?, Aq, Wt, St, In, AW) are nearly unlimited, and these provide similar structure. Popular options include white Egyptian lotus (*Nymphaea lotus*) and crested floatingheart (*Nymphoides cristata*), the latter considered aggressive if it escapes.

Waterlilies attract numerous insects, such as this darner dragonfly, to garden water features.

Peppers and Lizard Tails

Lizard's Tail (*Saururus cernuus*)—Na, Ss, Aq, Wt, St, In, AS

These small freshwater plants survive extremely well in garden water features, providing water-edge cover. Their fragrant white flowers on drooping stalks bloom from summer through fall, attracting pollinating insects and their bird predators, especially warblers and vireos. Their leaves are used by frogs, anoles, and spiders; their tubers are eaten by waterfowl, although this is an unlikely backyard garden event. They are so adaptable to water features they are best grown in pots to keep them in line.

Cinnamon Bark (*Canella winterana*)—Na, Sh/Tr, Bt, Pr, St, In, Fr, Nc, AS

Also called wild cinnamon, cinnamon bark has a long human history, having been taken from the West Indies to Europe by the first Spanish explorers. Blooming for much of the year, the fragrant ⅛-inch flowers are purple to red, occurring in terminal clusters, a few opening at a time. They attract bees, wasps, butterflies, and humming-birds. The ½-inch soft, red to yellow fruits persist on the plant, providing food for wintering birds. Although in the West Indies they can be good-sized trees to 30 feet, in South Florida they tend to be slow-growing shrubs or small trees to 15 feet. Open ascending branches provide good cover for perch sites. Natively, they are part of the subcanopy or shrubby edges of coastal hammocks in the Keys and provide structure within or at the edges of tree plantings. Other landscape uses are as small specimens, informal screens, or even patio plants. At the northern edge of its natural range in South Florida, cinnamon bark is Florida-listed endangered.

Lizard's tail is a highly adaptable plant that survives well in garden water features, providing cover for birds like this female Northern Cardinal.

Cinnamon bark's fragrant flowers attract humming-birds, as well as numerous insects for other birds to eat.

Laurels

Red Bay (*Persea borbonia*)—Na, Sh/Tr, Pr, St, In, Fr, AW

These adaptable, variable, dense, and broad-crowned evergreen trees provide exceptional cover for birds, as well as high-energy fruit. Inconspicuous yellow-green flowers appear in spring (although sometimes later), followed by tiny ½–1-inch dark blue to purple mini-avocado fruits available mostly in fall. The high-energy fruits are eaten by mockingbirds, thrashers, cardinals, jays, crows, bluebirds, and bobwhites, as well as by warblers and vireos, especially on fall migration. The fruits also attract raccoons, deer, and squirrels. The leaves are densely packed together and provide food for insects, including caterpillars of palamedes and spicebush swallowtail butterflies and io moths. Natively they are hammock plants reaching 20–30 feet tall, smaller in pinelands. They have complete canopies with many internal twigs and drooping branches that reach the ground, providing ample structure. For birds, they are best used in mixed-tree plantings or as large specimens; to retain structural value, they should not be trimmed or shaped. In addition to its use in gardens, red bay should be considered for commercial and even roadside plantings, although there is concern about the potential impact of a new disease, laurel wilt, caused by a fungus (*Raffaelea lauricola*) spread by redbay ambrosia beetles (*Xyleborus glabratus*). The similar but smaller native swamp bay (*Persea palustris*) can be used in wetter settings.

Avocado (*Persea americana*)—Nn, Tr, Pr, St, In, Fr, AW

Avocados are one of the most important bird trees in South Florida. They support numerous insects, likely because avocados are related to native species and have been selected in horticulture. Insectivorous birds work the branches and leaves year-round. Among the bird prey hosted by avocados are swallowtail caterpillars, mites (*Oligonychus yothersi*), scale insects (*Aspidiotus*), whiteflies (*Trialeurodes floridensis*), thrips (*Selenothrips rubrocinctus, Heliothrips haemorrhoidalis*), leaf hoppers (*Empoasca minuenda*), leafrollers (*Gracilaria perseae*), geometer moths (Geometridae) such as avocado spanworm moths (*Epimecis detexta*), ambrosia beetle borers (*Xylosandrus*), ants, and termites. Tiny but abundant greenish flowers attract honey bees, thought to be their main pollinator, as well as avocado lace bugs (*Acysta perseae*), wasps (*Polistes*), mirid bugs (*Dagbertus*), house flies (*Musa domestica*), other flies, and thrips (*Franklimélla*). Clearly avocados present an array of insects for birds to eat. Although summer to fall fruits are too large for birds to eat whole, Red-bellied Woodpeckers and squirrels dig holes in the hanging fruit. Once open, the fruit is fair game for jays, orioles, and many other birds. Up to 60 feet tall and broad, avocados are often among the tallest trees in the neighborhood, providing high canopy structure and perching sites. For birds, they should not be trimmed. As with its relatives, there is concern about the future impact of laurel wilt.

Lancewood (*Ocotea coriacea*)—Na, Sh/Tr, Pr, St, In, Fr, AS

Although a tropical plant, lancewood can be used in gardens along the entire South Florida coastline. Impressive arrays of small ½-inch white spring flowers attract the

Lancewood's small white flowers, leaves, and branches attract countless invertebrates that in turn lure birds. The small avocado-like fruits are also bird attractors.

same variety of insect pollinators as do avocados, especially honey bees. The ½-inch purple-black fruits, produced in late summer through winter, are eaten by mockingbirds, catbirds, cardinals, jays, thrushes, bluebirds, robins, and bobwhites, as well as by squirrels and raccoons. They host a diverse insect community, including swallowtail caterpillars, and their broad leaves provide good cover. As hammock canopy trees, they typically grow to 20–30 feet and should be considered for mixed-tree hammock-like plantings. They also work as buffer plantings and in commercial settings.

Magnolias

Pond Apple (*Annona glabra*)—Na, Aq, Wt, Ns, Pr, St, In, AS

Related to tropical fruits such as soursop (*Annona muricata*) and custard apple (*Annona reticulata*), this swamp tree takes readily to garden settings. Its 1-inch flowers are pollinated by flies, and the bark supports numerous insects and spiders. It is an exceptional tree for epiphytic bromeliads and orchids. Insectivorous birds, especially blackbirds, grackles, and Common Yellowthroats, work through the canopy. Its most distinctive feature is its 3–5-inch apple-like fruit, eaten after it falls by raccoons, turtles, and alligators but not often by birds. In wetlands, waterbirds often place their nests in the stout branches of pond apple trees. In garden settings, they grow variably 10–20 feet tall and so are large shrubs to trees. They can be accent trees but look best overhanging a small pond where their apples dangle intriguingly for many weeks.

Sweetbay (*Magnolia virginiana*)—Na, Sh/Tr, Pr, St, In, Sd, AW

Locally called sweetbay magnolia or swamp magnolia, this stunning tree is native to South Florida north of the Keys. Fragrant white flowers in spring and summer turn to conelike clusters of red seeds that last into winter, or until eaten by Red-bellied Woodpeckers, mockingbirds, catbirds, thrashers, crows, towhees, Eastern Kingbirds,

Red-eyed Vireos, squirrels, raccoons, or native rats and mice. Once on the ground, seeds are eaten by turkeys and bobwhite. Long thick leaves and multiple branches provide cover and also provide an exceptional supply of insects, spiders, and other invertebrates, including caterpillars of the eastern tiger and palamedes swallowtails. In South Florida, sweetbays are trees of damp ground and so in gardens do best in moist organic soils. Although tall, up to 30 feet in South Florida, they have a relatively narrow, single-trunked growth form and so can be used as large specimen trees or within mixed-tree plantings where they may sucker into thickets. The farther north, the taller and more deciduous the plants become. The more sensational southern magnolia (*Magnolia grandiflora*) is rather rare in cultivation in South Florida but can be grown with care in a garden setting.

Water Plantains

Bulltongue Arrowhead (*Sagittaria lancifolia*)—Na, Aq, Wt, In, AS

These emergent aquatic plants have beautiful white, 1-inch flowers that from spring through fall attract pollinator insects including bumble bees, sweat bees, small butterflies, wasps, flies, and beetles. The leaves, to 3 feet long, attract chewing insects, especially grasshoppers and caterpillars such as the Cattail Borer. They also support spiders, and frogs hide in the leaves. All these attract birds, especially Red-winged Blackbirds, warblers, wrens, and vireos. These are plants to use at pond edges and in shallow garden water features.

Bulltongue arrowhead grows well in shallow water features and attracts numerous insects, spiders, and other invertebrates.

Screwpines

Common Screwpine (*Pandanus utilis*), Beach Screwpine (*Pandanus sanderi*)—Nn, Tr, Wt, Ns, Pr, Fr, Sd, AS

These Old World tropical trees with ribbonlike leaves and prop roots produce an internally open structure, providing perches for owls, hawks, mockingbirds, mynas, and many other birds. Trunks are used by cavity-nesting birds. Their compound fruits are eaten by Amazons and macaws and also ants, bees, and flies on the tree, and once on the ground by raccoons, iguanas, and land crabs. Screwpines go well at the edges of water features, where they can form open jungles of branches providing cover for birds.

Lilies and Lily Relatives

Perfumed Spiderlily (*Hymenocallis latifolia*)—Na, Ss/Sh, Wf, St, In, AW

These beautiful plants are fast growing and hardy, reaching 2–3 feet high and equally wide. Their foliage provides cover for insects, snails, slugs, millipedes, and other invertebrates. These attract ground- and low-foraging birds, as well as frogs, lizards, and snakes, which also can be bird food. Sensational white, fragrant, 5-inch-long flowers, blooming spring to fall, attract pollinating insects including sphinx moths and hawk moths. The leaves attract grasshoppers and support sphinx moth caterpillars, also known as hornworms. Rather than as specimens, these lilies are best used as tall ground cover and at the shrub zone edge. Occurring naturally over a wide habitat breadth, including beach dunes, they are quite drought and sand tolerant, will reseed, and can be planted from bulbs. In nearly any situation, they provide excellent cover for birds.

Greenbriers (*Smilax*)—Na, Vn, St, In, Fr, AR

These thin, painful climbing vines have fragrant flowers that attract bees, wasps, and butterflies. Their ¼-inch blue to black fruits, which remain on the vine from late summer through winter, are eaten by all the fruit-eating birds, especially mockingbirds and catbirds, but also vireos, warblers, and woodpeckers. Despite their value, greenbriers are not often available for sale because of their thinness and unattractive thorniness, but in fact, their wide-ranging, sharp-thorned stems are an added value for birds within the tree canopy. In addition to climbing, they can creep along the ground within a diverse lawn. Bamboo vine (*Smilax laurifolia*), also called laurel greenbrier, has a wide range in North America and is well adapted to South Florida. Earleaf greenbrier (*Smilax auriculata*) occurs natively in drier pineland sites. Everglades greenbrier (*Smilax havanensis*), a threatened species in Florida, is found in North America only in South Florida. Other species of greenbriers have similar values in the bird garden. Once established, greenbriers develop a starchy root, once eaten by native Indians and pioneers, and so are quite hardy. Greenbriers can be grown from seed and do best in partial sun, planted where they can climb up tree trunks.

Left: Earleaf greenbriers provide both fruit and thorny protection for birds high in the canopy.

Right: The poisonbulb, or grand crinum lily, is an impressive garden plant with elegant flowers and an imposing size (up to 5 feet high and more wide), providing substantial cover for birds as well as a home for insects, spiders, and snails.

String-lily (*Crinum americanum*)—Na, Ss/Sh, Aq, Wt, St, In, AS

Native to freshwater swamps in the southeastern United States, this amaryllis provides excellent cover in water features, drainage areas, and other moist soils. It grows 2–3 feet high and nearly as broad, and its large leaves are a favored food of lubber grasshoppers. Sphinx moths pollinate the 10-inch-diameter fragrant white flowers in their spring-to-fall blooming.

Poisonbulb (*Crinum asiaticum*)—Nn, Ss/Sh, Wt, St, In, AW

Also more attractively called the grand crinum lily, this is a larger version of the native swamp lily and is popular with landscapers because it is both sensational and virtually indestructible. Its leaves are 4–5 feet long and grow in a rosette from a pseudostem the size of a small tree trunk anchored by a similarly huge bulb. A plant is typically 5–6 feet wide, and suckering plants can increase clump size almost indefinitely. It flowers year-round with sweet-smelling 6-inch tubular white flowers clustered by the dozens into magnificent 12-inch inflorescences that attract ants, bees, and butterflies. Debris collects within its leaf bases, and these and the humid, protected space under the plant provide cover for a diverse community of ants, grasshoppers, spiders, and especially snails, slugs, and millipedes. Although the plant is known for being poisonous to consume, it provides exceptional cover and food for a bird garden, serving as a hedge, edge, or spectacular focal point.

Agave (*Agave*)—Na/Nn, Ss/Sh, St, Nc, AW/AS

Agaves or century plants are impressive, fierce plants with sharply pointed leaves that in some species reach 5 feet long. Plants themselves can stand as tall as wide, and the fruiting stalk in some species reaches 20–30 feet. They are highly recommended in bird-friendly, cat-unfriendly gardens, especially when placed within hedges or garden edges, and near feeding stations. Although natively bat pollinated, the flowers provide large quantities of nectar and so attract nectar-seeking birds such as hummingbirds and orioles as well as many insects including honey bees. The American century plant (*Agave americana*), originally from Mexico, has several cultivars. Sisal hemp (*Agave sisalana*) has a history in South Florida as it was introduced from Mexico more than a hundred years ago as a commercial crop by Henry Perrine, who was killed by Indians for his efforts. This agave has naturalized in the Keys and along the southern Florida coast and can be a bit aggressive. False sisal (*Agave decipiens*) is uncommonly found in the wild in South Florida from the Keys north along the coasts. In South Florida, the wild century plant (*Agave weberi*) occurs in sand and shell mounds in Lee and Palm Beach counties. It is generally considered a rare Florida endemic but could instead be a cultivar introduced by the Spanish several hundred years ago. Many other agaves, non-natives of various sizes and shapes, are available and provide similar bird sheltering. Most agaves require little care and no fertilization or irrigation.

Spanish Bayonet (*Yucca aloifolia*)—Na, Sh/Tr, St, In, AS

Like agaves, these dry-site natives have viciously pointed leaves and for that reason are useful in bird gardens where bird protection is desired, such as in hedges and near feeding stations and nest boxes. In summer, their fragrant, white, bell-shaped flowers in large sprays attract symbiotic yucca moths (*Tegeticula yuccasella*) that both pollinate and later feed on the seeds. They seldom fruit in South Florida, likely because of a paucity of the correct moths, but they do support lots of other insects, including weevils, mealybugs, and thrips, which are hunted by small birds. They are usually 5–10 feet tall, but can reach 20, and can form formidable thickets.

Orchids—Na/Nn, Ep/Ss, St, In, AW/AS/AR

Gardeners know and appreciate orchids for their intriguing long-lasting flowers, but they are also useful additions to bird-friendly gardens because they increase physical complexity and attract insects and other invertebrates to their root masses. Their flowers, evolved to attract pollinating insects, similarly provide food for birds. The South Florida garden is special in North America because orchids can be used so profusely. More than two dozen epiphytic orchids are native to South Florida, the most widespread and adaptable being the Florida butterfly orchid (*Encyclia tampensis*). Other well-known natives include the clamshell orchid (*Prosthechea cochleata*), night-scented epidendrum (*Epidendrum nocturnum*), cigar or cowhorn orchid (*Cyrtopodium punctatum*), and vanilla orchids (*Vanilla* species). Florida's native orchids have suffered from overharvesting, habitat loss, and non-native pests and are not allowed to be collected from the wild, but some are cultivated and may be purchased.

Orchids provide much more than beauty in a bird garden. Their flowers are highly specialized to attract pollinators, and, as epiphytes, they create additional insect and bird habitat on tree trunks. This *Oncidium sphacelatum*, native to Central America, is effective at creating habitat. It can be quite large with cascading sprays of flowers.

Further, thousands of non-native orchids and hybrids are available. Schomburgkias, vandas, dendrobiums, cattleyas, as well as non-native encylias and oncidiums, do well when installed on appropriate South Florida trees, especially live oak, buttonwood, and fruit trees. All these increase the bird-friendly space within a garden.

Palms

Coconut Palm (*Cocos nucifera*)—Nn, Tr, Ns, Pr, St, In, Fr, AW

Coconut palms are such symbols of South Florida gardens as to be a requirement. Certainly every garden aiming to attract birds needs a few. Although native to the Indo-Pacific, they have been planted in South Florida for more than 150 years and so add historic value as well. The old-time South Florida coconut palm of picture postcards, the Jamaica Tall variety, achieves a height of 80 feet, often wonderfully bent by the wind. Owing to disease, these have mostly been replaced by smaller, straighttrunked golden and red Malayan coconut varieties and the Malayan-Jamaican hybrid 'Maypan.' Dwarf varieties are now also available, but taller is better for birds.

Flowers provide nectar and attract honey bees and other insects, although they are also wind pollinated. The flowers also attract orioles and hummingbirds for nectar, and parrots and bulbuls eat the flowers directly. Coconut palms are known mostly for their fruit. When small, the fruits are eaten by crows, Amazon parrots, and macaws. When large and still on the tree, squirrels chew them to expose the pulp, which is then eaten by woodpeckers and other birds. The palm's canopy, composed of live and dead leaves, inflorescences, fruit, and accompanying detritus, is a cornucopia of insects, other invertebrates, and small vertebrates, all of which can be eaten by birds. The canopy provides high nesting sites for Red-shouldered and Cooper's Hawks, owls, and Monk Parakeets. The high fronds are perching sites for hawks, mockingbirds, starlings, crows, grackles, vultures, mynas, and other birds.

As discussed previously, coconut palms in a bird-friendly garden should not be trimmed of dead fronds or remnant bracts as these provide insect food and roost sites

South Florida's original coconut palm, the Jamaica Tall variety, towers up to 80 feet high.

Coconut palm is one of South Florida's most important bird plants. Its trunk provides nesting cavities, its leaves provide insects, and here a Red-bellied Woodpecker picks the remaining coconut meat after an eastern gray squirrel has opened the nut.

for bats and are important for the tree's health. Nor should coconuts be trimmed off, unless of course for the gardener's harvest or for protecting passersby. The fronds and fruit will fall when they are ready. This, actually, is the only real issue with planting coconut palms: they need to be planted where falling coconuts and their massive leaves will not hit people or do other damage.

An important value of coconut palms to gardens lies in their trunks, the number one source of natural nesting cavities in South Florida. Red-bellied Woodpeckers and Yellow-bellied Sapsuckers excavate cavities that are then used by other species, such as Great Crested Flycatchers, parakeets, conures, and starlings. Coconut palms, alive and dead, attract all these species to a garden. They are best planted where they can be left standing when they die to be used by birds for many years.

Florida Royal Palm (*Roystonea regia*)—Na, Tr, Ns, Pr, St, In, Fr, AS

Among the more spectacular native plants in South Florida, royal palms should be in the mixed-tree zone of most bird gardens. They can grow 60–100 feet tall, the crowns reaching above surrounding canopy, providing important and well-used high perch sites. Red-bellied Woodpeckers are commonly seen clinging to the top of the still un-furled newest leaf standing upright above the palm. Royal palms have tiny pink and white flowers on impressive many-branched flower stalks, occurring at any time of year but mostly in spring. These attract bees, butterflies, and other insects. The flow-ers are followed by ½-inch dark purple fruits, peaking in summer through winter and favored by the larger fruit-eating birds, including crows, Red-bellied Woodpeckers, mockingbirds, robins, jays, and Amazon parrots. The complex crown of leaves, in-florescences, and fruit support many insects and other invertebrates, including its own royal palm bug (*Xylastodoris luteolus*), as well as tree frogs, anoles, and snakes. Red-bellied Woodpeckers, Eastern Phoebes, grackles, jays, starlings, parrots, and mi-grating and wintering warblers feed in the crown. Monk Parakeets build their nests there as well. Strong fronds offer high perches for owls, hawks, mockingbirds, grack-les, crows, vultures, mynas, and many other birds. Dead trees become exceptionally important for cavity-nesting species because Red-bellied and Pileated Woodpeckers excavate chambers in their trunks.

Impressively tall and sturdy, the crown of royal palm hosts many perching birds and provides high nest sites. Larger birds, such as this Red-Shouldered Hawk, nest in the canopy, and cavity-nesting species use the trunk.

Attracting Birds to South Florida Gardens

They should be planted where their very heavy falling fronds do not pose a danger to passersby or property. It is generally recommended that royal palms not be planted in small yards, but rather be reserved for large estates with long driveways. We disagree; when the palms are adult and towering over a garden, the only thing at eye level is the trunks, and even these disappear at eye level when planted within a mixed-tree setting. Meanwhile, they will be used by every bird in the neighborhood.

Although native to the extreme southern end of Florida, they are surprisingly cold hardy and can grow throughout South Florida. Their taxonomy is confusing, but most royal palms available are derived from West Indian stock rather than from Florida native stock; however, they can be told apart. The Cuban royal palm has a bulging trunk whereas the Florida royal palm is more straight. Either provides exceptional, nearly indispensable, value to birds in a South Florida garden.

Everglades Palm (*Acoelorrhaphe wrightii*)—Na, Sh/Tr, St, In, Fr, AW

This clumping palm is an incredibly useful plant for South Florida bird gardens. It forms clusters of multiple trunks at differing heights up to 30 feet, with 2–3-foot-wide fan-shaped leaves on thorny stems. This hedge offers superior protection. Thorny-stemmed leaves remain on the tree well after dying, adding to the clump's barrier qualities and to its bird value. It is quite important that these not be trimmed off, for both the birds and the palm. In late winter through spring, their ⅛-inch flowers on 4-foot inflorescences attract large numbers of insects, especially flies and bees. Small ¼–½-inch fruits, first orange then black, available in fall and winter, are eaten by mockingbirds, cardinals, grackles, and jays. Also called paurotis palm, they naturally form fringing thickets between low tree islands and adjacent marsh and so are perfectly situated adjacent to lakes, rock pits, canals, or large garden ponds, as well as bordering structures. In any situation, they need a good supply of water, and also manganese supplements if growing directly on limestone or near concrete. Although native to extreme South Florida, they can survive farther north over much of the South Florida area.

Clumped Everglades palms form an attractive yet nearly impenetrable garden hedge, excellent shelter and protection for birds.

Cabbage Palm (*Sabal palmetto*)—Na, Sh/Tr, Ns, Pr, St, In, Fr, AW

Also called sabal palm, this excellent bird plant is found natively in various habitats throughout Florida, and in fact is the state tree. It is adaptable to many garden situations. Fragrant summer flowers attract honey bees, bumble bees, wasps, flies, and butterflies, which in turn are pursued by woodpeckers, flycatchers, and other insectivorous birds. In late summer to fall, massive displays of ⅓–½-inch fruit provide food for resident, migrating, and early wintering birds, including cardinals, mockingbirds, flickers, woodpeckers, phoebes and other flycatchers, catbirds, grackles, thrashers, jays, turkeys, bobwhites, blackbirds, robins, conures, and Amazons, also squirrels, opossums, and raccoons. Persistent leaf bases (called boots) provide detritus-filled cups for epiphytes such as hand fern (*Ophioglossum palmatum*), golden polypody, shoestring fern, whisk fern (*Psilotum nudum*), and strangler fig, all of which support insects, spiders, millipedes, anoles, frogs, and snakes. Leaves host caterpillars such as monk skippers and cabbage palm caterpillars (owlet moth, *Litoprosopus futilis*), also the palmetto weevil (*Rhynchophorus cruentatus*), North America's largest weevil. The complex crown structure of fan-shaped leaves, stems, inflorescences, and old boots provides ample substrate for the large nests of owls and hawks.

The leaves should not be trimmed. They will break off when ready, leaving the boot behind, and needless to say, the food-supplying boots should be left on until they fall off on their own. Cavities are made in trunks by flickers and Red-bellied and Pileated Woodpeckers and are then used by Amazon parrots and parakeets. Their growth form is variable, from small shrubs to trees upward of 80 feet, more commonly 30 feet in South Florida. They can be used as specimens or in mixed-tree plantings, preferring organic soil. They can be purchased at almost any size for instantaneous gratification.

One of the many assets of cabbage palm is the detritus pockets that naturally occur along its trunk, providing substrate for insects and epiphytes like these golden polypody ferns. Birds forage on the community of insects and other animals living in the detritus, as well as on the palm's fruit.

Dwarf Palmetto (*Sabal minor*), Scrub Palmetto (*Sabal etonia*)—Na, Sh, St, In, Fr, AS

These are two shorter-growing palmettos, reaching about 5 feet tall. Small ¼-inch flowers on long, many-branched stalks (up to 6 feet long in *minor*, 2–3 feet lying on the ground in *etonia*) bloom mostly in spring and attract bees, wasps, ants, and butterflies in large numbers. Small ⅓–½-inch black berries, in fall, are eaten by mockingbirds, cardinals, thrashers, turkeys, and bobwhites, as well as by raccoons, foxes, squirrels, deer, and opossums. Dwarf palmettos have huge leaves for their size, up to 5 feet wide, whereas the leaves of scrub palmetto are about 3 feet. Both species lack serious aboveground stems and so can be used to create edge or understory. Either, when clumped, provide excellent cover for ground- and low-foraging birds, especially thrashers that often nest in low-lying palms.

Sargent's Cherry Palm (*Pseudophoenix sargentii*)—Na, Sh/Tr, St, In, Fr, AS

Also known as buccaneer palm, this is now the rarest native palm in the wild in South Florida. It has large inflorescences periodically throughout the year, followed by bright red ¾-inch fruits. The flowers attract an array of insects, and the fruit is eaten by Red-bellied Woodpeckers, mockingbirds, cardinals, jays, grackles, and others. The palms occur naturally in coastal scrub and hammocks in South Florida but were once reduced to a small population on Elliott Key, before being rescued and introduced to cultivation. They are single stemmed, up to 15 feet tall, look in some ways like a small royal palm, and can be used similarly in small gardens. For birds, they are best planted at the edge of a mixed-tree stand where their growth form can be appreciated.

Sargent's cherry palms were nearly extirpated in South Florida but are now widely cultivated, and the fruits are well loved by birds.

Manila Palm (*Adonidia merillii*)—Nn, Sh/Tr, St, In, Fr, AW

Also known as the Christmas palm or simply as adonidia (also sometimes listed in the genus *Normanbya* or *Veitchia*), this palm has been a common component of traditional South Florida landscaping for many decades. It is a single-trunked, medium-sized palm to about 15–25 feet high and can be used as a mini royal palm. Its value in a South Florida bird garden is its 1–2-inch red fruits, available in fall and winter—thus the name Christmas palm. The fruits are attractive to parrots, which eat the skin and underlying pulp. This palm does well in alkaline soils and is relatively pest free although susceptible to lethal yellowing disease and to frost.

Areca Palm (*Dypsis lutescens*)—Nn, Sh/Tr, St, In, Fr, AW

Also known as bamboo palm, this multistemmed clump-forming palm is a common house and garden plant in South Florida. In the bird garden, it can grow to 30 feet high and create a thick hedge providing excellent bird protection. Its foliage and yellow summer flowers attract insects, including caterpillars and mealybugs. More importantly for birds are its 1-inch red fruits that are quite persistent on the plant, nearly year-round. In South Florida it especially attracts mockingbirds, parrots, and parakeets.

Florida Silver Palm (*Coccothrinax argentata*)—Na, Sh/Tr, In, Fr, AS

Understory palms of native pine rocklands, their small, white, spring to summer peaking flowers attract nectarivorous insects and their dark fruits, a bit larger than ¼-inch, are consumed by White-crowned Pigeons, jays, mockingbirds, and cardinals. These palms support a diverse insect fauna in their crown and bark, including monk skipper caterpillars. Having the capacity to attain 30 feet elsewhere in its Caribbean range, silver palms are mostly much shorter in South Florida, less than 8 feet. They do best unencumbered by competition, planted more or less by themselves at the outer edge of a shrub zone.

Florida Thatch Palm (*Thrinax radiata*)—Na, Sh/Tr, In, Fr, AS

Found natively in extreme South Florida and the Keys, their large inflorescences attract bees, flies, and beetles, in turn attracting insectivorous birds. White ⅓–½-inch fruits, peaking in abundance in spring and summer, are eaten by mockingbirds, grackles, jays and Red-bellied Woodpeckers, as well as by white-tailed deer and raccoons. Their dense crowns provide cover and structure for insects and host monk skipper caterpillars. These palms grow 10–30 feet on single trunks with fan-shaped leaves 2–3

Left: Proliferations of insect-attracting flowers followed by fruit make Florida thatch palm a bird attractor. Once ripe, the white fruits will be rapidly stripped from these stems.

Right: Saw palmettos clump to create dense shrub layers, as shown in this native landscaping. Their recumbent stems also create a protected environment in which birds can forage, roost, and nest.

feet in diameter. They are best used as part of the tree zone or, given their attractiveness to birds and wildlife, as specimens. They can even be used in containers.

Key Thatch Palm (*Thrinax morrisii*)—Na, Sh/Tr, In, Fr, AS

This palm is native to the Florida Keys and is also known as silver thatch palm and brittle thatch palm. Its more appropriate scientific name is *Leucothrinax morrisii*. This palm adapts well to gardens in the southern portion of South Florida. Dense crowns provide space and cover for insects, other invertebrates, anoles, and frogs. They bloom primarily in spring with long-arching inflorescences of small fragrant flowers that attract numerous insects, which then attract birds. White ⅓-inch fruits in large clusters peak in fall and are eaten by mockingbirds, grackles, jays, Red-bellied Woodpeckers, cardinals, many more birds, and raccoons, opossums, and Florida box turtles. Although growing to 20 feet, in South Florida these palms are more typically 8–12. Silvery leaf undersides make these very attractive in a garden.

Canary Island Date Palm (*Phoenix canariensis*)—Nn, Tr, Ns, St, Fr, AW

These palms have lots going against them as they are large, broad, with dangerous spines, and often peculiarly trimmed to look like giant pineapples, but in their untrimmed condition, they have a lot going for them, making excellent cover for birds. Although taller elsewhere, they tend to be 20–30 feet in South Florida. Monk Parakeets preferentially nest among their thorny branches. They have small, white, wind-pollinated flowers and 1-inch orange to yellow dates that are eaten by larger birds, such as parrots and macaws, when they ripen in early summer. The taller Senegal date palm (*Phoenix reclinata*) has similar bird garden value.

Saw Palmetto (*Serenoa repens*)—Na, Sh, Ns, St, In, Fr, AS

These short-statured palms have fragrant flowers that attract honey bees and other small bees, their primary pollinators. They also attract flies, wasps, and butterflies, including hairstreaks and atala. Saw palmetto leaves and stems support a large insect fauna, including palmetto and monk skipper caterpillars, Florida tortoise beetles (*Hemisphaerota cyanea*), ants, and wasps. Their ¾–1-inch black fruits, which peak in late summer, are eaten by turkeys, bobwhites, thrashers, mockingbirds, grackles, and parrots, also by gopher tortoises, Florida box turtles, raccoons, opossums, deer, and (it is hoped outside the garden) black bear. Florida Scrub-Jays and others use their fibers for nests. Most saw palmettos have recumbent stems that spread along the ground, and this creeping habit forms clumps of thorny leaf stems, creating one of the best safe havens for birds from predatory cats. The cover is used by nearly all low-foraging birds, such as bobwhites, thrashers, warblers, vireos, thrushes, catbirds, and sparrows. Thrashers and bobwhites often nest under them. Growing in much of the southeastern United States, they are hardy plants. When stems are recumbent, they are shrub-sized, 4–6 feet, but in situations where their stems grow vertically they can achieve 15 feet. Saw palmettos are best in mass plantings where they can create hedges, accent clumps, and shrub zone edges, all of which are effective barriers. A distinctive form native to coastal South Florida has attractive silvery leaves.

Spiderworts

Dayflowers—Na/Nn, Ss, Ln, Wf, In, Sd, AW/AS.

Several species of dayflowers, named because their flowers tend to last through the morning only, occur in South Florida. Pollen in their 1-inch blue flowers attracts insects, especially syrphid flies, honey bees, and bumble bees. The plants also attract beetles, bugs, and moths. Both insects and seeds attract ground-feeding birds, making these important components of a natural South Florida lawn. Whitemouth dayflower (*Commelina erecta*), the only South Florida native, has stems ascending 10 inches from a common base, forming a dense clump. Florida has two non-native subspecies of the pantropical climbing dayflower (*Commelina diffusa*). These creeping, mat-forming herbs grow to only 3 inches, with ½-inch blue flowers and ⅛-inch seeds. Considered by some gardeners to be an annoyance, it is in fact an excellent citizen of diverse lawns. Jio (*Commelina benghalensis*; Nn, X), more commonly known as wandering Jew, Benghal dayflower, or Indian dayflower, is an aggressive non-native to be avoided, and removed when found.

Pickerelweed (*Pontederia cordata*)—Na, Aq, Wt, In, AS

These shallow-water emergent plants are common in South Florida's interior wetlands. Attractive blue flowers in spring and summer attract insects, especially their primary pollinators, large bees, but also beetles, skippers, sulphurs, and dozens of other butterfly species. Pickerelweed does well in shallow garden ponds, generally in submerged pots with organic soil.

Above: Sometimes considered a weed, the climbing dayflower is a fine addition to any diverse lawn for its attractiveness to insects.

Left: Pickerelweed is an excellent water feature plant that attracts many insects, including this gulf fritillary butterfly, and provides housing for frogs and other small vertebrates as well.

Bromeliads

Bromeliads—Na/Nn, Ep/Ss, St, In, AW/AS

Like the orchids, many bromeliads are epiphytic and most have attractive inflorescences. Bromeliads can also be planted directly on the ground or on low rocks and wood to create flowerbed-style plantings. South Florida bird gardeners are fortunate to be in a climate that favors growing bromeliads outdoors. Bromeliads add physical niches, most accumulate debris, and some collect water within their spiral rosette of leaves, called tanks or phytotelmata, all of which shelter communities of invertebrates and small vertebrates. Although bromeliad faunal communities are more famously diverse in the tropics, Florida bromeliads have their share. Flies, aquatic beetles (Dytiscidae), and ostracods are the more common inhabitants. Also to be found are earthworms, ants, wasps, flies, scale insects, thrips, whiteflies, weevils, other beetles, mosquito larvae, copepods (including the mosquito-eating copepod *Mesocyclos*), spiders, snails, tree frogs, anoles, ribbon snakes, and bats, the latter especially in Spanish moss. More than 160 insect species have been documented on Spanish moss alone. Bromeliads having tubular flowers attract hummingbirds and butterflies. The pale flowers of the cardinal airplant (*Tillandsia fasciculata*) open in evening, attracting moths. Given the prey base, there is little surprise that birds, especially warblers, vireos, and gnatcatchers, frequently forage among bromeliads. Spanish moss (*Tillandsia usneoides*) is used for nest lining by many birds (which accounts in part for its wide distribution); Yellow-throated Warblers and Northern Parula depend on it.

In some gardens, rough-barked trees will accumulate native epiphytic bromeliads on their own, especially if plants are already in the neighborhood. The cardinal airplant, Spanish moss, and ballmoss (*Tillandsia recurvata*) are historically the most

Above: Spanish moss is the most widespread bromeliad in Florida and one of the most prolific for producing bird food. Birds like this Black-throated Blue Warbler are drawn to Spanish moss for its invertebrates.

Right: Cardinal airplants may voluntarily recruit to rough-barked trees, like this buttonwood. Bromeliads vastly expand a canopy's structural complexity.

widespread habitat generalists, and the most likely to volunteer in a garden. Other natives that might establish themselves include twisted airplant (*Tillandsia flexuosa*), southern needleleaf (*Tillandsia setacea*), giant airplant (*Tillandsia utriculata*), and hoary airplant (*Tillandsia pruinosa*). Alternatively, gardeners can themselves install bromeliads on trunks, branches, walls, fences, snags, rocks, pots, and hanging baskets. Spanish moss and its more compact relative ballmoss, especially, should if at all possible be in South Florida bird-friendly gardens. Bromeliads introduce a truly tropical native component to the garden. Ten of Florida's native bromeliad species are listed as threatened or endangered, at risk from overharvest, habitat destruction, and more recently the Mexican bromeliad weevil (*Metamasius callizona*). Listed native bromeliads cannot be collected without a state-issued permit and written permission from the landowner. Native bromeliads in general should not be collected from the wild, unless as part of a rescue.

Many non-native bromeliad species serve similar structural functions as native species and can be readily purchased, often rather cheaply. Bromeliads tend not to escape from the garden and so pose little threat to native habitat. Various species and cultivars available include the achmeas, billbergias, vriesas, guzmanias, and tillandsias. Portea (*Portea petropolitana*), grown either as an epiphyte or ground cover, has large sprays of flowers that attract large butterflies and hummingbirds. Many references and bromeliad societies can provide access to information on bromeliad horticulture and conservation.

Grasses and Sedges

Nutgrass (*Cyperus rotundus*)—Nn, Ln, In, Sd, AR

Nutgrass or purple nut sedge is considered by many the worst weed in the world because of the near impossibility of removing it from sod lawns, beds, and containers once it gets there; however, as part of a diverse bird-friendly lawn, nut sedge need not be detested. Its tiny seeds, only slightly larger than 1/16-inch, attract small seed-eating birds. It also supports moth caterpillars, thrips, leafhoppers, billbugs, and flea beetles. Nut sedge usually volunteers as part of a diverse lawn, spreading by rhizomes and producing small nutlike tubers, which themselves may be eaten by dirt-scratching birds such as fowl. Native alternatives include fragrant flatsedge (*Cyperus odoratus*) and flatleaf flatsedge (*Cyperus planifolius*), both of which can be started by seed and also tend toward weedy.

Hairawn Muhly Grass (*Muhlenbergia capillaris*)—Na, Ss, Wf, St, Sd, AS

Almost always called pink muhly or muhly grass, this bunch grass blooms from September to December with ethereal pink flowers on plumelike stalks, making a superior display in any South Florida garden. The flowers are followed in winter by seeds that attract Indigo and Painted Buntings, sparrows, and cardinals. Dense although thin blades provide excellent cover along bed margins and host a variety of insects, especially skippers. Natively, muhly grows in seasonally wet prairies and pinelands and so endures a wide range of garden situations. Its spectacular fall flowering on bunches 2–3 feet tall is sufficient to merit planting at corners of driveways, as borders, or almost anywhere.

Elliott's Lovegrass (*Eragrostis elliottii*)—Na, Ss, St, Sd, AR

This bunch grass, native to South Florida's pinelands, grows 1–2 feet high, making clumps about as wide. It is drought tolerant, doing best in sandy soil. Showy white flowers are produced in fall, continuing into winter, when the seeds attract buntings and sparrows. The clumps can be used alone, as ground cover, or among herbaceous mixed plantings, providing cover for birds at the edges of lawns.

Lopsided Indiangrass (*Sorghastrum secundum*)—Na, Ss, Bt, St, In, Sd, AS

This perennial bunch grass has attractive bright yellow flowers and gold to brown seeds, making for an interesting display. Its fall-available seeds are eaten by sparrows and buntings. It also attracts insects, including skippers (swarthy, Delaware, eufala, and twin-spot), and it hosts their caterpillars. From 3 to 6 feet tall, this grass provides cover for birds, especially when planted adjacent to shrubs. In South Florida, it is a pineland native but occurs widely over an extensive natural range. It is also used in pastures. Dormant in winter, it is not good as an accent but can be part of a wildflower or butterfly garden.

Hairawn muhly grass is a particularly stunning border plant during its fall flowering, when it creates a pink wash. Later in winter, birds seek out its seeds.

Fakahatcheegrass (*Tripsacum dactyloides*)—Na, Ss, St, In, Sd, AS

Also called eastern gamagrass, this clump grass has many uses in South Florida bird gardens. It has very attractive reddish seeds that attract seed-eating birds in summer and fall. It spreads by rhizomes, creating clumps usually 2–3 feet tall, although some can be 4–5 feet and are taller when in bloom. Its leaves host skipper caterpillars. Occurring natively in marshes and wet prairies and at the margins of hammocks and ponds, it is useful for providing cover for ground-foraging birds at the edge of water features and edges of lawns. Florida mock gamagrass or Florida tripsacum (*Tripsacum floridanum*) (Na, Ss, St, In, Sd, AS) is a similar but endangered species from South Florida pinelands. It has thinner blades, 2–3 feet tall.

Sand Cordgrass (*Spartina bakeri*)—Na, Ss, St, In, Sd, AS

This clump grass occurs natively in both dry and wet habitats and so has garden versatility. It can grow to 5 feet tall and can spread by rhizomes into clumps as wide as 20 feet across. Fall flowers are small, but the persistent small seeds on 6-foot stems are eaten by buntings and sparrows in winter. Cordgrass provides excellent cover as borders and at the edges of water features.

Sod grasses—Nn, Ln, In, AW

Several sod grasses are used in South Florida, the most common being St. Augustine-grass (*Stenotaphrum secundatum*). It is almost native, occurring indigenously along the Gulf Coast on sandy beach ridges, edges of marshes, and shorelines. Propagated vegetatively for 200 years, this grass's limited genetic diversity makes it susceptible to pests, meaning it produces bird food. The pest/food list is huge, including caterpillars of Carolina satyr, numerous skippers (whirlabout, fiery, clouded, eufala, and sachem), southern broken-dash, tropical sod webworm, fall armyworm, cutworm, grass looper, also ants, bees, wasps, and crane flies (*Tipula*). Bermudagrass (*Cynodon dactylon*) is a warm-climate perennial used for sports fields. It too hosts skippers. If left to seed, the seeds are eaten by sparrows and buntings. Three species of zoysia grass (*Zoysia japonica*, *matrella*, and *pacifica*) are warm-season sod grasses native to China, Japan, and Southeast Asia. We emphasize in this book that the best lawn for birds is not a monoculture of sod, but a diverse lawn of many species of bird-friendly plants. These sod grasses can be included as part of this diversity as they add structure, insects, and seeds.

Sod grasses can be important components of a bird-friendly diverse lawn thanks to their insect pests. This small patch of grass alone is hosting a southern skipperling, a small spider on its web below, a wolf spider in the upper left corner, and a tiny hopper insect, to the lower right of the skipperling.

Southern Cattail (*Typha domingensis*), Broadleaf Cattail (*Typha latifolia*)—Na, Aq, Wt, Ns, St, In, AS

Cattails are common South Florida natives, often ignored as garden plants. Cattails, growing to 10 feet, provide structure in water features and lots of insects. Caterpillars are particularly abundant at times, including cattail caterpillar moths, pyralid moths, shy cosmets, and Henry's marsh moths. Grasshoppers are also common, characteristic being the cattail toothpick grasshopper (*Leptysma marginicollis*). Ants, wasps, and spiders are in great abundance. Cattails near water sources provide shelter for tree frogs and anoles. Red-winged Blackbirds are cattail specialists. Other users are grackles, mockingbirds, meadowlarks, Tree Swallows, wrens, warblers, especially Common Yellowthroats, and flycatchers. Cattails in sufficiently large stands are preferred nesting habitat for Red-winged Blackbirds, Boat-tailed Grackles, Common Yellowthroats, Pied-billed Grebes, Common Gallinules, and Green Herons.

Gingers

Bird of Paradise (*Strelitzia*)—Nn, Ss/Sh, Bt, St, In, Nc, AW

These banana-leaved plants have distinctive flowers that are visited by nectar-seeking birds throughout the tropics. Originally from South Africa, the plants evolved with sunbirds (Nectariniidae); in the New World, hummingbirds and other species take advantage of this nectar source. The orange bird of paradise (*Strelitzia reginae*) is traditionally the most common. About 4 feet tall, its flowers have orange sepals and blue petals emerging from a beaklike sheath, or spathe, that holds the nectar. Most prominent in summer, some flowers are still available to hummingbirds when they arrive in fall. Leaf and flower structure provide ample insect- and spider-sheltering niches. The white-flowered white bird of paradise (*Strelitzia alba*) grows 6–10 feet tall; the giant white bird of paradise (*Strelitzia nicolai*) grows to 30 feet.

Banana (*Musa*)—Nn, Sh, St, In, Fr, AW

Many varieties of bananas are grown in South Florida and have been for two centuries. These well-known herbaceous plants have leafy pseudostems 3–20 feet tall, depending on variety. The flowering stalk emerges from the center, exposing 2-inch tubular flowers, the earliest being functionally female and becoming the banana fruit. Ants, bees, wasps, fruit flies, and spiders are attracted to the fruit and then attract warblers and vireos. The fruit is eaten while on the plant by woodpeckers, grackles, and squirrels. For birds, bananas are best planted in clusters, which spread and maintain themselves by rhizomes. Banana patches (the traditional South Florida name) provide cover and shelter, and the high reaching leaves are used for perching by many birds.

While flowering, bananas provide food for insect-seeking birds and as the fruit ripens for fruit-seeking birds. Bananas also provide ample shelter when planted in clusters, locally called banana patches.

Pinks and Cacti

Cacti—Na/Nn, Ep/Ss/Sh, St, Fr, Nc, AW/AS

Cacti are so common as houseplants and so tied in imagination to the desert that they tend to be overlooked in outdoor gardening in South Florida. In fact, many species of cacti are native to South Florida and grow well, even prolifically, in bird gardens. Flowers attract nectarivorous insects, bats, and, if flowering in winter during the daytime, hummingbirds. Fruit is eaten especially by woodpeckers and cardinals, as well as by Florida box turtles, gopher tortoises, and raccoons. Cacti support a variety of insects that in turn attract flycatchers, gnatcatchers, and warblers. Spiny stems provide birds with the ultimate protection. For birds, cacti are best grown in the ground in mixed plantings, placed in sensitive locations such as around bird feeders and nest boxes, or used within mixed barriers and hedges to discourage outdoor cats.

The most common native cactus is the pricklypear (*Opuntia*), which includes natives, ornamentals, and the edible *Opuntia ficus-indica*. Depending on taxonomic preferences, six to nine pricklypear species are native to Florida, found mostly on beach strands and sandy areas. Erect pricklypear (*Opuntia stricta*) and pricklypear (*Opuntia humifusa*) occur on the coast, and cockspur pricklypear (*Opuntia pusilla*) is widespread in the southeastern United States. Semaphore pricklypear (*Opuntia corallicola*) is a naturally localized South Florida endemic but grows well in South Florida gardens. These are not easy to find, but many other non-native pricklypears and cultivars are readily available for purchase. *Cereus* cacti are upright tubular plants; *Acanthocereus* are vining night-blooming cacti. Triangle or dildo cactus (*Acanthocereus tetragonus*) is a state-listed threatened species from the Keys. Epiphytic cacti can be grown on garden trees in South Florida. The epiphytic mistletoe cactus (*Rhipsalis baccifera*) is native. The most commonly available non-native epiphytic cacti (named

Cacti, like this South Florida endemic semaphore pricklypear, can be attractive additions to a garden, providing thorny protection for birds against predators, particularly cats.

after their flowering season) are Christmas cactus (*Schlumbergera bridgesii*), Thanksgiving cactus (*Schlumbergera truncata*), and Easter cactus (*Hatiora gaertneri*). Many other non-native species are available for gardens, although the high rainfall and high humidity in South Florida make outdoor gardening with many cacti a challenge, a reason to seek out the native species. Cacti, wherever they are used, are extremely valuable in providing security and protection for birds in a garden.

Common Chickweed (*Stellaria media*)—Nn, Ln, AR

Generally considered a weed, this European carnation relative has ground-hugging stems that root at periodic nodes, forming mats. A valued constituent of diverse lawns in South Florida, it has ¼–½-inch white bilobed flowers that produce prodigious numbers of fruits and seeds in summer.

Bougainvillea (*Bougainvillea glabra*)—Nn, Sh/Vn, Ns, St, In, Nc, AW

Nothing says the tropics like bougainvillea, as this South American native now decorates gardens throughout the tropical world. Its well-known, brightly colored bracts surround tiny white to yellow flowers that attract insects, especially butterflies and bees. Bougainvillea also provides excellent cover because of its vining habits and (for some varieties) formidable thorns. A thick stand of bougainvillea is one of the best nest sites for mockingbirds, cardinals, and thrashers. Depending on variety, bougainvillea can be trained into shrubs, vines, or something in between. As a whole, it

Mangrove skipper is just one of the many pollinators attracted to flowering bougainvillea. This plant also provides exceptionally protected nesting sites.

blooms year-round but is most prolific in the dry season. *Bougainvillea glabra* is the most usual species, but bougainvillea has been in cultivation for centuries, so many cultivars and hybrids are available.

Blolly (*Guapira discolor*)—Na, Sh/Tr, Ns, St, Fr, AS

Also known as longleaf blolly, beeftree, and *Guapira longifolia*, in spring and summer its small green tubular flowers attract bees, butterflies, and other pollinators. The tiny ⅓-inch bright pink to red fruits attract White-crowned Pigeons throughout this bird's range, and they are additionally eaten by all the fruit-eating birds, including mockingbirds, catbirds, warblers, and tanagers, as well as by green iguanas. Blolly flowers and fruits over an extended time, even in the same flower cluster, so both are available from summer through early winter. Natively, blollies are 10–30-foot trees of South Florida's coastal hammocks and, more rarely, small shrubs in Miami-Dade's pine rocklands; however, they can be used in gardens throughout South Florida and are especially good in coastal sandy locations. Growth forms are genetically determined, so the bird gardener should select plants with dense, broad, rounded compact crowns for excellent cover. Blolly does best in sunny spots within mixed-shrub zones, planted in clusters so as to have both male and female plants.

American Pokeweed (*Phytolacca americana*)—Na, Sh, Fr, AR

Generally considered a weed because it is widely dispersed by birds and survives in disturbed soil, pokeweed is welcomed in bird gardens. Tiny ¼-inch green and pink flowers bloom year-round and produce ½-inch purple fruits that attract mockingbirds but also cardinals, thrashers, doves, woodpeckers, catbirds, robins, phoebes, towhees, bluebirds, thrushes, orioles, Blackpoll and other warblers, vireos, flycatchers (Eastern Kingbird, Great Crested Flycatcher), grackles, titmice, chickadees, Carolina Wrens, waxwings, and native and House sparrows, as well as raccoons and opossums. In South Florida, pokeweed natively occurs at the edges of hammocks and in pinelands, growing 8–10 feet, and so is best placed at edges of shrub or tree zones. The locations of plants are chosen mostly by birds defecating the seeds, so if one comes up in an opportune space, let it stay; if in an inopportune space, it can be moved before its taproot develops.

Rougeplant (*Rivina humilis*)—Na, Ss/Sh, Bt, Wf, In, Fr, AS

Also called rougeberry or bloodberry, these are plants for borders of shrub and tree plantings where they will likely volunteer anyway if they are in the neighborhood. They flower year-round on stalks of ⅛-inch white to pink flowers that attract insects. Warblers commonly search the stems. Their ⅛–¼-inch red fruit tends to peak during fall and winter, attracting migrating and wintering warblers, especially Black-throated Blue Warblers and American Redstarts, as well as other fruit-eating birds. Rougeplants are scraggly short-lived herbs to small shrubs to 4 feet tall. Natively, they occur at the edges of hammocks and dunes but also colonize roadsides and weedy places, so are at home along any sunny garden edge where they fill in spaces between the ground and low plants. They do well as part of wildflower plantings. Once in the garden, they will volunteer prolifically, and gardeners must decide which plants go and which stay; but for birds, the more rougeplant in a garden the better.

Cape Leadwort (*Plumbago auriculata*)—Nn, Sh/Vn, Bt, St, In, Nc, AW

Also known as plumbago, this South African plant can be used in any South Florida bird garden protected from freezes. Blue ¾-inch flowers in 4-inch clusters are present all year, though they are less prevalent toward the end of winter. Providing nectar, they are exceptional butterfly attractors. Plumbagos also support foliage insects, such as caterpillars of the cassius blue butterfly. The whiplike, semiwoody stems form loose rounded mounds 3–10 feet high with a similar spread, a structure providing excellent cover for small birds. Alternatively, plumbagos can be trained into compact mounded shrubs or into vines scrambling over supports. White and intense blue varieties are available. A native species called doctorbush (*Plumbago zeylanica*) (Na, Vn, Bt, In, Nc, AS), also known as wild plumbago and *Plumbago scandens*, is an attractively white-flowered, thin-stemmed wide-ranging vine or viny bush.

Left: Northern Mockingbirds are one of the many fruit-eating birds that eat and distribute American pokeweed.

Right: Rougeplant attracts many fruit-eating birds, such as this Palm Warbler, for both fruits and insects.

Seagrape (*Coccoloba uvifera*)—Na, Sh/Tr, St, In, Fr, AW

A characteristic plant of South Florida's beaches and coastal hammocks, seagrape is distinguished by its huge leaves and massive, wide-spreading tree form. Tiny spring flowers on 8-inch stalks attract hordes of honey bees, bumble bees, flies, and butterflies, including Florida duskywing, Julia, swallowtails, and fulvous hairstreak. Clusters of ½-inch fruit are available primarily in summer and fall (although actually year-round overall). As the fruits ripen individually within their clusters, they are sought out day after day by mockingbirds, Red-bellied Woodpeckers, White-crowned Pigeons, jays, crows, Amazon parrots, raccoons, and gray squirrels (which can strip trees of still-green fruit). The canopy is a complex community of spiders and insects, including beetles, bugs, flies, wasps, ants, termites, weevils (*Euscelus*) that roll up leaves, and caterpillars such as the seagrape borer that live in twigs. This fauna attracts birds year-round but even more so during migration and winter when seagrapes are continuously worked over by gnatcatchers, warblers, vireos, flycatchers, mockingbirds, catbirds, jays, Red-bellied Woodpeckers, grackles, and crows. Their leaves and open branching provide excellent cover for birds. Trees can grow to 40 feet but more generally top out near 25 feet. In their natural beachfront habitat, they endure trimming by salty sea breezes, so they can be trimmed into large shrubs or rough hedges. They are deciduous in the spring dry season, annoyingly so with their huge blower-resisting leaves. Mass plantings that resemble native beachside strands provide superior cover and structure for birds. They can be used in mixed-tree plantings, where their otherwise unmanageable leaves end up as natural mulch and their ever-sprawling growth can be constrained by competition from neighboring trees.

Left: One of South Florida's best bird trees, seagrape provides structure, insects, and fruit for many birds, like this female Black-throated Blue Warbler.

Right: Blue-gray Gnatcatchers are one of the many birds that hunt for insects on pigeon plum.

Pigeon Plum (*Coccoloba diversifolia*)—Na, Sh/Tr, St, In, Fr, AS

Among the most common trees in South Florida's native hammocks, pigeon plums have ¼-inch white flowers clustered on spikes, most abundantly in late winter and early spring. They attract honey bees, flies, and large butterflies such as large orange sulphurs and swallowtails. Dark purple ⅓-inch fleshy fruits, ripening in late summer through winter, are eaten by the namesake White-crowned Pigeon, as well as by mockingbirds, Red-bellied and Pileated Woodpeckers, and crows, also by catbirds and robins in winter. Pigeon plums host a diversity of spiders and insects, at times

being nearly defoliated by weevils (*Diaprepes*). Insects attract gnatcatchers, warblers, vireos, and flycatchers. Reaching 10–30 feet in South Florida, taller in more southerly locales and even taller in the Caribbean and Central America, they grow narrowly on a single trunk but can also sucker to form a thicket, especially in response to storm damage. Sturdy branches and large leaves provide cover and security for birds and their nests. Pigeon plums are best used as part of mixed-tree zones but can be accents or specimen trees, especially in tight spaces, or even container plants.

Grapes

Virginia Creeper (*Parthenocissus quinquefolia*)—Na, Vn, Ns, St, Fr, AS

Virginia creeper, also known as woodbine, is one of the very best plants to attract birds to a garden, as good as poison ivy without the dermatological drawbacks. This vine has clustering ¼-inch fruit available from summer through fall, sometimes lasting into the winter. The fruit is consumed by all small fruit–eating birds, including woodpeckers, Great Crested Flycatchers, Red-winged Blackbirds, bluebirds, mockingbirds, cardinals, thrashers, jays, and wintering thrushes, warblers, vireos, and robins. The vines can grow in sun or shade, winding their way up trees, becoming woody with age, and filling in canopy spaces to provide cover. Once in the neighborhood, they will volunteer.

Muscadine (*Vitis rotundifolia*), Summer Grape (*Vitis aestivalis*), Calloose Grape (*Vitis shuttleworthii*)—Na, Vn, Ns, St, Fr, AS

Muscadine (also called southern fox grape and *Muscadinia rotundifolia*), summer grape, and calloose grape are the native wild grapes of South Florida. In spring, small yellow wind-pollinated flowers also attract insects, including beetles, moths, and wasps. The clusters of dark fruit (½–1 inch for wild muscadine, less than ½ inch for

Virginia creeper fruits are favorites of many fruit-eating birds like this Red-eyed Vireo.

Wild muscadines attract fruit-loving birds once fruits are dark and ripe. In the meantime, insectivores visit for insects like the whitefly seen on one leaf here. Many birds take advantage of the vine's protective cover.

the others), produced summer through fall, attract migrating orioles and also Downy Woodpeckers, Carolina Wrens, vireos, cardinals, mockingbirds, and bluebirds. Ripe fruit also attracts wasps, bees, and leafroller caterpillars of moths. Grape vines planted to grow up trees or trained along fences, hedges and trellises create tangles of stems and leaves that provide excellent cover, especially for nesting. The older the vine, the more woody and rampant it can become and the more valuable to birds. Wild stock is probably best for birds since cultivated varieties tend to be too large and too thick-skinned for most native birds and do not grow well in the southern parts of South Florida; indeed, the common non-native grape vine of cultivation (*Vitis vinifera*) does not grow in South Florida.

Lignumvitae

Holywood Lignumvitae (*Guaiacum sanctum*)—Na, Sh/Tr, Pr, St, In, Fr, AS

Historically occurring in coastal hammocks in extreme South Florida through Central America, lignumvitae very early in European settlement was overharvested for its heavy wood and its medicinal properties. Flowers and fruit appear together throughout the spring and summer. The ¾-inch blue flowers produce orange ¾-inch fruits that split open to expose black seeds covered by red fleshy coats. Flowers attract butterflies and bees; fruit is eaten by mockingbirds, catbirds, vireos, and cardinals. Lignumvitae has a straight trunk with thin, spreading, drooping branches with many

Holywood lignumvitae merits planting along an edge or some other visible spot in the garden for aesthetic enjoyment. For the birds, it provides structure, insects, and fruit.

small leaves, creating a rounded to flat canopy, providing cover in which birds forage and perch. Fissured bark supports epiphytes and leaves host insects such as lyside sulphur caterpillars, and spiders. Although they have the capacity to reach 25 feet, in mainland South Florida holywood lignumvitae are more common as shrubs under 10 feet. As hammock plants, they do well as part of mixed-shrub zones or at the edges of tree zones where details of their flowers and seeds can be appreciated. They also make interesting specimen trees. A West Indian relative, roughbark or common lignumvitae (*Guaiacum officinale*), is faster growing with a less dense canopy than is holywood lignumvitae. Both kinds of lignumvitae can be planted as far north as coastal Palm Beach in cold-protected sites.

Maidenberries

Maidenberry (*Crossopetalum rhacoma*)—Na, Ss/Sh, Fr, AS

Also called rhacoma and poison cherry, maidenberry has tiny $\frac{1}{32}$-inch flowers year-round, followed by ¼-inch bright red fruit. The cherry-like fruit attracts mockingbirds, catbirds, jays, grackles, and other birds. Variably, maidenberries can be tall shrubs to 6 feet with drooping branches and shiny leaves or sprawling ground cover less than 2 feet tall. This is a native plant of South Florida's pine rocklands and hammock edges and best planted in mixed-species borders.

Christmasberry (*Crossopetalum ilicifolium*)—Na, Ss, Wf, Fr, AS

Also called quailberry and looking like a miniature holly, christmasberry is a slow-growing woody ground cover reaching no taller than 1 foot. Excellent for low flower gardens, rock gardens, and pineland plantings, it is best at the edges of other plantings in the sun. Tiny green flowers appear year-round, followed by attractive ¼-inch red fruit eaten by many birds, especially mockingbirds.

West Indian False Box (*Gyminda latifolia*)—Na, Tr, Fr, AR

Ranging through the West Indies and Mexico, in North America it occurs only in the Keys. A small tree to 25 feet, West Indian false box is native but rare and endangered in Florida. The plant is little known. It has tiny green flowers and is of potential interest for bird gardening because of its dark blue ⅓-inch fruit.

Euphorbs and Relatives

Cocoplum (*Chrysobalanus icaco*)—Na, Sh/Tr, St, In, Fr, AW

Because it is widely cultivated, malleable, has attractive evergreen leaves and obvious fruit, cocoplum is likely to be in every South Florida bird garden, and it should be. Spikes of fragrant, ¼-inch, nectar-rich white flowers attract bees, especially honey bees and bumble bees, flies, and butterflies. Fleshy purple or white fruits, 1–2 inches, are too large for most birds to eat whole, but White-crowned Pigeons and crows do, and cardinals, grackles, jays, Red-bellied Woodpeckers, and squirrels eat them a bite at a time. Cocoplum can fruit year-round but produces mostly in summer. Thick leaves on multiple closely spaced stems provide cover and harbor significant crops of insects. In winter, warblers and vireos continuously work the canopy. Naturally plants of hammock edges in swamps, terrestrial hammocks, and beaches throughout South Florida, cocoplums tolerate a wide range of soil, salt, and temperature conditions. There are several natural and cultivated growth forms. As shrubs or trees, they can reach 10–20 feet tall, and these are best for birds as part of mixed plantings. Cocoplum can also be trimmed into stand-alone shrubs or tame hedges. A dwarf variety only 1–2 feet tall, derived from shore-zone plants, can be used as ground cover or edge.

Cocoplum may have purple or white fruit; either is large, fleshy, sweet, and loved by birds like this Northern Cardinal.

Attracting Birds to South Florida Gardens

Pitchapple (*Clusia rosea*)—Na, Ep/Sh/Tr, Pr, St, In, Fr, AW

Also known as autograph trees because of their thick etchable leaves, pitchapples make interesting garden features, providing significant cover especially when massed. They originated from the lower Florida Keys, where the native stock was likely extirpated, and the nearby Bahamas, where they remain quite common along the shore. But pitchapples have been reintroduced and planted widely in South Florida gardens. They can self-seed as bird-deposited epiphytes in palms and oaks, assuming a strangling habit, which a gardener might need to guard against. Although potentially very tall trees, in South Florida they are usually shrubs to 10 feet with dense spreading crowns of large dark green leathery leaves. Large, 2–3-inch white to pink flowers open at night, and apple-like 1½-inch fruits persist on trees for months. Ripe fruits open to expose red seeds surrounded by black resin, both eaten by a wide variety of birds. It is considered by some to be an aggressive plant because of its epiphytic character and so is unwelcome in gardens. As a result, it should be used with caution, but it remains a valuable bird plant.

Left: The thick, leathery leaves of pitchapple provide a protective veil for secretive birds like this Gray Catbird.

Right: Bastard copperleaf is a hardy ground-cover plant that incorporates well into a bird-friendly diverse lawn.

Bastard Copperleaf (*Acalypha chamaedrifolia*)—Na, Ln, In, AR

Native to pine rocklands of Miami-Dade and the lower Keys, these perennial spurges are only 2–4 inches tall, with prostrate stems running out a foot or more. As part of a diverse lawn, their minute, spring-to-summer reddish flowers attract bees and other insects.

Mendez's Sandmat (*Chamaesyce mendezii*)—Na, Ln, In, Sd, AR

These ground-hugging euphorbs have small green leaves and even smaller ¹⁄₁₆-inch white flowers that become tiny seeds. Their flowers and leaves attract insects, and birds feed on both insects and seeds. They thrive on disturbed dry sites and roughly tended fields. They will self-establish and reseed in a diverse lawn. They form mats of ground-running stems several feet wide. The spotted sandmat (*Chamaesyce maculata*) is similar.

Mascarene Island Leafflower (*Phyllanthus tenellus*), Gale-of-wind (*Phyllanthrus amarus*)—Nn, Ss, Ln, AR

Gardeners generally consider leafflowers to be flowerpot weeds, but this is an example of how bird gardening differs. These small plants are excellent components of diverse lawns from summer through fall. Tiny greenish-white flowers produce miniscule round fruits that attract small birds.

Pineland Croton (*Croton linearis*)—Na, Ss, Bt, In, AS

This croton's white, ¼-inch flowers attract flies, bees, and a long list of butterflies, including skippers, blues, Florida duskywing, and hairstreaks. Tiny capsule-like seeds attract buntings. Crotons are small, thin, edge plants, 1–3 feet tall, 6 feet maximum. The thin leaves and branches provide little cover but do host an array of insects, including Horace's duskywing caterpillars and red-banded hairstreak butterflies and sometimes the rare Bartram's scrub-hairstreak and Florida leafwing butterflies. These insects attract low-foraging birds, including mockingbirds, Black-throated Blue Warblers, and American Redstarts.

Pineland croton attracts many types of insects as well as buntings to its seeds.

Guiana Plum (*Drypetes lateriflora*)—Na, Tr, Fr, AR

Ranging primarily through Central America and the West Indies, Guiana plum is a rare native plant of hammocks on the Miami Rock Ridge and South Florida coasts. In spring and summer, small green-white flowers produce ⅓-inch red fruits, eaten by small birds. It is the larval host for the Florida white butterfly (*Appias drusilla*). A shrub to small tree to 25 feet, it remains rare in cultivation. Similar milkbark (*Drypetes diversifolia*), having white fruit, occurs in North America only in the Keys. These species deserve a larger role in native bird gardens.

Crabwood (*Gymnanthes lucida*)—Na, Tr, St, Fr, AS

Also known as shiny oysterwood, crabwood is a common tree of intermediate stature in tropical hammocks. It has a tall narrow growth form and dense leaves, providing structure for birds by filling small spaces in the canopy of mixed-tree plantings. Growing to 20 feet, it can be used as a specimen; its thick leaves make good buffers and cover for birds. Green male flowers are on spikes adjacent to red female flower stalks. These produce ½-inch, brown to black seed capsules that are eaten, although not preferentially, by birds. The natural range in South Florida is restricted to the Keys and Miami-Dade, but it can be planted north of Miami.

Crabwood's dense leaves provide structure for birds and insects, like this hammock skipper.

Paintedleaf (*Poinsettia cyathophora*)—Na, Ss/Sh, Ln, Wf, St, In, Fr, AS

These miniature Christmas poinsettias have ¹⁄₁₆-inch flowers set within red-based leaves, attracting bees, butterflies, especially gulf fritillary, and other insects, year-round. Their ¼-inch fruits are eaten especially by Mourning Doves, buntings, and sparrows. Usually herbs ½–2 feet tall but sometimes more like shrubs to 4 feet, they are best used as edge fillers, ground cover, and butterfly plants, all providing low structure for small birds. They can be mowed high within diverse lawns and will volunteer. A rare relative, pineland spurge (*Poinsettia pinetorum*), is endemic to Miami-Dade and Monroe.

Paintedleaf attracts many insects, such as ants.

Long Key Locustberry (*Byrsonima lucida*)—Na, Sh/Tr, St, In, Fr, AS

Better known simply as locustberry, this attractive plant blooms from spring to summer. The ½-inch flowers of locustberry occur in clusters that start off white then turn pink before becoming red, showing multiple colors in a single cluster. The flowers attract a diversity of butterflies and other pollinators. Oil bees (*Centris*) extract oil from glands under the petals. The ¼-inch red to brown fruit, persisting on the plants through summer, is consumed by nearly all the fruit-eating bird species, including mockingbirds and parrots, as well as by box turtles. Thick, shiny, upright leaves provide habitat for spiders and insects, especially caterpillars such as the Florida duskywing butterfly. Locustberries are naturally thick, multistemmed, wide-spreading shrubs peaking at 10 feet tall, although trimmable to single-trunked trees or dense shrubs useful as barriers. They provide excellent cover for birds, especially if planted in clusters, and are used for nesting by cardinals and vireos. Stocks from the Keys develop into larger plants than those from the mainland. Natives of pine rocklands and hammock edges, they are best used as shrubs at the edges of mixed plantings. Although from very southern South Florida, they can be grown farther north if afforded cold protection.

Long Key locustberry flowers host many pollinating insects and then yield fruits eaten by all frugivorous birds.

Barbados Cherry (*Malpighia emarginata*)—Nn, Sh/Tr, St, In, Fr, AW

Also known as acerola, West Indian cherry, *Malpighia glabra*, and *Malpighia punicifolia*, this West Indian plant bears fruit that has become well appreciated in the healthcare field for its vitamin C content and is similarly appreciated by birds. From spring to fall, its ½-inch, red to pink flowers attract bees, but it is the bright red, 1-inch fruit, available summer through winter, that really attracts birds. Somewhat large, the fruits are eaten in pieces by mockingbirds, catbirds, grackles, and woodpeckers. Although the Barbados cherry can be trimmed to a central-trunked tree, its more normal form is that of a large spreading shrub with many thin branches, reaching to 10 feet and providing good cover. Foliage supports skippers, Florida duskywing and cassius blue caterpillars, stink bugs, and Caribbean fruit flies (*Anastrepha suspensa*). Miniature holly (*Malpighia coccigera*) is a spiky-leaved Caribbean species that gets only about 3 feet tall and 5 feet wide with ½-inch pink spring to summer flowers, followed by ½-inch orange fruit. It attracts fruit-eating birds as its larger relative does.

Corkystem Passionflower (*Passiflora suberosa*)—Na, Vn, Bt, St, In, Fr, Nc, AS

These wonderful vines have flowers and fruit nearly year-round. The ½-inch green flowers provide nectar to Ruby-throated Hummingbirds in winter, as well as to large carpenter bees, honey bees, flies, butterflies, and ants. Birds pick off small insects that get stuck to the flower bracts. Small, ¼-inch dark purple fruits are readily eaten by any of the fruit-seeking birds. Because of this attractiveness, once established, it will self-seed, compliments of the birds. The vines are larval hosts for gulf fritillary, Julia, and zebra longwing butterflies, adults of which are often quite visible near the plants. Other insects include scale insects, spider mites, and whiteflies. As a result of these insects, the vines are well worked by warblers, vireos, and gnatcatchers. Stems are thin, although they thicken with age, and may climb high into trees, sprawl over low structures, or run prostrate on the ground, incorporating themselves into a diverse lawn. Preferring sun to light shade, they are natively found on the edges of hammocks and in pinelands, but are readily available from native plant sources. They should be planted in similar situations where they can climb uninhibitedly.

Pineland Passionflower (*Passiflora pallens*)—Na, Vn, Bt, St, In, Fr, Nc, AS

Also called pale passionflower, this white-flowered native vine is a good choice for a garden in the southern portion of South Florida for both its structure and its fruit. Blooming year-round, the 2-inch flowers attract carpenter and other bees, as well as the usual array of passionflower butterflies and other insects. The 2-inch yellow fruits are broken into by larger birds while on the vine or after they fall. Once the fruits have opened, the seeds are sought by many birds. Found across the West Indies, in South Florida pineland passionflower is naturally rare and considered endangered, occurring only in hammocks and tree islands of Miami-Dade, Collier, and Monroe counties. But it is increasingly available for gardeners. In a garden, its flowers and fruit make for an interesting display, and its vines and leaves can rapidly and thoroughly fill, or even overfill, available space.

Left: Corkystem passionflower is well loved by butterflies and birds alike. Once the plant is established in a neighborhood, birds will quickly distribute it to their favorite stomping grounds. This passionflower may vine into the trees or creep along the ground, becoming part of a diverse lawn.

Right: Pineland passionflower is naturally rare and endangered in South Florida but can do well in gardens.

Purple Passionflower (*Passiflora incarnata*)—Na, Vn, St, In, AS

Also known as maypop, wild passion vine, or apricot vine, this passionflower has showy 2–4-inch purple flowers and 2-inch edible yellow-green fruit (called the maypop). Once the fruits are opened, the seeds attract birds. The vine supports the typical community of passionflower butterflies. A well-known garden plant, its native range extends south only to Central Florida. It nonetheless can grow in South Florida; preferring a seasonal cold period, it grows more persistently in the northern portions.

Passionfruit (*Passiflora edulis*)—Nn, Vn, St, In, Nc, AS

The edible passionfruit of commerce grows well, sometimes too well, in South Florida and has since prehistoric times. Unlike the native species, it flowers very seasonally and tends to be poorly pollinated, producing few temporally scattered fruits. Vegetatively, however, it thrives, tending to go rampant over, under, and through the garden, in the process providing superior cover for nesting birds. It supports the typical passionflower insects and, when in flower, provides nectar. For massive cover, this species can hardly be beat, and in fact its vigor may beat the gardener. We have had to remove edible passionfruit vines several times from our own garden.

Red Mangrove (*Rhizophora mangle*)—Na, Sh/Tr, Aq, Wt, Ns, Pr, St, In, AS

Found nowhere else in North America, mangroves are South Florida's primary bird habitat along hundreds of miles of coastline. Because it is wind pollinated and water distributed, red mangrove's primary bird value is in its complex structure. Along the coast, it is used as roosts and nest sites by herons (especially Green Herons), ibis, Osprey, Bald Eagles, Yellow and Prairie Warblers, Black-whiskered Vireos, Mangrove

Right: The edible passionfruit grows remarkably well in South Florida—abandoning trellises for nearby trees, roofs, or any other substrate it can find. This particular vine was pleased to take over the roof.

Below: Red mangroves provide structure, cover, and insects, like this common buckeye. Occurring natively along the coast, they can be planted inland in gardens and freshwater features.

Cuckoos, cardinals, mockingbirds, and flycatchers. The smaller birds, snakes, green iguanas, and anoles also frequent the canopy for insects. Red mangrove grows well on edges of freshwater canals and lakes and can be planted in large garden ponds or in containers.

Coastalplain Willow (*Salix caroliniana*)—Na, Sh/Tr, Aq, Wt, Ns, Pr, St, In, Nc, AS

These plants natively surround ponds and wet hammocks in South Florida's interior wetlands. Multiple rough-barked stems and numerous thin leaves provide cover to an extensive community of ants, termites, spiders, and caterpillars, including io moth and viceroy butterfly, for which they are the only native larval host, as well as frogs, lizards, and snakes. Their prolific catkin flowers attract even more insects, including honey bees, as well as foliage-searching and stem-gleaning birds. These include Common Yellowthroat, wrens, White-eyed Vireos, blackbirds, grackles, other warblers, titmice, phoebes, Indigo Buntings, mockingbirds, and catbirds. The nectar-rich flowers are consumed directly by orioles and, in the wetlands, by Purple Gallinules. In South Florida, willows are shrubs to small trees, generally 15–30 feet tall, having an irregular, spreading shape and providing excellent structure for birds. Although wetland plants, they have a wide range of soil tolerances. They are best used as back screens for ponds and small marshy areas.

Legumes and Relatives

Bay Cedar (*Suriana maritima*)—Na, Sh/Tr, Bt, St, In, AS

These interesting-looking coastal shrubs have inconspicuous yellow flowers and ¼-inch fruit. The flowers attract bees, and the fruit, although primarily water dispersed, attracts fruit-eating birds. Dense ascending branches provide ample cover for invertebrates, including spiders, walking sticks (*Aplopus*), and caterpillars of mallow scrub-hairstreak and martial scrub-hairstreak butterflies. Usually 6–10-foot shrubs amenable to trimming and hedging, they alternatively can grow to 25-foot trees. They are natives of coastal dunes of South Florida and more broadly of sandy and rocky coast in the Caribbean, so bay cedars grow well in dry places.

Bay cedar's flowers and dense leaves attract many insects and insectivorous birds.

Royal Poinciana (*Delonix regia*)—Nn, Tr, Pr, St, In, Sd, AW

Originally from Madagascar, this sensational tree is a symbol of old Florida. Glory comes in May–June when in some years flowering extravaganzas set its canopy ablaze. The 3-inch yellow to orange to red flowers provide nectar and pollen. In the Old World they are pollinated by sunbirds (Nectariniidae), but in South Florida only very early flowers overlap with the residency of hummingbirds. Here, they attract mostly bees and butterflies. Termites, ants, and other bark insects seem to thrive on poincianas, and insectivorous birds, especially migrating and wintering warblers and vireos, are often seen working the branches. Poincianas are big trees, 30–40 feet tall and spreading to 60 feet wide. Their large, hard seedpods are too much for native birds, but Amazon parrots, macaws, and squirrels gnaw the seeds out. Nearly all arboreal birds use the open spreading branches as perches. Big, messy, large-rooted, and old fashioned, these trees are seldom recommended for gardens these days, even though existing trees in flower never cease to amaze. If space is sufficient or if a poinciana preexists, it most certainly should be considered an excellent bird tree for a garden.

Historically a mainstay of South Florida landscaping, royal poinciana hosts a lively community of invertebrates and birds. Its fiery blossoms are a treat.

Sensitive Plants—Na/Nn, Sh/Tr, Bt, St, In, Sd, AS

These leguminous shrubs, also known as sennas and cassias, provide showy yellow flowers through the winter, attracting small bees, ants, and sulphur butterflies. Branches and leaves host ants, spiders, and sulphur and hairstreak caterpillars. All these insects attract mockingbirds, cardinals, warblers, vireos, and flycatchers. Seeds are eaten by birds as well. Cassias are multistemmed, short-lived, brittle-branched perennial shrubs, fast growing and salt tolerant. Given their limited lifespan, it is good to have several trees of different ages going. There are several species to consider. The native Chapman's wild sensitive plant (*Senna mexicana*) sprawls along the ground to 3 feet tall. This plant is a naming nightmare; the genus can be found as *Cassia* or *Senna*, species can be *chapmanii*, *mexicana* var. *chapmanii*, or *bahamensis*; English name might be Bahama senna or Mexican senna. By whatever name, it is an excellent bird plant and the preferred nectar and host plant of the orange-barred sulphur butterfly. Privet wild sensitive plant (*Senna ligustrina*), a bit more erect at 3–8 feet, is good

in shrub plantings or edges of mixed-tree plantings. Partridge pea (*Chamaecrista fasciculata*) is a robust native annual (usually), occurring as a weed on disturbed sites. Growing to about 3 feet, it often sprawls along the ground.

The most famous of the non-native cassias is the golden shower (*Cassia fistula*). This tall tree, growing to 60 feet and historically important in Southeast Asian culture and medicine, has been widely planted in the tropics around the world and long been a part of South Florida's tropical plantings. Blooming in late spring, the tree becomes covered with yellow flowers. Valamuerto (*Senna pendula*), which has been called by many names including *Senna bicapsularis,* is a vigorous and aggressive plant well distributed in gardens throughout the tropics, including in South Florida. These 10–12 foot trees are invasive in some parts of the world, although not in South Florida. Large leaflets and multiple branching provide good structure for birds and are excellent as backdrops for butterfly/hummingbird gardens. The candlestick (*Senna alata*) has sensational-looking 6-inch candle-like flower clusters. The pink shower tree (*Cassia bakeriana*) is a medium-sized pink flowering tree. Any of these cassias has similar benefits for birds and could be considered for bird-friendly gardens.

Hong Kong Orchid Tree (*Bauhinia* × *blakeana*)—Nn, Tr, St, In, Nc, AW

These non-native trees, part of the old-time South Florida yard flora, have several endearing characteristics to recommend them: fragrant purple orchid-like flowers, extraordinary attractiveness to Ruby-throated Hummingbirds, and sterility. Winter-blooming flowers attract hummingbirds, orioles, warblers, Amazon parrots, bees, wasps, and butterflies, particularly large swallowtails. These insects attract warblers, vireos and flycatchers. Several species of bauhinias are available to the South Florida gardener, but Hong Kong orchid trees are generally best to plant for birds, because they do everything and don't spread. The dwarf orchid tree (*Bauhinia acuminata*) (Nn, Tr, St, In, Nc, AW) is used by hummingbirds but is less attractive than the Hong Kong tree. The butterfly orchid tree (*Bauhinia divaricata*) (Nn, Tr, St, In, Nc, AW) grows about 10 feet tall with elongated, year-round, pink and white hummingbird-attracting flowers. The orchid tree (*Bauhinia variegata*) and purple orchid tree (*Bauhinia purpurea*) are excellent trees for bird gardens, but are considered invasive and it is recommended they not be planted where they might invade natural areas.

Cinnecord (*Vachellia choriophylla*)—Na, Sh/Tr, Ns, St, In, AS

Also called spineless acacia, tamarindillo, *Acacia choriophylla* and *Acacia choriophylloides*, this legume has fragrant ½-inch yellow powderpuff flowers on long stalks, present for much of the spring and summer and attracting bees, wasps, flies, and butterflies, and insect-eating birds. Cinnecords can have multiple stems or can be trained as small trees to 20 or even 30 feet, but because their branches are spreading and brittle, they tend to break down much before that height. Either growth form provides open branches under cover of leaves. A Florida endangered species, cinnecord occurs naturally but rarely in hammocks of the northern Florida Keys but does well north of this range.

Sweet Acacia (*Vachella farnesiana*)—Na, Sh, St, In, AS

These very thorny acacias require good drainage but provide superior cover. Their fragrant powderpuff flowers, occurring most abundantly in spring when the plant is leafless, attract flies, bees, wasps and butterflies. They are followed by seedpods containing ¼-inch seeds. The pineland acacia (*Vachella farnesiana* var. *pinetorum*) is smaller leaved and shorter statured, growing to about 5–6 feet. It is best used as a thorny edge.

Pineland acacia works well as a thorny, protective barrier against cats.

Stickpea (*Calliandra*)—Nn, Sh, Bt, St, In, Nc, AW

These Neotropical shrubs, known locally as powderpuff, have fuzzy flowers that attract nectarivorous insects, especially butterflies and bees and, in winter, Ruby-throated Hummingbirds. Amazon parrots shred the entire flower to get at its sweet core. Foliage attracts mealybugs, thornbugs, and caterpillars such as statira sulphur. Drooping thorny branches provide shelter for small birds. The Surinam pink powderpuff (*Calliandra surinamensis*) has prolific 3-inch pink flowers with white stamens. They bloom year-round, peaking in winter and spring, attracting nectar-sipping wintering birds. They tend to be droopy-branched multitrunked shrubs to 15 feet high and 10 feet wide. Powderpuff tree (*Calliandra haematocephala*) grows to 15 feet and has long-lasting red flowers. The pink powderpuff (*Calliandra emarginata*) grows to only 5 feet. All provide nectar, insects, and cover.

White-eyed Vireos, like this immature bird, and many other migrating and winter resident birds, forage along insect-rich false tamarind trunks, leaves, and branches.

False Tamarind (*Lysiloma latisiliquum*)—Na, Tr, Ns, St, In, Fr, AS

More widely known as wild tamarind or lysiloma, this is one of the more important native bird-friendly South Florida trees, especially for small insect-seeking birds. Fragrant ½-inch powderpuff flowers, produced spring to summer, attract nectar-feeding insects such as bees and cassius blue butterflies and mangrove skippers. The pods produce small black seeds eaten by flycatchers, gnatcatchers, warblers, grackles, crows, and jays, while the foliage and stems support ants, bees, wasps, termites, thorn bugs (*Umbonia crassicornis*), moth and butterfly caterpillars (cassius blue, large orange sulphur, mimosa yellow, and tiny hairstreak), and the rare and threatened native liguus tree snail (*Liguus fasciatus*). Given this invertebrate fauna, they are among the best garden trees for insectivorous birds, especially migrants and winter residents such as gnatcatchers, American Redstarts and other warblers, vireos, and various flycatchers. They are also excellent nesting trees. They can become big fast, 30–50 feet in South Florida, with trunks exceeding 3 feet in diameter, and so are best in mixed-tree zones where shrubs can grow beneath.

Florida Keys Blackbead (*Pithecellobium keyense*)—Na, Sh/Tr, Ns, St, In, Fr, Sd, AS

This large shrub to small tree has everything: interesting leaves, pretty flowers, protracted spring through fall blooming season, insects, fruit, and cover. Its ½-inch, fragrant, powderpuff flowers (pink in the Keys and white on the South Florida mainland) attract bees and more than a dozen butterfly species. When coiled pods open, exposing ½-inch seeds encased in sweet red arils, birds are attracted to both the seeds and the arils. It is the larval host for cassius blue and large orange sulphur butterflies. Natively found in coastal hammock thickets, it prefers well-drained sandy or limestone soils. In South Florida, blackbead is usually a shrub or small tree less than 10 feet tall but can grow to 20 feet. Trunks with multiple branches create an irregular crown, providing ample cover for birds. It works well as a specimen or for buffer plantings, and especially for birds as part of mixed-shrub or mixed-tree plantings.

Catclaw Blackbead (*Pithecellobium unguis-cati*)—Na, Sh/Tr, St, In, Fr, Sd, AS

Also called cat's claw, this thorny plant is related to Florida Keys blackbead, and its flowers and fruit hold the same value for birds since it is the host plant for a number of insects. It is a viny, thorny, wide shrub or tree. While this is not a plant for walkways, its thorny branches provide excellent bird protection, especially when put in mixed-tree and mixed-shrub stands.

Monkeypod (*Pithecellobium dulce*)—Nn, Tr, Ns, Pr, St, Fr, AS

Formerly widely planted in South Florida, this large tree, to 50 feet, has 2-inch flowers in clusters that produce 4–8-inch pods with black seeds surrounded by a white aril, both of which are eaten by grackles and Fish Crows. It has spreading spiny branches, providing protected perching space. Its susceptibility to hurricane toppling has led to its being less frequently planted, but it remains a good tree for birds.

Monkeypod provides fruit that Fish Crows flock to, literally.

Gray Nicker (*Caesalpinia bonduc*)—Na, Sh/Vn, Ns, Pr, St, In, AS

A viciously rampant vine native to South Florida beach hammocks and dunes, as well as to much of the tropical world, this aggressive thorny plant provides superior structure and cover for birds. Blooming most of the year in South Florida, its clusters of 1-inch yellow flowers attract bees and flies. The hard seeds within 4-inch pods are not eaten by birds; they are spread by water as "sea beans." It is a host plant for the very rare Miami blue butterfly. Its main bird value is in the incomparable protected space it provides. Nickerbean spreads to 20 feet, covering the landscape with a 4-foot-tall canopy of leaves, stems, and thorns up to 2 inches long. The yellow nicker (*Caesalpinia major*) also occurs in South Florida, having somewhat larger leaves and similar bird value. A gardener who chooses nickerbean is one truly devoted to the comfort of birds over personal pain and suffering.

Attracting Birds to South Florida Gardens

Tamarind (*Tamarindus indica*)—Nn, Tr, St, In, Fr, Sd, AS

This African native has been in cultivation in tropical countries for centuries. It was introduced by early settlers to South Florida, where examples are still to be found at old home sites. A large tree, to 40 feet in South Florida, its clusters of 1-inch red to yellow flowers attract bees, especially honey bees. Fruiting in South Florida occurs during the February–May dry season. The 3–5-inch pods containing edible pulp and seeds are widely used in tropical cuisines, and in South Florida are eagerly consumed by parrots, jays, and grackles. The bark and especially the seedpods support a fauna of ants, weevils, beetles, borers, caterpillars, and aphids. Given all these food opportunities, tamarinds can be counted on to attract birds and are a welcome addition to a tropical fruit tree planting, given sufficient room.

Left: Gray nicker forms a dense, thorny cover that provides superior bird protection.

Right: Host to many insects, white moneywort is a good diverse lawn addition.

White Moneywort (*Alysicarpus vaginalis*)—Nn, Ln, In, AR

Also known as alyce clover, false moneywort, and other names, moneyworts are small short-lived perennial herbs that run along the ground. Historically having widespread use in pastures and soil improvement projects, these proteinaceous plants are excellent additions to diverse lawns, although somewhat invasive. Moneywort is host plant for numerous insects, including beetles, leaf miners (Agromyzidae), and long-tailed skipper caterpillars. Year-round, 6-inch stems emerge from the foliage bearing red, ½-inch flowers that attract bees and other insects.

Trefoil (*Desmodium*)—Na, Ln, In, Sd, AR

These sprawling legumes occur natively in hammocks and pinelands and on disturbed roadsides and lots. They are excellent components of diverse lawns. They are rather well known (often as beggarticks), as their segmented seedpods break off and cling to shoes and clothing. As a result, they are readily recruitable to a lawn. Trefoil flowers attract bees and butterflies, and the foliage serves as host plant for hairstreak and skipper butterflies. Both seeds and insects are eaten by ground-feeding birds. The most common is zarzabacoa comun (*Desmodium incanum*), which is a name no one

Right: Trefoils, like this zarzabocoa comun, also called creeping tick trefoil and beggar's tick, serve well in a diverse lawn.

Far right: This syrphid fly is one of the many nectar-seeking insects attracted to the blooms of powderpuff, or sunshine mimosa. Powderpuff can be used well as a ground-cover plant or as part of a diverse lawn.

uses. It is more commonly called beggar's tick or Spanish clover and also creeping beggarweed and creeping tick trefoil. It is a year-round blooming perennial with pink to purple ¼-inch flowers and seedpods about ¼-inch long. It generally grows quite low, especially if mowed in a lawn. Threeflower ticktrefoil (*Desmodium triflorum*) is a small plant having ⅛-inch pink-purple flowers and ½-inch seedpods. Dixie ticktrefoil (*Desmodium tortuosum*), frequently used in pastures, is an annual with ½-inch purple flowers.

Powderpuff (*Mimosa strigillosa*)—Na, Ss, Ln, Wf, In, Sd, AW

This native legume, also called sunshine mimosa and sensitive plant because its leaves close when touched, is a beautiful and useful addition to a diverse lawn or ground cover. It spreads widely along recumbent stems that root at nodes. Pink powderpuff flowers on 6-inch stalks attract butterflies and other nectar-seeking insects. It is also host for mimosa yellow caterpillars. It can grow to 9 inches but is kept shorter by mowing. This plant should be in every diverse lawn in South Florida.

Jamaican Dogwood (*Piscidia piscipula*)—Na, Tr, Ns, St, In, Nc, AS

This distinctive tree, locally called Florida fishpoison tree, has ¾-inch white to pink, pealike nectar-rich flowers borne in clusters when the tree is leafless in spring, making an obvious display that attracts birds, butterflies, ants, and bees, including honey bees. The 2–3-inch winged seedpods are apparently wind and water distributed and not very attractive to birds. Jamaican dogwood is, however, an excellent caterpillar tree, supporting, among other species, cassius blue, fulvous hairstreak, and hammock skipper butterflies, also the nest-making psyllid (*Euphalerus nidifex*). Although capable of growing taller, in South Florida, Jamaican dogwoods tend to be about 20–30 feet, their multiple internal stems providing significant structure under the cover of a complete canopy. They are best used in a mixed-species setting that also hides their periodic defoliation.

Attracting Birds to South Florida Gardens

Coralbean (*Erythrina herbacea*)—Na, Sh/Tr/Vn, Bt, In, Nc, AS

Also called Cherokee bean, coral bean derives from southern North America and likely co-evolved with the Ruby-throated Hummingbird. Bright pink to red, tubular, 2-inch-long flowers clustered on top of stems are perfectly shaped and positioned for hummingbirds, although they also attract large butterflies. Blooming in South Florida occurs in early spring, as hummingbirds are preparing to return north, into the core of the coralbean's range. Black seedpods open in fall, exposing bright red seeds that remain for weeks until eaten by birds. Coralbeans tend to be deeply rooted, sun-seeking, viny trees in South Florida, sprawling upward into the canopy 15 feet on spindly thorny trunks. The branches are brittle and require canopy support.

Painted Buntings, like this immature male, are among the many birds and insects that seek refuge on Jamaican dogwood trees.

Coralbean flowers are perfectly designed for Ruby-throated Hummingbirds. Hummingbirds encounter flowering plants in South Florida in spring just before their departure.

Yellow Necklacepod (*Sophora tomentosa*)—Na, Sh, In, Sd, Nc, AS

This interesting shrub has beautiful yellow, 1-inch, pealike flowers on foot-long spikes that are visited in winter and early spring by Ruby-throated Hummingbirds, butterflies, moths, and bees, including honey bees. The plants themselves host a range of invertebrates, especially ants, spiders, and gray hairstreak caterpillars. Warblers and vireos work the thin branches and leaves for these invertebrate prey. When the 6-inch pods open, the seeds are eaten by catbirds, mockingbirds, and others. Necklacepods are lanky 5–10-foot-high shrubs with multiple ascending stems that tend to fill spaces in the subcanopy of mixed-tree and shrub stands. The South Florida native variety (*Sophora tomentosa* var. *truncata*) has smooth instead of fuzzy leaves.

Cheesytoes (*Stylosanthes hamata*)—Na, Ln, Wf, Sd, AS

Better known by the more attractive name of pencil flower, these short legumes, to 5 inches tall, spread along the ground on thin woody branches. They have tiny yellow flowers year-round that attract small butterflies, ¼-inch seedpods, and foliage that hosts ants, grasshoppers, and the barred yellow butterfly. A native of coastal areas from South America into South Florida, it has been cultivated in many other countries as a forage crop and in South Florida can be part of a diverse lawn.

Live Oak (*Quercus virginiana*)—Na, Tr, Ns, Pr, St, In, Fr, AW

The number one overall bird plant in South Florida, live oak provides ample food and structure for birds. In spring, inconspicuous wind-pollinated flowers produce copious pollen that is eaten by Ruby-throated Hummingbirds. In fall and winter, the small acorns, ½-inch in diameter, attract neighborhood ducks, bobwhites, Sandhill Cranes, Chestnut-fronted Macaws, Amazon parrots, Red-bellied Woodpeckers, Blue Jays, Brown Thrashers, crows, Boat-tailed Grackles, towhees, wrens, squirrels, raccoons, and deer. In "mast years," these acorns can litter the ground. Pollen and acorns aside, the great value of live oaks is the community of insects hidden in their tight dense leaves, rough fissured bark, and epiphytes. Hundreds of species of insects have been recorded from oaks in the United States; caterpillars particularly abound, including oak moth, tussock moth, polyphemus moth, Horace's duskywing, red-banded hairstreak, gray hairstreak, great purple hairstreak, and white M hairstreak. Other characteristic insects are scale insects, aphids, flies, bees, and wasps, including gall-making cynipid wasps. Nearly every bird species that seeks insects in trees is attracted to live oaks, especially woodpeckers (Red-bellied Woodpeckers, Northern Flickers, Yellow-bellied Sapsuckers), phoebes and other flycatchers, gnatcatchers, Northern Parula, Yellow-throated and other migrating and wintering warblers, vireos, jays, tanagers, orioles, and titmice. Stout branches provide strong support for nesting Great Horned Owls, Cooper's and Red-shouldered Hawks, Gray Kingbirds, mockingbirds, jays, and Monk Parakeets. As branches break off and holes develop, they are expanded by Red-bellied Woodpeckers and flickers into nesting cavities that are later used by Eastern Screech-Owls and other species. Live oaks are large trees. Those in South Florida generally can reach about 40, perhaps 50, feet tall and about as wide, although in more northern parts of the area the potential is 60–80 feet tall

If there is space in a yard, live oak is the single best bird plant in South Florida. Stout branches, dense leaves, fissured bark, pollen, acorns, and epiphytes all translate into protection and food. Birds like this Yellow-rumped Warbler throng to the venue.

with spreading horizontal branches potentially reaching out 100 feet. Despite a temperate zone origin, live oaks are among the dominant trees in South Florida's tropical hammocks and do exceptionally well for birds as part of mixed-tree plantings in bird gardens. This is where to put the screech-owl box. If gardens are large enough, oaks can be planted as specimens, and many yards have preexisting oaks that can continue to be featured within planned plantings.

Chapman's Oak (*Quercus chapmanii*), Sand Live Oak (*Quercus germinata*), Dwarf Live Oak (*Quercus minima*)—Na, Sh/Tr, St, In, Fr, AS

These small-growing oaks are native to South Florida's sandy pinelands, naturally reaching their southern range limits in the sandy soil of northern Miami-Dade and Collier counties. They provide cover, insects, and fruit, playing similar roles in the garden to live oak but at a smaller scale. Chapman's and sand live oaks can grow 15–30 feet in South Florida and are best used in mixed-species stands. Dwarf live oak is less than 3 feet tall, forming spreading clumps best used as ground cover or edges. All have acorns that are eaten by wildlife and a stature smaller than that of the live oak.

Wax Myrtle (*Myrica cerifera*)—Na, Sh/Tr, St, In, Fr, AS

The most important bird-friendly feature of wax myrtle is the ¼-inch waxy fruit. Persistent on the plant through fall and winter, so available to wintering birds just before their return migration, these high-energy morsels attract many species. Yellow-rumped Warblers and Tree Swallows are particularly attracted to wax myrtle as they have physiological and biochemical adaptations to efficiently digest the saturated long-chain fatty acids making up the wax. The ability of these species to eat winter-available fruit allows them to remain more to the north in the winter than related species. Other wax myrtle devotees are cardinals, catbirds, titmice, and Cedar

Waxwings, and many other species eat the berries, although perhaps at lower efficiency. These include bobwhites, flickers, Red-bellied Woodpeckers, Downy Woodpeckers, thrushes, mockingbirds, thrashers, Ruby-crowned Kinglets, Carolina Wrens, Palm and other warblers, vireos, bluebirds, robins, towhees, and jays. Thick foliage, rough bark, and catkin flowers provide insects, including ants, termites, bees including honey bees, and caterpillars of Horace's duskywing, viceroy, and red-banded hairstreak butterflies. The dense, leafy crown on multiple stems and branches and lots of internal space provide cover. As a fast-growing pioneer and edge plant of both damp and high-ground habitats, it survives a wide range of cultivation conditions in South Florida. For bird fruit, both male and female plants should be planted. Fast growing, suckering, and nitrogen fixing, they can form thick, multistemmed shrubs as part of mixed-shrub plantings, or they can be trimmed into rough hedges, barrier screens, or small trees 8–15 or even 25 feet tall.

Hackberry

Sugarberry (*Celtis laevigata*)—Na, Sh/Tr, St, In, Fr, AS

This tree is also known as southern hackberry, but the name sugarberry suggests why the fruit is well dispersed by birds. A temperate North American tree, southern sugarberry is found in South Florida north of the Keys, primarily in damp peaty hammocks and on Indian mounds. In spring, tiny greenish flowers attract bees and in late summer produce sweet, edible ¼–⅜-inch dark red fruit. Fruits persist through the winter, making them available to both migrant and wintering birds, including mockingbirds, catbirds, thrashers, towhees, waxwings, flickers, bluebirds, Red-bellied Woodpeckers, phoebes, sapsuckers, titmice, and robins, also to squirrels and deer.

Sugarberry hosts an exceptional number of insects, including caterpillars of io moth, and tawny emperor, question mark, hackberry emperor, and American snout butterflies (the only South Florida host), also mealybugs, gall-forming psyllids, whiteflies, lace bugs, and wood-boring, long-horned, and bark beetles. This huge community of insects attracts the attention of all the insect-eating birds, particularly warblers, vireos, and mockingbirds. They are fast-growing trees with thick, spreading crowns of drooping branches and occasional suckering, all providing cover. Although 60-foot trees elsewhere, they seldom reach 25 feet in South Florida and are best used within mixed-tree settings on organic soil. Alone it has a broad canopy and can be used as a specimen. It is used for commercial, park, and roadside landscaping throughout the South.

Colubrina

Greenheart (*Colubrina arborescens*)—Na, Sh, In, Fr, AS

Also called coffee colubrina, this endangered native has inconspicuous 3/16-inch green to yellow flowers, appearing in clusters most of the year, although peaking in spring. The highly fragrant flowers are attractive to armies of bees, wasps, flies, butterflies, and diurnal moths. Insects also use the fuzzy leaves, stems, and flaking brown trunks. Insectivorous birds are intensely attracted during flowering, especially Eastern Kingbirds, and other flycatchers, gnatcatchers, winter and migrating warblers, and vireos. Tiny 1/8–1/4-inch capsule-like fruits are eaten by vireos and warblers. This open-canopied Caribbean plant is a fast-growing shrub, to 15–20 feet tall. Natively it is found at edges or in partial sun in coastal hammocks in southern South Florida, most commonly in the Keys but can be planted as far north as Palm Beach. It is best for birds at edges of mixed-shrub plantings or as a screen. The similar latherleaf (*Colubrina asiatica*) is a non-native, invasive plant to be shunned.

Soldierwood (*Colubrina elliptica*)—Na, Sh/Tr, St, In, Fr, AS

Also called nakedwood and snakebark, this tree is widespread in the West Indies and tropical America, but in North America occurs only in South Florida. Insignificant 1/8-inch green to yellow flowers occur year-round, peaking in spring to summer. These flowers are its primary value as a bird plant as they attract a large number and diversity of insects, just in time for migrating tanagers, orioles, warblers, and vireos. This species has recently attained some local fame for its bird-attracting ability. The rough, flaky bark is also a good substrate for insects. Fruits, available during fall migration, are 1/8-inch, greenish becoming red to orange, and famously exploding open when totally ripe, though often eaten by birds beforehand. Soldierwood natively occurs in the rockland hammocks of the Upper Keys (Monroe and Miami-Dade, where it is rare and endangered) but can be planted in gardens farther north. Tall trees in the West Indies, they tend to be understory or edge shrubs 10 feet or less in South Florida but provide significant structure owing to thick branching. They are best for birds as part of mixed-shrub or tree plantings, placed where the abundant bird activity can be readily observed.

Rose Relatives

Nettletree (*Trema micrantha*)—Na, Sh/Tr, In, Fr, AS

This species is also called the Jamaican nettletree but in South Florida is known almost universally as Florida trema or just trema. The nettletree flowers year-round, the tiny yellow to green flowers appearing along the thin stems. These are followed by ¼-inch orange fruit, peaking in summer and fall and also lining the branches. Flowers attract insects, and the tiny fruits are eaten by resident mockingbirds, cardinals, thrashers, doves, towhees, titmice, and Red-bellied Woodpeckers, as well as by win-

Overlooked by humans most of the year, nettletree, or Florida trema, draws attention when its branches are covered in tiny, bright orange fruit.

tering and migrant gnatcatchers, warblers, vireos, bluebirds, flycatchers, catbirds, flickers, sapsuckers, and early arriving waxwings. Trema is host for a diverse collection of ants, mealybugs, scale insects, weevils, spiders, and caterpillars such as the martial scrub-hairstreak and io moth. It is more common in the southern portions of South Florida where it is a shrub or small tree no more than 10–20 feet tall, although it has the capacity to reach 30 feet. Natively this is an early successional hammock edge and tree gap plant that seeds easily and grows quickly, sprawling into open space and so is best in mixed-shrub zones or as a rough screen.

Black Ironwood (*Krugiodendron ferreum*)—Na, Sh/Tr, St, In, Fr, AS

Also called leadwood but most commonly in South Florida simply ironwood, this is a dense-wooded tropical tree that occurs natively in hammocks along the Atlantic Coast. It produces small, inconspicuous nectar-bearing flowers in spring that attract bees and wasps. Its ¼-inch purple/red to black fruits, available late summer to fall, attract fruit-eating birds, including migrating warblers. Within its leaves, branches, and trunk, ironwood supports an abundance of insects and spiders, including Sri Lanka weevils (*Myllocerus undecimpustulatus*), which cause its characteristic leaf notching, and Cuban May beetles (*Phyllophaga bruneri*), which cause its periodic defoliation. The invertebrates attract flycatchers, gnatcatchers, winter and migrating warblers,

vireos, and other insectivorous birds. Small, narrow-crowned, and densely branched, ironwood provides excellent cover for birds. While growing to 30 feet, it is more usually a shrub in South Florida and slow growing. Having glossy dark leaves, it is very attractive as a specimen and is used as such in commercial settings. For birds, it is better in sunny situations within mixed-shrub areas.

Left: Hammock skippers are one of the many insects attracted to black ironwood.

Right: Strangler figs are one of South Florida's most important bird plants. This Cape May Warbler is one of many birds that eat its fruit during migration.

Strangler Fig (*Ficus aurea*), Wild Banyan Tree or Short-leaf Fig (*Ficus citrifolia*)—Na, Tr, Pr, Ns, St, In, Fr, AW

These two native figs are among the most important bird trees in South Florida. The inconspicuous flowers attract and are pollinated by fig wasps (*Pegoscapus mexicanus* and *Pegoscapus tonduzi*, respectively). The wasps also lay their eggs within the fruit, from the interior. With dead wasps inside, the ⅓-inch figs provide both protein and sugar, attracting fruit-eating birds, which spread the tiny seeds. Fruiting tends to peak during fall migration season, but individual trees fruit on varying schedules from year to year. Any fruit-eating bird might be attracted to figs, including White-crowned Pigeons, woodpeckers, mockingbirds, catbirds, cardinals, orioles, conures, Amazons, thrushes, jays, thrashers, gnatcatchers, vireos, flycatchers, and many of the migrating and wintering warblers and wintering Cedar Waxwings. Native figs support a significant community of bird-attracting insects including wasps, mites (*Amblyseius*), ficus whiteflies (*Singhiella simplex*), rove beetles (*Charoxus*) (which eat the pollinating wasps and larvae inside the fruit), ants (attracted to nectaries), and caterpillars, including ruddy daggerwing and wasp moth (*Lymire*).

Both fig species can be very big, 40–60 feet tall for strangler fig and 30–50 feet for short-leaf fig, and nearly as wide. Because of their height and breadth, they provide exceptional structure and cover for perching, roosting, and nesting. They are trees of hammocks and so are best used at the rear of mixed-species tree areas where their excessive size can be incorporated into the canopy. Short-leaf figs are more tame than strangler figs in terms of aggressive spreading, and unlike strangler figs they don't start off as epiphytes. Strangler figs, germinating on other plants, especially cabbage palms, can eventually wrap around and kill their host; however, strangler figs can also germinate in the ground and need no support. Either native fig can be a valuable stand-alone specimen tree if garden room is sufficient. With due consideration for keeping it in control, at least one native fig tree should be part of a South Florida bird garden.

Red Mulberry (*Morus rubra*)—Na, Sh/Tr, In, Fr, AW

This native fruit-bearing and insect-attracting tree is a superior bird plant. Deciduous in winter, it blooms with greenish-white flowers simultaneously with spring leaf-out. Although primarily wind pollinated, the flowers attract flies, butterflies, wasps, and bees, also insectivorous birds, especially vireos, warblers, and flycatchers. Related to white mulberry (*Morus alba*), the famous silkworm host, this mulberry too supports tent caterpillars (Lasiocampidae) as well as a wealth of other insects, including mulberry leafrollers (*Diaphania pulverulentalis*), scale insects (*Pulvinaria*), whiteflies, mites, mealybugs (*Pseudococcus*), and stem-borers including beetles (*Dora schema*) and snout mouths (*Euzophera*). The 1-inch-long purple fruit, available mostly spring through summer, attracts any frugivorous bird in the neighborhood, including Downy, Red-bellied, and Pileated Woodpeckers, doves, Eastern and Gray Kingbirds, Great Crested Flycatchers, mockingbirds, catbirds, thrashers, cardinals, jays, crows, grackles, titmice, Carolina Wrens, tanagers, and orioles, also opossums, raccoons, and squirrels, and once on the ground, quail and box turtles. In South Florida, they natively are hammock trees that become 30–40 feet tall and so do well in mixed-tree settings where their spreading, thin branches can insinuate into the larger canopy. They can also be used as specimens, although messy ones. These plants attract birds to a garden for many months of the year and are highly recommended.

Darlingplum (*Reynosia septentrionalis*)—Na, Sh/Tr, Fr, AS

Found throughout the Caribbean, in North America this is a South Florida specialty, occurring natively only in the coastal hammocks of the Keys in Monroe and Miami-Dade counties. Also called red ironwood, it is a shrub to small tree, generally shorter than 10–15 feet. It has miniscule yellow-green flowers that lack petals and

Native to coastal hammocks in South Florida, darlingplum fruits are consumed by many birds.

1-inch purple fruits, which are quite edible and attract doves, pigeons, and smaller birds that eat them in pieces. Its branches and leaves are rather irregularly positioned and overall provide shelter and stout nesting sites for species seeking low cover such as vireos and cardinals. It is best as part of a mixed-species shrub or tree area but can be grown in containers.

West Indian Cherry (*Prunus myrtifolia*)—Na, Tr, St, In, Fr, AS

Also known as *Laurocerasus myrtifolia*, myrtle cherry, and myrtle laurelcherry, this is South Florida's only native cherry tree, one derived from the tropics. In winter, tiny but fragrant ¼-inch white flowers form large clusters that attract bees. The clusters develop in summer into showy clustered masses of ½-inch glossy dark red to orange-brown fruits that, although considered poisonous to humans, are eagerly sought out by birds, especially mockingbirds, cardinals, and Red-bellied Woodpeckers, also squirrels. In South Florida, they tend to be trees to about 25 feet, occasionally reaching 45 feet, and provide significant cover for birds. Natively from the pine rocklands and hammocks of Miami-Dade, they are fast-growing and well adapted to local limestone soils and the annual dry season. They can be used as part of mixed-tree areas, specimen trees, or hedgy buffers, and are to be encouraged in commercial plantings.

Loquat (*Eriobotrya japonica*)—Nn, Tr, Pr, St, In, Fr, AW

Cultivated for more than a thousand years, the loquat produces 1-inch white flowers in large terminal clusters in fall and early winter. These fragrant blossoms attract many bees, flies, and butterflies, and in turn the insectivorous birds that feed among the blooms. By late winter, they produce pulpy 1–2-inch yellow fruits that are eaten in bits by Red-bellied Woodpeckers, mockingbirds, cardinals, grackles, and jays. Long in cultivation, loquats have many "pests" that birds seek out, including fruit flies, beetles, weevils, scale insects, carpenter bees, and thrips. These trees can be 30 feet tall, although there are dozens of cultivated varieties around the world, including dwarf varieties and the Wolfe, developed in South Florida. Their thick leaves conceal an open internal structure providing good perching opportunities for birds and squirrels. Orchids seem to do well on them, providing additional structure.

Myrtles

Black Olive (*Terminalia buceras*)—Na?, Tr, Ns, Pr, St, Fr, AW

More commonly called *Bucida buceras* and also oxhorn bucida, the black olive arguably occurred natively in the Keys but in any case is a West Indian tree that has been widely planted in South Florida for decades in both garden and commercial settings. Having fallen into local horticultural disfavor, it more than deserves rehabilitation for bird gardens. Its ¼-inch seed-capsule fruits are eaten by a variety of frugivorous birds, but the tree's value is mostly as roosting and nesting habitat. Black olive has a dense, rounded, wind-resistant canopy, thickly set leaves, and thorns, all of which provide significant cover and nesting sites for hawks, doves, mockingbirds, Common Grackles, Blue Jays, and Gray Kingbirds. Grackles, crows, parrots, doves, and House Sparrows use the trees as night roosts. In South Florida, black olives are generally 20–30 feet tall, but old specimens, of which there are many in the region, can achieve 50–70 feet. Tall trees are invaluable as nesting sites for larger birds such as Cooper's Hawks. They are recommended as specimen trees for gardens, roadsides, and parking lots, where they are exceptionally good at providing shelter among the asphalt. The spiny black olive (*Terminalia molinetii*) (Na, Sh/Tr, Ns, Pr, St, Fr, AS), also known as dwarf

Gray Kingbirds are one of the birds that take advantage of the protective canopy of black olives for nesting.

black olive and *Bucida spinosa*, is also a native to Miami-Dade County but no longer occurs in the wild; it is readily available from nurseries, however. Although smaller and less dense than black olive, when left to its own devices in a garden (and not turned into a bonsai), it can reach 25 feet. It also provides exceptional cover in its canopy of complexly organized thorny branches.

Buttonwood (*Conocarpus erectus*)—Na, Sh/Tr, Ns, Pr, St, In, AW

Buttonwood is among the more important of South Florida's bird trees. The flowers, which can appear year-round but peak in summer, look like tiny greenish fuzz balls with the entire flower head being no more than ½ inch. These attract numerous

Buttonwood's healthy invertebrate population is one of its many bird-friendly attributes. Here a Northern Parula hunts in a rolled buttonwood leaf. Buttonwood is one of the most important bird trees in South Florida.

insects, including butterflies, honey bees, and other bees. Dispersed by water, the ½-inch conelike fruits burst open when ripe, but the fruits, as well as leaves and rough epiphyte-friendly bark, support a vast community of insects and spiders. Among buttonwood's typical insects are martial scrub-hairstreak and tantalus sphinx moth caterpillars, non-native Sri Lanka weevils, buttonwood flea beetles (*Chaetocnema brunnescens*), bagworms (*Biopsyche*), ants, termites, and flies. All this arthropod life attracts flycatchers, gnatcatchers, wintering and migrating warblers, vireos, mockingbirds, catbirds, Red-bellied Woodpeckers, grackles, and jays. They are also favorite perches for hummingbirds. There is usually a bird or two working any large buttonwood tree. A natural variation, the attractive light-leaved silver buttonwood (var. *sericea*) is readily available and widely planted. In any garden, buttonwoods are among the trees most used by birds, particularly during migration season and in winter. In South Florida gardens, they are quite flexible. Best on limestone-derived soils, they can quickly grow 20–50 feet tall and are exceptional as specimens. This is one tree that attracts birds solo.

Pineapple Guava (*Acca sellowiana*)—Nn, Sh, St, In, Nc, AS

Also known as feijoa and *Feijoa sellowiana*, these South American plants have been in cultivation for a century and are common in traditional South Florida gardens. Blooming in spring and summer, their single or clustered 1-inch flowers have bright red stamens emerging from purple-tinged white fleshy petals. Bees eat the petals and so pollinate the flowers. The petals are also eaten by mockingbirds, jays, starlings, and mynas. Fruits are 3–4 inches, too large for birds, so tend to fall to the ground overripe in winter. Their round, dense growth form provides ample structure for small birds.

Crimson Bottlebrush (*Callistemon citrinus*)—Nn, Sh, Bt, In, Nc, AW

Loved by hummingbirds, the bottlebrush's red, bristly 4-inch flowers provide nectar for wintering Ruby-throated Hummingbirds, as well as for butterflies, honey bees, wasps, flies, and other nectar-feeding insects. Red-whiskered Bulbuls, Amazons, conures, and Monk Parakeets eat the flowers directly. The rough bark often hosts epiphytic plants and associated insects, which attract mockingbirds, catbirds, grackles, flycatchers, warblers, and vireos. Bottlebrush is generally maintained as a shrub, 10–15 feet tall, usually as a specimen planting, but it can be used in screens, hedges, or even espaliered. It is also called *Melaleuca citrinus* and *Callistemon lanceolatus*. A drooping form called weeping bottlebrush or just bottlebrush (*Melaleuca viminalis*) is widely planted in South Florida but considered potentially invasive and should be used with caution in gardens.

Spicewood (*Calyptranthes pallens*)—Na, Sh/Tr, St, In, Fr, AS

These thick shrubs to small trees, also called pale lidflower, have everything for birds. Fragrant white-pink flowers borne in attractive terminal clusters attract butterflies and bees in late spring to summer. Human-edible, ¼-inch orange turning dark purple-black fruits ripen in fall and winter and are long lasting as dry fruit on the plant. These are eaten by mockingbirds, catbirds, cardinals, thrushes, grackles, and jays. The plants have an intricate growth form with multiple trunks and orderly branching, producing complex rounded shrubs or small trees up to about 15–25 feet high. Natively hammock plants that grow in partial shade, they are excellent under and at the edges of mixed plantings. They can be made into small trees by trimming, but the normal growth form tends toward use as screens and rough hedges. They are useful in commercial settings.

Myrtle-of-the-River (*Calyptranthes zuzygium*)—Na, Sh/Tr, Pr, St, In, Fr, AS

This attractively foliaged shrub or tree has fragrant and exceptionally showy, fuzzy green-white flowers in spring and summer that attract insects. Its small ¼-inch fruits are red turning dark blue-purple and highly attractive to birds. It is a shrub to tree 20 feet tall but capable of achieving 40 feet. Its thick, irregular canopy provides good cover. It is best in mixed-tree or mixed-shrub plantings, especially when mixed with stoppers. Its native North American range is restricted to southeastern Florida. It is listed as endangered in Florida and worth planting for plant conservation purposes in the southern end of the state.

Florida Clover Ash (*Tetrazygia bicolor*)—Na, Sh/Tr, In, Fr, AS

Actually no one uses this name; some call it West Indian lilac, but to most gardeners this species is simply tetrazygia. Its clusters of fragrant white to pink flowers bloom in spring and summer, attracting legions of nectarivorous insects, especially bees includ-

The intricate flowers of Florida clover ash, more commonly called tetrazygia or West Indian lilac, attract pollinating bees and other nectarivorous insects.

ing honey bees. Dark purple/black ½-inch fruits peak in spring but stay on the plant through late summer and fall, when they are eaten especially by mockingbirds, but also attract catbirds, thrushes, and thrashers. Tetrazygia are shrubs or small trees, typically to 10 or perhaps 12 feet tall, but they can get taller. Natively from pinelands and hammocks in the extreme south of South Florida and thriving in organic soils, they are best for birds as part of untrimmed mixed-shrub or tree plantings; however, they can be nicely symmetrical accent plants and work in commercial settings as well.

Stopper (*Eugenia*)

Several native species of stopper should be heavily used in any South Florida bird garden; all are superior providers of insects, exceptional cover, and fruit. Flowers attract nectar-hunting insects, especially bees and butterflies. The small obvious fruit, available primarily in spring and summer but into the fall, is eagerly consumed by a variety of fruit-eating birds, especially mockingbirds, catbirds, thrashers, cardinals, warblers, vireos, and jays. The tight branch structure provides niches for insects and spiders that attract warblers, vireos, and other midlevel-foraging insect-eating birds. Tight canopies provide ample cover and, when large enough, nest sites. Several stopper species in a garden provide a succession of fruit. Natively they are part of the understory and hammock edge and are best used in similar situations. Although stoppers grow 15–20 feet, in gardens they are usually maintained as shrubs and for birds are best massed as part of diverse shrub zones. They can also be used as hedges and barrier plantings.

Spanish Stopper (*Eugenia foetida*)—Na, Sh/Tr, Ns, Pr, St, In, Fr, AS

Also known as boxleaf stopper, this is a tallish, densely leaved, narrow shrub that can be used for barriers, screens, or hedges but has the capacity to be a large tree, 30–40 feet tall. The tiny summer flowers produce similarly tiny ¼-inch black fruits in later fall and winter, which despite their size attract birds. Spanish stopper is somewhat cold tolerant and can be used throughout South Florida.

Spanish stopper produces an abundance of fruit, attracting frugivorous birds.

White Stopper (*Eugenia axillaris*)—Na, Sh/Tr, Ns, Pr, St, In, Fr, AS

Also endearingly called skunk wood in South Florida, white stopper provides *the* typical fragrance of South Florida's tropical hammock. It has fuzzy, small white flowers in summer, and the red-purple turning to black ¼–½-inch fruits persist on the shrub for some time, so is available to birds over a long period. A dense, symmetrical growth habit provides cover for birds. Since the species naturally ranges northward into Central Florida, it can be grown throughout South Florida.

Red Stopper (*Eugenia rhombea*)—Na, Sh/Tr, Ns, Pr, St, In, Fr, AS

A natively rare plant from the Keys, it is now widely planted in gardens. The ¼-inch fruit turns from orange to red to black.

Redberry Stopper (*Eugenia confusa*)—Na, Sh/Tr, Ns, Pr, St, In, Fr, AS

Also called ironwood and redberry eugenia, this is perhaps the most attractive of the native stoppers. It is a Florida endangered species because of its restricted natural range but still available to gardeners. This stopper can be used for shrub hedges to about 6 feet or as tall thin specimen plants to 18 feet tall. As the name implies, it has bright red ¼-inch berries that turn blacker as they ripen.

Mangroveberry (*Mosiera longipes*)—Na, Sh/Tr, Ns, Pr, St, In, Fr, AS

Also referred to as *Psidium longipes* and more commonly called long-stalked stopper or Bahama stopper, this is another Florida-listed species available for gardeners. It is a small shrub, generally under 3 feet tall. Tiny white flowers produce dark berries that are attractive to birds.

Surinam Cherry (*Eugenia uniflora*)—Nn, X?, Sh, Ns, St, Fr, AW

Once South Florida's traditional hedge, this South American stopper has fallen into disfavor, but it remains a bird favorite. Its ½–1-inch orange/red fruits, peaking in spring, are eaten whole by larger birds and in pieces by smaller birds. Mockingbirds, grackles, crows, and late-staying catbirds are at the top of the dining list. Hedges, if made dense by trimming, are readily used for nesting. In fact, this is an excellent bird plant. Unfortunately, it is now considered an invasive exotic because birds distribute its seeds so widely. As a result, it is advocated that it not be planted in bird-dropping range of natural hammocks.

Left: Like those of all native stoppers, the nectar-rich flowers of white stopper entice many insects and will be followed by bird-friendly fruit.

Right: Red stopper, like other stoppers, provides structure for nests such as this cardinal nest.

Simpson's Stopper (*Myrcianthes fragrans*)—Na, Sh/Tr, Ns, Pr, St, In, Fr, AS

This plant is called twinberry outside of South Florida. Here, though, historically and to the present, it is inevitably called Simpson's stopper. Most South Florida gardeners cherish this name as honoring Charles Torrey Simpson, one of the greatest of South Florida's early naturalists. Ironically, the name actually honors his brother, a plant collector. This is a narrow shrub to small tree having small tight leaves, attractive bark, and strongly buttressed base. The tight strong branches provide excellent cover and nesting sites. Fragrant white flowers are produced prolifically, most commonly in spring but variably. Orange to red ¼–½-inch fruits appear mostly in summer to early fall attracting mockingbirds, which will defend them vigorously. Simpson stoppers are among the more cold hardy of the native stoppers and so can be planted throughout South Florida. They can be shrubs to 6 feet or become trees to 20 feet. For birds they are particularly good in massed plantings, providing thick fall and winter shelter, such as near feeders.

Attractive both visually and to the birds, fruits of Simpson's stopper and the other native stoppers attract fruit-eating birds.

Bitterbush

Florida Bitterbush (*Picramnia pentandra*)—Na, Sh/Tr, In, Fr, AS

In spring and summer, tiny white flowers clustering on drooping terminal stems attract insects for nectar and pollen and are followed by ½-inch attractively hanging fruits in winter. The fruits, which start green and turn scarlet then black as they ripen, are eaten readily by mockingbirds, cardinals, catbirds, Red-bellied Woodpeckers, grackles, and jays, as well as by squirrels. The foliage supports numerous insects, including caterpillars of the dina yellow butterfly. Occurring in North America only in South Florida, they natively are fast-growing postfire invaders of coastal hammocks. Usually shrubs no more than 10 feet tall, they can be flexibly planted in mixed-species tree settings, as accent trees, in small clusters of shrubs, or as hedges.

Capers and Papaya

Jamaican Capertree (*Capparis jamaicensis*)—Na, Sh/Tr, Ns, Pr, St, In, Fr, AW

A striking plant in all respects, Jamaican capertree, or more usually called Jamaica caper, has fragrant spring-blooming 3-inch flowers that turn from white to pink as they mature, attracting bees, flies, and butterflies. Later in summer, ¼-inch seeds in 10–12-inch capsules are eaten by Mourning Doves, jays, cardinals, and mockingbirds. The foliage also feeds many insects. Jamaica caper is typically an 8–10-foot shrub but can grow to 20 feet. Densely branched with thick, dark green leaves along the canopy edge and more open on the inside, its structure provides exceptional cover for birds. Jamaica capers are favored for mockingbird and cardinal nests. Native plants of high-ground hammocks near the coast, they do well both in mixed-shrub settings and in partial shade. They are especially recommended as rough native hedges, although the more trimming, the fewer the flowers.

Impressive flowers and dense leaves make Jamaican capertree an ideal hedge, providing privacy for both people and birds.

Bayleaf Capertree (*Capparis flexuosa*)—Na, Sh/Vn, St, In, Sd, AS

Also called limber caper, its fragrant summer flowers open in the evening, likely to attract moths, but its fruit is eaten by Mourning Doves, jays, mockingbirds, grackles, and many other birds. Natively, this is a vining shrub in coastal hammock, sprawling its woody stems 10–25 feet into the canopy. It is best used within a mixed-tree planting. Its foliage supports caterpillars of white butterflies and other insects, while its growth habit provides structure and cover for birds within its canopy.

Virginia Pepperweed (*Lepidium virginicum*)—Na, Ln, In, AR

Although actually native to South Florida, Virginia pepperweed is a common winter weed in lawns elsewhere. Also known as pepper-grass or poor-man's pepper, it is a self-seeding annual that starts from ground-hugging florets but in spring and summer sends up 1–2-foot flowering stalks bearing ⅛-inch flowers that attract bees and butterflies, and it serves as a larval host plant for several white butterflies. This is an excellent plant for diverse lawns, maintained by high mowing.

Papaya (*Carica papaya*)—Nn, Sh/Tr, Vg, In, Fr, AW

Papayas are tropical American plants that have occurred in South Florida for a millennium and have been used by inhabitants since that time. Their flowers, atop tree-sized stems 10–20 feet tall, are usually pollinated by moths. They bear year-round fruit that attracts insects, including bugs, moths, whiteflies, scale, mites, and especially the huge papaya fruit flies (*Toxotrypana curvicauda*). Migrating warblers and wintering mixed flocks of birds search papaya leaves and stems. Fruit is eaten directly by woodpeckers and parrots, and once the fruit is open the pulp and seeds are fair game for any fruit-eating birds, which is why the plant spreads so readily. Papayas are easily added to vegetable gardens (from the seeds of store-bought fruit) or as a culturally accurate element of a South Florida hammock planting. Some consider them intrusively invasive, but they have been so for a thousand years.

Bombax and Hibiscus

Bombax Trees—Nn, Tr, Pr, St, In, Nc, AS

These several species are distinctive and impressive trees, a centerpiece of any garden they occupy. These include the floss silk tree (*Ceiba speciosa*), kapok (*Ceiba pentandra*), and red silk cottontree (*Bombax ceiba*). They are very tall trees in the South Florida context; the kapok at 80 feet towers above most other South Florida plants. These trees are deciduous in winter and while still leafless cover themselves with masses of flowers that are highly attractive to nectar-feeding birds and insects. Orioles, late-staying hummingbirds, and bees flock to the flowers. The trees provide superior structure for birds year-round, and most have thorny trunks that discourage climbing predators. Many species of birds forage along the branches, but they seem to be particularly attractive to mynas in winter and parrots in summer.

Left: Planting papaya in a garden supplies many birds with insects and some with fruit and seeds.

Right: Flocks of Yellow-chevroned Parakeets are attracted to the floss silk tree, consuming both fruits and flowers.

Common Wireweed (*Sida ulmifolia*)—Na, Ln, In, AR

More commonly known as teaweed and *Sida acuta* but also called broomgrass and common fanpetals, this pantropical weed has ½-inch yellow flowers that attract year-round bees, skippers, and fritillary butterflies. Its nutritious foliage is eaten directly by bobwhites and turkeys. Wireweed is a larval host for a number of caterpillars, including gray hairstreaks, mallow scrub-hairstreaks, and common and tropical checkered-skippers. Plants reach 3 feet tall but can be high-mowed into an excellent diverse lawn weed.

Common wire-weed flowers attract insects, and the leaves are eaten directly by some birds. It is a valuable addition to diverse lawns.

Swamp Rosemallow (*Hibiscus grandiflorus*)—Na, Sh, Wt, Bt, Nc, AS

Also known as swamp hibiscus, this native hibiscus sports 5-inch flowers, white to pink with reddish-purple interiors, that attract Ruby-throated Hummingbirds and orioles. Swamp rosemallow is a shrub 6–9 feet tall in summer, with stems dying back in the winter. As a swamp plant, it does best in damp sites and water features. The scarlet rosemallow (*Hibiscus coccineus*) occurs naturally to Central Florida and western South Florida and is widely planted for its remarkable red, 6-inch summer flowers that attract butterflies.

Non-native Hibiscus (*Hibiscus*)—Nn, Sh, In, Nc, AW

Cultivated hibiscus are omnipresent around the tropics, and it would seem impossible to have a garden in the South Florida subtropics without one. Fortunately, they are good bird plants for their insects and for their flowers, which have nectar reserves deep within their calyxes. Simple flowers attract Ruby-throated Hummingbirds and orioles. Multiple-petaled flowers are not accessible directly by nectar-feeding birds, but the flowers of all varieties are eaten by parrots and green iguanas. Because hibiscus have been so long in cultivation and because related species are native in South Florida, they support a large and diverse insect world of ants, bees, sawflies, whiteflies, spider mites, grasshoppers, mealybugs, and caterpillars, including gray hairstreak caterpillars. Among the insectivorous birds that feed in hibiscus are warblers, vireos, orioles, mockingbirds, jays, cardinals, catbirds, Indigo Buntings, and Red-winged Blackbirds. Most gardeners battle hibiscus insects with chemicals (often hurting the plants), but bird gardeners need to welcome these bugs for the birds, even if their hibiscus look a bit ratty at times.

Garden Rosemallow (*Hibiscus rosa-sinensis*)—Nn, Sh, Bt, St, In, Nc, AW

Actually no one calls this the garden rosemallow but rather just hibiscus. This is the most common cultivated hibiscus in South Florida, and in fact traditionally one of its more abundant flowers. It comes in hundreds of varieties, the old fashioned 'Painted Lady' being South Florida's tradition. Most plants are kept as shrubs under 6–8 feet tall. Highly trimmable, they can be used for hedges, specimen shrubs, butterfly/hummingbird gardens, or container plants—actually nearly anywhere. They do need care, especially newer varieties. Most new varieties can be temperamental, and they need fertilizer. For bird gardens, simple-flowered, old-time, hardy varieties are best.

Fringed Rosemallow (*Hibiscus rosa-sinensis* var. *schizopetalus*)—Nn, Sh, Bt, St, In, Nc, AW

This African species is naturalized on old home sites and shell mounds, attesting to its historical significance in South Florida. Usually called fringed hibiscus and considered a separate species (*Hibiscus schizopetalus*) from the common hibiscus, it grows as a single-stemmed shrub. The downward-hanging flowers, like the other hibiscus, supply insects and nectar.

Yellow Mahoe (*Talipariti tiliaceum* var. *pernambucense*)—Na?, Sh/Tr, Bt, St, In, Nc, AS; Sea Hibiscus (*Talipariti tiliaceum*)—Nn, X?, Tr, Bt, St, In, Nc, AW; Portia Tree (*Thespesia populnea*)—Nn, X?, Tr, Bt, St, In, Nc, AS.

Differentiating the three look-alike seaside hibiscus trees even puzzles experts. Yellow mahoe is a yellow-flowered plant (the flowers turning orange as the day progresses) that occurs along the South Florida coast, as well as in the West Indies and on the Atlantic and Pacific coasts of South America. Natively, it grows adjacent to mangrove swamps and on beach dunes. It is likely native to South Florida, or was introduced from tropical America by trade long ago. Most authorities now consider the American native plants a full species (*Hibiscus pernambucensis*), not a variety. Sea hibiscus, also known as mahoe, is from tropical Asia. Its flowers have red centers. The portia tree is a pantropical plant with initial yellow flowers with maroon centers. It is rarer than the others in South Florida.

Yellow mahoe provides insect food and exceptional cover for birds, although considered invasive in some circumstances.

All three are large shrubs to trees that grow along the shore, grow quickly, and create tangled thickets of branches and roots that provide excellent cover for birds. In addition, mahoe foliage hosts a community of insects, including aphids, whiteflies, mealybugs, caterpillars, and spiders. Butterflies, bees, ants, and flies are all attracted to the flowers. From a bird's perspective, mahoes are thus highly desirable plants, providing both structure and insects. They do well in damp, fresh to brackish soil conditions and were once widely endorsed for coastal planting by early South Florida naturalists, but today mahoes are in disfavor and considered aggressive, undesirable plants. Nonetheless, the thicket-like growth that is considered undesirable from some perspectives creates superior habitat for birds. In a controlled garden setting, they can be kept in check and provide excellent structure for birds.

Bahama Swampbush (*Pavonia bahamensis*)—Nn, Sh/Tr, Bt, Nc, AS
Swampbush (*Pavonia paludicola*)—Na, Sh, In, Bt, Nc, AS

These nectar-rich hibiscus are exceptional bird plants. Pollinated by hummingbirds and Bananaquits in their native Bahamas, they are gaining increasing attention from South Florida gardeners for attracting hummingbirds, warblers, and orioles to their small green-yellow flowers. They additionally attract nectar-seeking insects, providing another bird-food source. In South Florida, they are usually shrubs to 7 feet tall, providing cover within a thick crown. The native species (*Pavonia spicata*) is rare in South Florida. Increasingly available in horticulture, Bahama swampbush should not be overlooked when planting gardens intended for wintering hummingbirds.

Famous for attracting hummingbirds, swampbush also attracts other nectar-seeking and insect-seeking birds, like this Palm Warbler, to its miniature hibiscus flowers.

Turk's Cap (*Malvaviscus penduliflorus*)—Nn, Sh/Tr, Bt, St, In, Nc, AW

These are also called mazapan and *Malvaviscus arboreus*; in South Florida, as in their natural Central and South American range, Turk's caps bloom in winter and spring when Ruby-throated Hummingbirds are present. Their red or pink 3-inch flowers, looking like unopened hibiscus, hold a large supply of nectar, which hummingbirds access by piercing the bottoms of flowers. Painted Buntings, Spot-breasted and Baltimore Orioles, parrots, butterflies, moths, bees, wasps, iguanas, and raccoons are attracted to the flowers. Although less used now, Turk's cap was part of the old-time tropical plantings in South Florida and is well naturalized, persisting on disturbed sites. A shrub to small tree, 9 feet tall, it makes an excellent backdrop for butterfly areas.

Strawberrytree (*Muntingia calabura*)—Nn, X?, Tr, St, In, Fr, AS

Also called Jamaica cherry and many other names where it has been naturalized world-wide, this Central American and Caribbean native has white, ½-inch flowers that occur from spring through fall. The flowers attract bees, including honey bees, ants, and flies. The ½-inch red or yellow fruit is sweet, juicy, seedy, and very birdy, also attracting insects, especially fruit flies in South Florida. Catbirds, mockingbirds, jays, grackles and parakeets commonly eat the fruit, and all the insectivorous birds are attracted to the numerous insects. This is an exceptional bird tree. It is a pioneer plant and so is fast growing and short-lived, quickly becoming a wide-spreading tree to 30 feet tall and wide. It is seldom recommended for planting because the trees get to be big, messy, and fruit-fly ridden and also are potentially invasive because birds carry their seeds. But for a bird garden, a strawberry tree might be considered in situations where it will pose no harm to native habitats, as it will certainly attract many many birds.

Sumac, Citrus, and Relatives

Mango (*Mangifera indica*)—Nn, Tr, St, In, Fr, AW

Mango is certainly a tree a bird gardener wants, if at all possible, in any South Florida garden. Tiny yellow to red flowers are borne in large inflorescences that attract hordes of insects—wasps, flies, hoverflies, ants, and honey bees. As might be expected of commercial trees, leaves and trunks host legions of bird-attracting insects, such as bud mites, moth-borers, square borers (gray hairstreak and red-banded hairstreak caterpillars), scale insects, thrips, ambrosia beetles (*Xylosandrus*), banded cucumber

The mango tree is a South Florida icon that provides food and shelter to birds while also supplying the gardener with fruit.

beetles (*Diabrotica balteata*), and spider mites. As a result, birds are always working the canopy, especially during migration periods and in winter. Fruits on the tree are penetrated by woodpeckers, Chestnut-fronted Macaws, Amazon parrots, squirrels, and black rats, after which the pulp can be eaten by other birds. There are many mango varieties, including dwarf sizes, but the larger the tree, the better for the birds. All South Florida bird gardeners with space should consider one or more mangos—because nothing says a South Florida garden like a mango tree.

Eastern Poison Ivy (*Toxicodendron radicans*)—Na, Vn, St, Fr, AR

Despite its obvious downside, poison ivy's small, berry-like gray fruit is among the most sought after of all fruits by birds. Overall, about 50 bird species have been documented eating poison ivy, particular South Florida devotees include Downy Woodpeckers, flickers, Yellow-bellied Sapsuckers, Red-bellied Woodpeckers, warblers, vireos, titmice, wrens, robins, and bluebirds. In South Florida, fruits ripen in late summer and fall and some remain through winter, making them especially valuable to migrating and wintering birds. This vine volunteers after being dispersed by birds, so the bird gardener's choice once one arrives is whether to kill, transplant, or let it be. While poison ivy certainly would not be wanted where people easily come in contact, it is an extremely valuable bird plant when allowed to do its thing deep within plantings.

Poisonwood (*Metopium toxiferum*)—Na, Sh/Tr, St, Fr, AR

Poisonwood or Florida poisontree presents dermatological challenges in a garden, but it is a crucial part of the natural bird-plant landscape of South Florida. Its ¼–½-inch fruit, available in summer and fall, attracts nearly all fruit-eating species, including mockingbirds, cardinals, jays, grackles, and especially in South Florida, White-crowned Pigeons. Planting or allowing poisonwood trees is one way to attract these pigeons. Natively, these are shrubs or small trees of pinelands and early successional trees in hammocks, where they occasionally grow to 40 feet. They are best used in mixed-shrub or tree plantings. Of course, they need to be planted well away from where sensitive people might encounter them.

Despite its name, poisonwood provides copious fruit for birds and other wildlife, like gray squirrels.

Winged Sumac (*Rhus copallinum*)—Na, Sh, In, Fr, AR

Also known as shiny sumac or shining sumac, these are fast-growing, sun-loving pioneer plants. Their small, yellowish-green flowers occur in terminal clusters from spring to summer, attracting beetles as well as honey bees and flies. Large, drooping, terminal masses of ⅛-inch red fruit develop by fall and remain on the plants through winter, making them available to flocking frugivores such as waxwings, robins, and Tree Swallows. Sumacs provide important food for game birds and mammals such as squirrels, opossums, and deer, which also browse the stems and leaves. The flowers, fruit, and leaves all attract insects, sumac being the larval host for red-banded hairstreak butterflies. Open-structured shrubs generally 10–15 feet tall, they readily form thickets by suckering, providing cover for birds. They are deciduous, presenting an attractive red fall foliage, a rather atypical feature for a South Florida native plant. They naturally occur in pinelands but can tolerate a wide range of conditions, from containers to parking lots.

Gumbo Limbo (*Bursera simaruba*)—Na, Tr, Ns, Pr, St, In, Fr, AS

These widely planted trees are as characteristic of South Florida as are palms. They are briefly deciduous in the dry season of winter and early spring. In spring, tiny green to brown flowers occur on 6-inch panicles, attracting hordes of nectar-seeking insects, especially bees and wasps, and migrating insect-eating birds, including warblers, gnatcatchers, vireos, flycatchers, and thrushes. Their leaves host a variety of insects such as caterpillars (including the rare dingy purplewing butterfly), leaf beetles (*Blepharida*), and, more recently, rugose spiraling whiteflies (*Aleurodicus rugioperculatus*), which have turned out to be great attractants for migrating warblers. Gumbo limbo's ½-inch fruits are surrounded by red arils; both fruit and arils attract birds, especially White-crowned Pigeons but also Eastern Kingbirds, Gray Kingbirds, Great Crested Flycatchers, mockingbirds, vireos, Mourning Doves, Red-bellied Woodpeckers, cardinals, catbirds, grackles, jays, orioles, crows, warblers, Amazon parrots, and macaws. If a gumbo limbo is growing nearby, its seedlings will be found volunteering in a bird garden. They grow fast, quickly achieving 30–50 feet, although capable of attaining 80, being one of the tallest native trees. Shedding leaves, exuding sticky

Gumbo limbo provides both fruit and insects, such as the newly invading rugose spiraling whitefly. This Common Yellowthroat is one of the many birds that are attracted to infected trees to feed on the whiteflies.

sap, and hosting fungus-encouraging whiteflies have dimmed gumbo limbo's appeal to some gardeners. This is unfortunate because everything about these trees, including the whiteflies, is of value to birds. They are excellent planted in their native situation, in a mixed-tree setting, and also as specimens, although perhaps not over driveways and patios. Gumbo limbo trees are nearly essential in any South Florida garden aiming to attract birds, and they also do well as roadside plantings. The seeds are well dispersed by birds, so they likely will volunteer in the garden if present in the neighborhood. The important point is to plant them where their negative characteristics are not a bother and their many positive characteristics can enhance a bird garden.

West Indian Mahogany (*Swietenia mahagoni*)—Na, Tr, Ns, Pr, St, In, AW

These trees have tiny flowers that develop into large woody capsules up to 4 inches long and hard as rocks. While their fruits are not for birds, mahogany's insects are. The variety of insects that inhabit the canopy include flies, bees, ants, termites, beetles (such as Cuban May beetles), and caterpillars (such as mahogany webworms, *Macalla thyrsisalis*). Insect-eating birds are always working the canopy, including gnatcatchers, migrating and wintering warblers, vireos, flycatchers, grackles, and mockingbirds. Mahogany's closed canopy and multiple internal branches provide exceptional structure and cover for birds, and they are favored nesting trees for mockingbirds, jays, doves, grackles, and others. Natively hammock canopy trees, they can grow fast, to 30–40 feet, although they can reach 50 feet or taller. They can be installed as specimen trees, but they are deciduous in the spring and serve birds best in mixed-tree settings. Mahogany is native to the Keys and the extreme southeastern coast to Miami but has been planted successfully well beyond this range. There is some concern about planting it outside its natural Keys range as it can invade native

West Indian mahogany fruits are not suitable for birds until the pods crack open, but year-round the trees provide ample cover and insect prey, making them good bird-garden choices.

hammocks farther north, altering natural species composition. Miami-Dade County does have restrictions against planting mahoganies on non-residential land within 500 feet of natural rockland hammocks or pine rocklands, but this would not apply to most gardens. If appropriate, mahoganies should be part of a South Florida bird garden.

Left: Boat-tailed Grackles peck at citrus rind and spread the oils on their feathers to ward off parasites.

Above: Citrus flowers attract numerous insects, such as this honey bee.

Citrus (*Citrus*)—Nn, Tr, Ns, Pr, St, In, Fr, AW

Several species of citrus are traditional components of South Florida gardens and yards; other citrus relatives are native. Sour orange dates back to the Spanish era and key lime to the mid-1800s, and both are still found on old home sites, in old groves, and on Indian mounds and tree islands in the glades. Diseases, insects, freezes, changing agricultural economics, and totally irrational state-mandated pest-control measures have taken their toll, making backyard citrus somewhat less satisfying than previously. Nonetheless, citrus should be considered for any South Florida bird garden. Fragrant flowers attract hummingbirds, flies, bees, and butterflies, especially swallowtails, and also spiders and other predators. Leaves and stems host a characteristic fauna comprising both commercial "pests" and insects borrowed from native citrus relatives, including aphids, whiteflies, mealybugs, leaf-footed bugs, spider mites, scale insects, fruit flies, stink bugs, and swallowtail butterfly caterpillars. These invertebrates attract small birds, especially wintering warblers and vireos. The fruits themselves may be broken into by Red-bellied Woodpeckers, Amazon parrots, macaws, rats, and squirrels, opening them for others. Grackles pick the rind to use for feather maintenance. In larger plants, the complex branches, thorny in some species, provide excellent nesting locations, used especially by mockingbirds and jays. Depending on species, citrus can reach 20 feet tall in South Florida or can be trimmed to match the site. They can even be grown in containers. Because of their many issues, cultivation requires time and effort, including careful watching, specific fertilization to overcome micronutrient deficiencies, and periodic application of horticultural soaps and oils. If successful, the gardener may then be faced with the decision as to how the crop is to be shared with birds

Perhaps the most characteristic citrus of South Florida, or at least famed for its pies, is the key lime (*Citrus × aurantiifolia*). Introduced to South Florida from Mexico and called Mexican lime elsewhere, it has been part of South Florida culture ever since. It can grow most anywhere, including in containers. Sour oranges (*Citrus × aurantium*) are also part of South Florida history, having been planted on home sites by Indians who obtained them from the Spanish. These make interesting, useful, and folkloric additions to the South Florida bird garden. Several other typical citruses planted in South Florida gardens are grapefruit (*Citrus × paradisi*), sweet orange (*Citrus × sinensis*), calamondin (× *Citrofortunella mitis*), kumquat (*Citrus japonica*), Persian (Tahitian) lime (*Citrus × latifolia*), and lemon (*Citrus × limon*). All provide fruit and insects, and large specimens provide structure.

Orange Jessamine (*Murraya paniculata*)—Nn, X?, Sh/Tr, St, In, Fr, AW

This Asian plant, also called orange jasmine, chalcas, *Chalcas exotica*, and *Chalcas paniculata*, has fragrant, ¾-inch white star-shaped flowers. In South Florida, it blooms in spring and summer, attracting nectar-seeking bees, butterflies, and birds. The red, ½-inch fruit is available in fall, attracting various birds, especially mockingbirds. Orange jessamine is a tall, open shrub or small tree to 15 feet, but can be trimmed into desired sizes, hedge plants, or potted plants. It is vigorous and the seeds are dispersed by birds, so much so that planting is discouraged near natural hammocks. It should be used with caution. Its use in a bird garden will depend on risk in any location.

Sea Torchwood (*Amyris elemifera*)—Na, Sh/Tr, Ns, St, In, Fr, AS

Also called common torchwood, sea amyrus, or usually just torchwood, this citrus relative has fragrant, ³⁄₁₆-inch white flowers that grow in obvious clusters, attracting insects. It flowers year-round. Fruiting peaks in summer and winter. Aromatic, ¼-inch, purple/black, citrus-like fruits attract mockingbirds, cardinals, and Red-bellied Woodpeckers, also raccoons and squirrels. It is host to giant swallowtail caterpillars. As a tall shrub or small tree to 15 feet, its dense growth form provides good cover and nest sites.

Wild Lime (*Zanthoxylum fagara*)—Na, Tr, St, In, AS

Called pricklyash or lime pricklyash in the Caribbean, this intriguing-looking plant produces clusters of fragrant yellow flowers in spring and summer that attract

Wild lime, South Florida's native citrus, has recurved thorns that provide excellent bird protection, and it is an essential plant for attracting swallowtails to a yard.

butterflies and bees. Small dry fruits may be eaten by birds but seem not overly attractive. The foliage hosts swallowtail butterfly caterpillars. A feature soon noticed by gardeners is its awful recurved thorns, a valuable asset for a bird garden in a cat-infested neighborhood. It is usually a small tree about 10 feet high, although potentially 20–30 feet, and best planted on the edge of mixed-tree stands where the thin, thorny branches can sprawl through available space as they reach for the sun.

Lychee (*Litchi chinensis*)—Nn, Tr, St, In, Fr, AW

These fruit trees of southern China became commercially viable locally in the 1960s. Small white to yellow flowers are pollinated by insects, including bees (especially honey bees), flies, and wasps. Their 2-inch fruit, covered with thick pink-red skins, are too large and tough for most native birds but can be handled by parrots. A prime benefit of these trees is their dense canopy, providing excellent shelter, cover, and nest sites. As commercial trees, lychee have their share of insect pests and therefore bird food, including twig pruners, twig borers, leaf beetle larvae, ambrosia beetles, greenshield scale insects, stink bugs, and cotton square borer larvae (*Strymon metinu*). Small birds are often seen working the plant's interiors for these insects.

Inkwood (*Exothea paniculata*)—Na, Sh/Tr, St, Fr, AS

Also called butterbough, this tree has tiny white ¼-inch flowers in showy clusters at the ends of branches, resulting in similarly placed dark purple, ½-inch fruit available for birds in spring and summer. Growing to 30 feet, inkwood has dark glossy compound leaves on upright branches that create a dense, broad canopy. It is a hammock tree in South Florida, and in tropical forests elsewhere, so is best used as part of mixed-tree settings or, when young, as a multistemmed barrier plant.

Faux Persil (*Cardiospermum corindum*)—Na, Vn, In, AS

This vine, also called heartseed and most commonly balloonvine, has year-round 2-inch white flowers that produce 1–2-inch balloon-like fruit containing seeds. Its vining stems and leaves harbor numerous insects, such as soapberry bugs (*Jadera haematoloma*) and caterpillars of hairstreak butterflies and the rare Miami blue. Balloonvine occurs in coastal hammocks in Miami-Dade and Monroe counties, especially the Keys, where it is disputably native. It is best planted within mixed-tree or shrub settings.

White Ironwood (*Hypelate trifoliata*)—Na, Sh/Tr, St, In, AS

This rare and endangered native of hammocks of the lower Keys has tiny but pretty clusters of white flowers from late spring through late fall, attracting an array of insects, including bees, wasps, and small butterflies, that attract birds. Black ⅜-inch fruits, available in winter and spring, are eaten by mockingbirds, catbirds, thrushes, waxwings, cardinals, and jays. White ironwood can become a small tree to 20 feet, but more often stays as a shrub, the compound glossy leaves providing good bird cover.

Soapberry (*Sapindus saponaria*)—Na, Tr, St, In, AS

Also known as wingleaf soapberry and Florida winged soapberry, this species has a wide natural range, from southern North America through tropical America and even to Africa. In South Florida in fall and again in spring, this tree produces an exuberant display of white ¼-inch flowers borne on foot-long panicles covering the treetop. This display attracts bees, including honey bees, wasps, and butterflies, which attract birds, especially during migration. The yellow to brown ½–1-inch fruits, thought to be poisonous, are seemingly not very attractive to birds, but both fruit and bark attract insects, including soapberry bugs (*Jadera, Boisea*). These fast-growing single-trunked trees are generally tall, reaching 30–40 feet in South Florida, having a potential to 60 feet. The flaked bark, multiple spreading side branches, and winged leaves give the crowns a shrubby appearance, producing ample structure and cover for birds. The farther north, the more winter deciduous soapberries become. In South Florida they are trees of coastal hammocks and best used as part of mixed-tree stands but are also good in commercial settings, along highways, and as specimen trees.

Paradisetree (*Simarouba glauca*)—Na, Tr, Pr, Fr, AS

Also known as bitterwood, the paradisetree blooms in spring, producing terminal clusters of yellow to cream ¼-inch flowers. In late spring and summer, it copiously produces fleshy, red turning black, ¾–1-inch fruits that attract mockingbirds, cardinals, grackles, and Red-bellied Woodpeckers, which often eat unripe fruit. Although weak stemmed when young, the paradisetree grows straight with a single trunk usually 20–30 feet high, potentially to 50 feet. Its distinctively compound leaves, which start red before turning green, form an open canopy with good perches. Paradisetrees are deciduous in the dry season, need protection from cold, wind, and root disturbance, and need good drainage. Because both male and female trees are required for fruiting, several trees are best planted together within mixed-tree areas, preferably in organic soil.

Ericales

Impatiens (*Impatiens walleriana, Impatiens hawkeri*, hybrids)—Nn, Ss, Bt, Sd, Nc, AS, AW

Originally from East Africa and New Guinea, respectively, these two species of impatiens are common and well-appreciated bedding plants. They have been cultivated into many colors and growth forms for use in beds, as container plants, or in planted edges. In South Florida they are planted mostly in winter as annuals and tend to fail in most summers. In winter, hummingbirds are attracted to the flowers, preferring red forms. Seeds, which disperse by exploding from pods, are consumed on the plant by seed-eating birds such as cardinals, grosbeaks, and towhees. Impatiens needs water, and irrigating a bed of impatiens can distress plants nearby that do not need water, so placement and irrigation are important considerations.

Standingcypress (*Ipomopsis rubra*)—Na, Ss, Bt, Wf, Nc, AW

This phlox relative, sometimes known as Spanish larkspur, likely evolved with Ruby-throated Hummingbirds, their ranges nearly coinciding. At 2–4 feet tall, sometimes to 6, the extremely showy, red, tubular, 1½-inch-long flowers are perfectly positioned for these hummingbirds. In South Florida, standingcypress blooms in late summer, so some are still present when hummingbirds migrate into the area. They also attract larger butterflies, such as sulphurs. These plants are biennial, blooming in the second year.

Satinleaf (*Chrysophyllum oliviforme*)—Na, Tr, In, Fr, AS

This spectacular tree has ⅛-inch flowers from summer to fall, attracting insects, as do its bark and leaves (which are sometimes annoyingly curled by a mite, *Eriophyes chrysophylli*). Wintering gnatcatchers, Eastern Kingbirds, migrating redstarts, Yellow-rumped and other warblers, and White-eyed and other vireos often work its canopy. Edible, purple, ½–1-inch fruits, appearing in fall and winter, are eaten by the larger frugivorous birds, including White-crowned Pigeons, Red-bellied Woodpeckers, jays, mockingbirds, cardinals, catbirds, and grackles. They are natively hammock trees, tending to occupy canopy gaps to 30 feet in height. In gardens, they are best in mixed-tree plantings where the bronze undersides of their leaves can contrast with the otherwise green canopy.

Satinleaf gets its name from the soft, brown undersides of its otherwise shiny, dark green leaves. Aside from their stunning appearance, these leaves attract many insects for bird food as does the satinleaf fruit.

Wild Dilly (*Manilkara jaimiqui*)—Na, Sh/Tr, In, Fr, AS

Also called *Manilkara bahamensis*, wild dilly is native to hammocks in extreme South Florida, especially in the Keys. The 1-inch fruits containing large seeds, available from winter to spring, are eaten by the larger fruit-eating birds, such as crows, jays, and grackles, also by opossums, raccoons, and iguanas. The fruit also attracts insects such as fruit flies (*Anastrepha*), wasps, weevils, scarab beetles, and mealybugs. Wild dilly is an excellent wildlife plant best grown within mixed-tree settings.

Sapodilla (*Manilkara zapota*)—Nn, Tr, In, AS

The edible sapodilla is a larger tree than the dilly, and its thick canopy provides superior structure for birds. Although a longtime tree in South Florida, it is now considered invasive of native habitats, although in fact it spreads quite slowly. In gardens where it poses no threat to nearby hammocks, it is highly recommended for birds.

False Mastic (*Sideroxylon foetidissimum*)—Na, Tr, Pr, St, In, Fr, AS

Sometimes simply called mastic, this native tree produces fruit called jungle plums that are highly sought after by birds. The inconspicuous, rather foul-smelling yellow flowers, which can appear year-round, peaking in summer, attract large numbers of flies, which also become bird food. The 1-inch yellow to orange fruits are available in winter and attract larger birds, including mockingbirds, catbirds, thrushes, cardinals, and jays, also raccoons and opossums. It can be a large tree, reaching 70 feet in parts of the range but more usually about 30 in South Florida, which is still tall locally. It is relatively cold hardy and can be planted anywhere in South Florida. False mastic is excellent for mixed-tree stands, and despite its odor, it is also an excellent specimen tree in a large yard.

Willow Bustic (*Sideroxylon salicifolium*)—Na, Sh/Tr, In, Fr, AS

Also known as bustic, white bully, *Bumelia salicifolia,* or *Dipholis salicifolia,* this South Florida and West Indian native is a rather common tree of tropical hammocks and pine rocklands in southern South Florida. Large numbers of grape jelly–smelling, ¼-inch white to green flowers cluster along branches from winter through a peak in early spring, attracting butterflies, including duskywings and hairstreaks, bees, and flies. This sapodilla relative has sweet ¼-inch black fruit peaking in summer and eaten by cardinals, mockingbirds, grackles, jays, many other birds, and mammals. It hosts exceptional numbers of insects, especially webworms, beetles, and borers. Growing as a shrub or tree, generally 20–30 feet tall (although potentially taller), it is used as part of mixed-tree zones, in tall buffer screens, or as individual accent plants. It is quite suitable for small gardens, narrow spaces, and commercial applications.

Common hammock and pineland plants in southern South Florida, willow bustic attracts birds with its insects and fruit.

Attracting Birds to South Florida Gardens

Tough Bully (*Sideroxylon tenax*)—Na, Sh/Tr, St, In, Fr, AS

Also called tough buckthorn bully, tough bumelia, silver buckthorn, Florida bully, and *Bumelia tenax*, this tree occurs natively mostly in coastal hammocks of Central and North Florida but also reaches the more northern portions of South Florida. It has ⅛-inch fragrant white flowers that cover the plants in spring and summer, attracting hordes of insects, especially bees and wasps. Edible, ½-inch, pulpy black fruits are produced in fall and eaten eagerly by any of the fruit-eating birds and mammals. Although deciduous, it is an ideal cover-providing plant with beautifully bicolored leaves and spiny branches. In South Florida, individuals range from shrubs, spreading by suckers into thickets, to small trees, 5–15 feet tall. Tough bully is best as part of mixed-tree areas where it can provide thorny cover for birds within the canopy.

Saffron Plum (*Sideroxylon celastrinum*)—Na, Tr, St, In, Fr, AS

Also known as bumelia and *Bumelia celastrina*, this tree has fragrant white flowers year-round, peaking in spring and again in fall, attracting many pollinating insects, especially bees. Its ¾-inch black fruits are similarly available over much of the year, peaking in summer and winter, and are highly prized by fruit-eating birds and other wildlife. Naturally reaching 20 feet in hammocks of southern and western South Florida, it can be used as a specimen or as part of mixed-tree plantings, attracting fruit-eating birds in either situation. Thorniness creates excellent bird cover.

Myrsine (*Myrsine cubana*)—Na, Sh/Tr, St, Fr, AS

This widespread tropical American shrub is both interesting and bird friendly. The ⅛-inch green flowers cluster year-round along the previous year's stems. Although not attracting insects, flowers yield ¼-inch black fruits, peaking in fall and winter. Fruits start green, turning black on ripening, sometimes desiccating and staying on the branch for many months. Although the fruit is available to all wintering birds, resident species seem particularly attracted to it, including Red-bellied Woodpeckers, jays, cardinals, and thrashers. In South Florida, myrsine occurs naturally in the understory of hammocks and pinelands, growing 10–15 feet but capable of becoming a tree to 30 feet. It is seen mostly as an erect, single-trunked, open, thin-branched shrub that can be planted as part of shrub areas, at the edges of tree plantings, as a specimen, or, with trimming, as buffering hedges. Both male and female plants are needed for fruiting, so it is beneficial to plant multiples in clusters, which also provide better cover, especially if they sucker. Not particularly cold sensitive, myrsine can be planted in most of South Florida. The name for this species has not settled. It may be listed as *Myrsine guianensis*, *Rapanea guianensis* (incorrectly), *Myrsine floridana*, *Rapanea punctata*, or *Myrsine cubana*. There are related species for sale, but there is only one species of myrsine native to South Florida, so it is important to get the right one.

Marlberry (*Ardisia escallonioides*)—Na, Sh/Tr, St, In, Fr, AS

Like the related myrsine, this plant provides exceptional bird fruit. It has a nearly year-long blooming season, with ¼-inch fragrant flowers in terminal clusters, sometimes massively covering much of the plant and attracting numerous nectar-feeding insects, especially bees and wasps. The ¼-inch dark fruits last from fall into winter and so are available to migrating and wintering birds, as well as to residents, including warblers, vireos, Red-bellied Woodpeckers, cardinals, catbirds, thrashers, and mockingbirds. Their dense growth form provides significant cover for midlevel foraging birds. This shrub to small tree, 12–15 feet or rarely to 20, occurs naturally in the understory and does well in shade and more poorly in the sun. Given their sparse and thin branching, they provide best cover when planted in masses in the understory or edges of mixed-tree plantings. Be aware that invasive non-native ardisias are available for purchase, including Japanese ardisia (*Ardisia japonica*), which needs to be used carefully, as well as China-shrub (*Ardisia solanacea*), scratchthroat (*Ardisia crenata*), and shoebutton (*Ardisia elliptica*), all of which need to be avoided.

Joewood (*Jacquinia keyensis*)—Na, Sh/Tr, Ns, Pr, St, In, Fr, AS

This wonderfully structured native plant has white, ½-inch, summer–fall, extremely fragrant flowers that attract an array of insects to their nectar. The yellow to orange, ½-inch, upright fruits are eaten by frugivorous birds, especially mockingbirds and Red-bellied Woodpeckers. Slow-growing, most get no more than 4–5 feet tall, although some max at 10 feet, making them ideal as specimens. Joewood has a thick trunk and drought-resistant leaves that create excellent canopy cover for birds, and the strong branches are used for nest sites. In South Florida it occurs naturally in coastal marl soils at the edges of coastal hammocks and in thickets next to mangroves, so it is hardy in gardens. Joewood is best in the partial shade at the edges of mixed plantings.

Below: Marlberry flowers attract many pollinating and nectar-seeking insects, like this southern carpenter bee, that in turn feed birds. Marlberries are also prolific providers of small fruit.

Right: Copious fruit and insect-attracting flowers make joewood popular with both frugivorous and insectivorous birds.

Borages

Bahama Strongbark (*Bourreria succulenta*)—Na, Sh/Tr, Bt, St, In, Fr, Nc, AS

This shrub to small tree is increasingly planted in South Florida for its bird and butterfly value. It produces fragrant, ½-inch, white tubular flowers for much of the year, peaking in summer and fall. Ruby-throated Hummingbirds are attracted to the flowers, as are bees and butterflies, especially sulphurs, swallowtails, and skippers. The insects attract warblers, vireos, and other insectivores. Attractive clusters of orange to red, fleshy, ½-inch fruit also are available for most of the year, peaking in fall and winter. The fruit attracts mockingbirds, catbirds, cardinals, doves including White-crowned Pigeons, grackles, and jays. Growth form is rather droopy, viny, and irregular, providing good structure and cover. Native to extreme southeastern South Florida, Bahama strongbark is cold sensitive but can be planted somewhat north of its native range. It is generally a shrub to 10 feet, more rarely small trees up to 25–30 feet, and does well in somewhat shaded situations. It is best for birds in mixed-shrub and tree settings. Naming of this species remains confusing and even contentious among local naturalists. It is also known in the local South Florida literature as Bahama strongback, bodywood, *Bourreria ovata*, and *Bourreria revoluta*. Its Caribbean name is pigeon berry, which is far better than any of the Florida and Bahamian alternatives.

Bahama strongbark has hummingbird- and insect-attracting flowers and berries enjoyed by many midsized birds.

Smooth Strongbark (*Bourreria cassinifolia*)—Na, Sh, Bt, In, Fr, Nc, AS

This shrub has white, ¼-inch, tubular, extremely fragrant flowers that attract butterflies, bees, wasps and Ruby-throated Hummingbirds. Warblers and vireos feed on the insects. The ½-inch orange fruits are eaten by many birds, including mockingbirds, catbirds, cardinals, Blue-headed and other vireos, warblers, and jays. Natively it occurs only at a few pineland sites in extreme southeastern South Florida; however, it is becoming more widely planted elsewhere in South Florida in bird and butterfly gardens. Smooth strongbark is a 5–8-foot shrub with somewhat weeping branches. It needs sun and can be spaced at edges of mixed-shrub zones or in butterfly gardens. It also can be an attractive, well-behaved accent plant, as it can be cautiously trimmed.

The gulf fritillary butterfly is one of many insects attracted to the flowers of smooth strongbark.

As with Bahama strongbark, names are a bit confusing as this species is also known in the local South Florida literature as little strongbark, dwarf strongbark, pineland strongbark, or pineland strongback.

Curacao Bush (*Cordia globosa*)—Na, Ss/Sh, Bt, St, In, Fr, Nc, AS

Also known as bloodberry but most commonly in South Florida as butterfly sage or butterfly bush, this is a superior insect plant, flowering and fruiting for much of the year. Clusters of small white ¼-inch, nectar-bearing flowers attract huge numbers of butterflies, including the rare atala, as well as bees, ants, wasps, flies, and many other insects, which in turn attract warblers, vireos, and flycatchers. The ³⁄₁₆-inch bright red fruit are eaten by frugivorous birds, especially mockingbirds and cardinals but also catbirds, thrashers, grackles, thrushes, and jays. Butterfly bush is a larval host for cloudless sulphur butterflies. Versatile in the garden, it can be trimmed and manipulated into short (2–4-foot), dense hammock-edge plants for use at boundaries or between taller plantings and lawn, or into more shrublike plants (4–8 feet). A Florida endangered species, butterfly bush is a well-known butterfly plant. It tends to volunteer and persist along open edges of plantings or can be easily planted by spreading its fruit.

Curacao bush, also known as bloodberry for its bright red fruit, is a superior insect-attracting bush and loved by birds for both the insects and the fruit.

Largeleaf Geigertree (*Cordia sebestena*)—Na, Tr, In, Nc, AS

This beautifully flowered tree has distinctive reddish-orange clusters of flowers attracting Ruby-throated Hummingbirds. It flowers from fall to spring, during the time hummingbirds are in South Florida. Flowers also attract nectarivorous insects, especially butterflies such as cloudless sulphurs and diurnal moths. Leaves and branches support insects and spiders, including specialist Geiger tortoise beetles (*Physonota calochroma floridensis*), which are sensational enough for gardeners to endure their periodic defoliation of the trees. All provide food for insectivorous birds, especially wintering and migrating warblers. The white 1–1½-inch fruits of largeleaf Geigertree are not usually eaten by birds in South Florida, being naturally distributed by water. Occurring natively in seaside hammocks, it can grow to 30 feet but in South Florida are usually to about 15–20. The Geigertree is likely, but not assuredly, native to the Florida Keys, perhaps even to as far north as the Brickell Hammock in Miami. IT is defoliated, sometimes even killed, by cold snaps. Because it tends to be straggly, it is best planted in clusters in ways that show off its flower displays.

Largeleaf Geigertree flowers attract hummingbirds and numerous insects, including several butterflies.

Scorpionstail (*Heliotropium angiospermum*)—Na, Sh/Ss, Bt, Wf, In, AR

The name scorpionstail comes from its tiny white ¹⁄₁₆-inch flowers on curling spikes, which bloom year-round. Although tiny, the flowers attract an amazing number and variety of insects, including butterflies—cassius blues, swallowtails, Florida and southern whites, gray hairstreaks, gulf fritillaries, queens, and ruddy daggerwings. All this insect attendance attracts birds. Fruits similarly are tiny, ⅛-inch. Scorpionstail occurs natively in coastal hammocks, but readily colonizes disturbed sites. Also called pineland heliotrope, it is a short-statured sprawling plant, 1–3 feet, but can also be a small shrub. It forms clusters and is excellent for butterfly gardens, wildflower gardens, and edges of shrub areas.

Coffee Relatives

Snowberry (*Chiococca alba*)—Na, Ss/Vn, St, In, Fr, AS

Also called milkberry, these dark green shrubs have tubular, white to yellow, fragrant summer flowers that attract butterflies, bees, and other insects. The white, ¼–½-inch summer fruit are highlights of any garden and are eaten by mockingbirds, thrashers, grackles, and Red-bellied Woodpeckers. The plants have a low, viny growth form that creeps along the ground, climbs into trees, or forms messy shrubs. In hammock and pineland plantings, they creep into gaps to provide additional canopy structure. Pineland snowberry (sometimes referred to as *Chiococca parvifolia* or *Chiococca pinetorum*) is a low-growing, small-leaved form from pinelands that can be used for borders.

Blacktorch (*Erithalis fruticosa*)—Na, Sh, St, In, Fr, AS

This shrub produces white, ¼-inch clustering flowers most of the year and, often simultaneously, black, ¼-inch fruit. It is highly recommended as a bird-attracting plant. The flower nectar attracts insects, especially bees and wasps. Fruit is eaten by many birds, especially mockingbirds, thrashers, grackles, and Red-bellied Woodpeckers. The small leaves and dense growth form provide excellent cover for small birds. Natively blacktorch is a shrub of Keys coastal hammocks, although it can be planted farther north. Growing 4–8 feet, it can be used in shrub areas, as small accent shrubs, or as buffers because of its compact growth.

One of the more important bird plants, blacktorch produces vast quantities of fruits eaten by many fruit-eating birds.

Rough Velvetseed (*Guettarda scabra*)—Na, Sh/Tr, St, In, Fr, AS

Also called roughleaf velvetseed or wild guava, this shrub provides an interesting addition to South Florida bird gardens. Blooming year-round with peaks in spring and summer, fragrant, tubular, white to red, ¼-inch flowers attract bees and butterflies. Half-blind adult sphinx moths (*Perigonia lusca*) are characteristic at the flowers and as caterpillars feeding on the leaves. Flowers develop into fuzzy, ¼-inch red fruits that ripen to near black and are eaten by many birds, especially attracting mockingbirds. Specimens range from shrubs to short trees 5–15 feet tall, although potentially to 30 feet, providing good structure for birds within their open canopy of ascending branches and rough green leaves. This West Indian plant natively occurs in hammocks and pinelands of the Keys and southern Florida mainland and so is best planted in mixed-tree or shrub areas where it can spread by rhizomes. The distinctive crown and leaves make it an interesting garden addition. A second native species, hammock velvetseed (*Guettarda elliptica*) (Na, Sh, St, In, Fr, AS) is also sometimes available to gardeners. It is usually a low, rambling shrub or small tree about 10 feet tall,

Rough velvetseed attracts birds with insect-attracting flowers and fruits and a protective canopy.

peaking at 20 feet. Like roughleaf velvetseed, it has an open canopy, tubular flowers (pink to white to red), and ½-inch fuzzy fruit (ripening from red to purple to black); both flowers and fruit are present all year, peaking in spring and summer.

Firebush (*Hamelia patens*)—Na, Sh/Tr, Bt, St, In, Fr, Nc, AS

An essential plant in any South Florida bird garden, firebush provides flowers and fruit for most of the year. Attractive red or yellow-orange 1-inch tubular flowers in terminal clusters are clearly adapted for the Ruby-throated Hummingbird's bill, and this is why it should be in every bird-oriented garden. Orioles will eat entire flowers directly. Flowers are also alive with wasps, bees including honey bees, flies, especially a small green fly (*Augochlora pura*), and butterflies such as black swallowtail, statira sulphur, zebra longwing, and atala, as well as the Pluto sphinx moth. Firebush also has aphids, grasshoppers, ants, and many other insects and their spider predators. As might be expected, these attract insectivorous birds, especially the smaller species such as gnatcatchers, warblers, vireos, flycatchers, and Indigo Buntings. The ¼-inch, dark red to purple fruits are eaten by mockingbirds, catbirds, Blue-headed Vireos, other vireos, and warblers. Firebush naturally grows as shrubs at the edges of tropical hammocks, filling the canopy with multiple tall stems and far-reaching branches. This is also its best use in a bird garden, allowing the branches to wind their way through the canopy, displaying their flowers high above. Usually shrubs, firebush can grow into thick, broad, small trees to 15 feet tall. But they are greedy and may choose to take over the yard. Firebush considers any gardeners' attempt at management to be a challenge to be conquered. Firebush does best in sunny alkaline conditions but is resilient and amenable to commercial and roadside plantings. It is sensitive to cold and wind but can nonetheless be planted throughout most of South Florida, being less hardy and shorter statured northward. Branches are too weak for

Firebush is a near essential plant for a South Florida bird garden. Flowers attract both hummingbirds in winter and butterflies like this zebra longwing for much of the year.

most bird nesting but provide excellent cover as hedges and especially when incorporated into a mixed-species tree canopy. There is much needless controversy about the native status of this plant. The red-flowered forms are native to South Florida, having light green 4–8-inch-long leaves with fuzzy undersides that are shed throughout the winter. *Hamelia patens* var. *glabra* from Mexico has smooth leaves and yellow, orange, and red flowers. Some authorities worry about the two hybridizing. From a bird's perspective, the non-native variety may be preferable because it is not deciduous and flowers longer, thereby providing more insects and nectar. Dwarf varieties, now available, are too short for hummingbirds. Bahama firebush (*Hamelia cuprea*) has larger, more bell-shaped yellow flowers. Firebush of some sort needs to be somewhere within every South Florida bird garden.

Common Buttonbush (*Cephalanthus occidentalis*)—Na, Sh, Wt, In, Fr, AS

This is a spectacular addition to any bird garden, with white, 1½-inch, globelike flowers that make fragrant "honey ball" displays in spring through early fall that attract

The fragrant "honey ball" flowers of common buttonbush entice a remarkable number of nectar-seeking insects, particularly bees like this honey bee.

beetles, a primary pollinator, as well as honey bees, bumble bees, butterflies, and a great many smaller insects. Clusters of tiny, bright red fruits remain on the plant through late summer and fall, attracting fruit-eating birds. Foliage supports numerous insects, including lygus bugs, leafhoppers, thrips, beetles, aphids, flies, and caterpillars such as titan and hydrangea sphinx moths. These insect hordes attract warblers, vireos, and flycatchers. Requiring moist soil, buttonbush is best used in damp places but can be placed in other, not overly dry, locations.

Wild Coffee (*Psychotria*)—Na, Sh, St, In, Fr, AS

South Florida's three native coffee species attract birds with their fruit and the insects that come to the flowers. They are thick shrubs that prefer partial shade and so can be used in the understory or at the edge of a mixed tree or shrub planting. They should be used as the core of shrub components for gardens aiming to attract birds. Small white flowers bloom year-round, peaking from spring to summer, attracting bees and butterflies, including atalas, great southern whites, Julias, black swallowtails, spicebush swallowtails, and especially zebra longwings. The yellow or red ¼-inch fruits ripen in summer to fall and attract mockingbirds, cardinals, catbirds, thrushes, grackles, jays, and many other species.

Wild coffee (*Psychotria nervosa*), the most commonly grown, is a thick shrub 4–6 feet tall. A shorter, 1–2 foot variety is also available. Its well-ribbed shiny leaves give it the alternative name of shiny-leaved wild coffee. Shortleaf wild coffee (*Psychotria sulzneri*), also called velvetleaf wild coffee, is generally 3–6 feet, although it can grow to 9 feet. It has distinctive velvety leaves and produces abundant fruit crops. Bahama wild coffee (*Psychotria ligustrifolia*) is usually 3–4 feet tall but can be 9–10. It is also called privetleaf wild coffee for its smaller leaves. Once in a garden, coffees may be reseeded by birds, providing seedlings that can be transplanted.

Wild coffees are near essential understory shrubs in a bird-attracting garden. Insects like this clouded skipper, along with coffee's fruit, provide food for birds.

Scarlet Jungleflame (*Ixora coccinea*)—Nn, Sh, In, Nc, AW

Among South Florida's traditional plantings and more usually known simply as ixora, these Asian plants are commonly seen throughout the tropical world. Showy flowers attract butterflies and other nectar-seeking insects, which then attract birds. They also house a good community of other insects, such as scale insects and bagworms. Left to their own devices, they are rounded shrubs to 12 feet tall and 8 feet wide creating excellent cover, but most gardeners unfortunately hedge them. They require acidifying fertilizer to overcome iron deficiencies in South Florida's lime soils. Of the many cultivars of differing growth forms, sizes, flower head sizes, and flower colors, it is thought that red-flowered and larger growth forms are best for bird gardens.

A standard tropical garden plant around the world, scarlet jungleflame, better known as ixora, has flowers that provide nectar for hummingbirds and butterflies.

Beach Creeper (*Ernodea littoralis*)—Na, Ss, Bt, St, In, Fr, AS

Also called golden creeper, wild pomegranate, and cough shrub or coughbush for its use as medicinal tea in its West Indian range, this plant is useful in a South Florida bird garden as ground cover or included in a short-statured planting. Pinkish-white, ½-inch tubular flowers attract insects, especially butterflies, year-round. Its ¼-inch, apple-tasting, golden-yellow fruits are eaten by many birds, especially mockingbirds and cardinals. Prostrate stems run along the ground, creating low cover, although they can also go vertical to 3 feet and become shrubbier. Natively plants of coastal strands, they have succulent leaves and provide excellent, matted ground cover in sunny areas. They are also good in wildflower, butterfly, and rock garden settings.

Tearshrub (*Vallesia antillana*)—Na, Sh, St, Fr, AS

Also called tearbush, pearlberry, and, incorrectly, *Vallesia glabra,* these rare and endangered white-fruited shrubs are natively from the Florida Keys. Their dainty, ¼-inch, clustering white flowers yield ¼-inch white fruits from spring to fall, attracting fruit-eating birds. They are dense, shrubby plants to 10 feet tall, with small, thickly spaced leaves providing good cover.

Golden Trumpet (*Allamanda cathartica*)—Nn, Vn, Ns, Pr, St, AW

Also called yellow allamanda, brownbud allamanda, or simply allamanda, this vine is part of the old-time South Florida flora. Introduced around the tropics, this plant is a perennial vine that blooms several times per year and is often covered with 3-inch trumpet-shaped flowers. It is generally used on a trellis or arbor or even climbing on trees, reaching 12 or more feet tall. It is its vining habit that makes it valuable for birds. Its viny stems and thick evergreen leaves provide significant cover, especially for roosting and for nests. The native wild allamanda (*Pentalinon luteum*) (Na, Vn, Ns, Pr, St, AS), also known as *Urechites luteus,* is a native species with 2-inch yellow flowers and a vining habit similar to that of golden trumpet and has similar value to garden birds.

Milkweed (*Asclepias*)—Na/Nn, Ss/Sh, Bt, Wf, In, Nc, AW/AR

Milkweeds are essential for South Florida butterfly gardens, where they host the three milkweed butterfly caterpillars found in South Florida: monarchs, queens, and soldiers. Birds are not particularly fond of these noxious caterpillars and butterflies, but milkweeds produce copious amounts of nectar that attracts innumerable other desirable insects. Wasps, bees, ants, other insects, and especially butterflies all visit milkweed flowers. Many South Florida butterflies use milkweed flowers, including monarchs, queens, swallowtails, painted ladies, admirals, fritillaries, hairstreaks, and clearwing moths. The accessible, terminal flowers are readily used by Ruby-throated

Scarlet milkweeds are the most common garden milkweed in South Florida, famously visited by monarch and queen butterflies, the latter pictured here.

Flowers of the native milkweed vine, white twinevine, attract a range of insect pollinators for birds to eat.

Hummingbirds. Milkweeds are best planted in masses so a succession of plants is available to compensate for caterpillar activity.

Several species of asclepias, both native and non-native, are worth adding to a bird garden. The non-native scarlet milkweed (*Asclepias curassavica*), also called Mexican milkweed and bloodflower, is the most common garden milkweed in South Florida. It has long been used for its butterfly and hummingbird attractions and is now probably the most important single species in South Florida supporting milkweed butterflies. It is hardy, with thick clusters of red and yellow flowers available all year. It spreads easily to disturbed soil sites, and its wind-dispersed seeds volunteer in a garden, if specimens are nearby. Growing to 3 feet tall, it is best in beds and at edges, where it usually self-seeds in any case.

Although not common, several native asclepias are sometimes available and should also be considered. Their benefits to butterflies and hummingbirds are similar to those of scarlet milkweed. The rarely available native butterflyweed (*Asclepias tuberosa*) can be planted on sandy but not limestone soil. It grows 1–2 feet tall with bright orange flowers in summer through early fall. Fewflower milkweed (*Asclepias lanceolata*) displays red and orange flowers but more sparsely than butterfly weed. Natively found in South Florida wet prairies, it does best in wet or pond edge settings. Longleaf milkweed (*Asclepias longifolia*), with white and purple flowers, and swamp milkweed (*Asclepias incarnata*), with pink flowers, also natively occur in damp soils. Other native asclepias are not often available for the gardener.

White Twinevine (*Sarcostemma clausum*)—Na, Vn, St, In, AS

Also called white vine and *Funastrum clausum*, this pantropical milkweed is also one of the most important South Florida plants for milkweed butterflies. The vine has clusters of ⅜-inch white flowers in fall and winter that attract bees, flies, butterflies, and other insects, and it hosts larval milkweed insects. Its vining habit allows it to create thick cover for birds within and on top of tree canopies. It prefers moist soil and is best planted within mixed-shrub or tree areas into which it can vine.

White Indigoberry (*Randia aculeata*)—Na, Sh, St, In, Fr, AS

Year-round but especially in spring, indigoberry's fragrant, ½-inch white tubular five-petaled flowers attract insects, especially butterflies. Its ⅓–½-inch green-white fruits with famously blue pulp are eaten by birds, especially mockingbirds, catbirds, and Red-bellied Woodpeckers. Closely positioned glossy green leaves host numerous insects, including caterpillars of the tantalus sphinx moth. Indigoberry is a hardy-branching, multistemmed, spiny shrub to 10 feet tall with attractive leaves, providing excellent bird cover and nesting sites. It occurs natively in open, grassy pinelands and at hammock edges, especially along the coast, where it tends to grow taller than inland. Indigoberry can be used in gardens in many ways, including as accent shrubs or as vines in mixed shrub and tree settings.

Sevenyear Apple (*Genipa clusiifolia*)—Na, Sh, Bt, In, Fr, Nc, AW

More often listed as *Casasia clusiifolia,* this is an interesting shrub with persistent 3-inch fruits that change from green to gold to black as they age. From the bird gardener's perspective, interest is in the tubular white 1-inch flowers that attract Ruby-throated Hummingbirds, as well as many bees and butterflies, including mangrove skippers. The flowers occur over a long period from spring to fall, overlapping both ends of the hummingbird's wintering period in South Florida. Sevenyear apple also hosts good supplies of insects in the foliage, including tantalus sphinx moth caterpillars. As the fruit ripens and softens, birds do eat at them. Red-bellied Woodpeckers and mockingbirds generally start the process, and other species follow. Once the fruits are on the ground, iguanas, opossums, raccoons, rats, and mice take over. The seemingly overripe, prunelike fruit is edible by humans, or so it is said. It natively occurs as a large shrub, 5–15 feet, on coastal dunes and in coastal hammocks, suggesting it would do best on sandy, well-drained sites and can tolerate salt air and spray and some degree of drought. It has many uses in gardens, as a specimen or accent, with other hummingbird plants, or included in buffers.

Sevenyear apple fruits are too big for native birds to eat whole but are eaten in pieces once ripe and softened.

Panama Rose (*Rondeletia leucophylla*), Fragrant Panama Rose (*Rondeletia odorata*)—Nn, Ss, Bt, Wf, Nc, AS

These pentas-looking plants, also called shrub pentas, are from Central America and the West Indies, respectively. They have 2-inch-long tubular flowers in 3–5-inch terminal clusters, pink on flowering roses and reddish orange with yellow throats on fragrant flowering roses. They attract butterflies and Ruby-throated Hummingbirds. As thick, tall shrubs (10–15 feet), they can be used as accents, edges, or even hedging plants.

Egyptian Starcluster (*Pentas lanceolata*)—Nn, Ss/Sh, Bt, Wf, Nc, AW

Almost always known as pentas, this East African plant is a notable bee, butterfly, and hummingbird attractor. Tubular, star-shaped flowers occur in prolific, terminal clusters, 2–3 inches wide, that in South Florida bloom nearly year-round, except after cold weather. They attract butterflies, flies, and bees, including honey bees, and Ruby-throated Hummingbirds. Tersa sphinx moths (*Xylophanes tersa*) also feed on flower nectar, and the plants host 3-inch hornworm caterpillars. They are useful components of South Florida butterfly or hummingbird gardens. The old varieties are tall, hardy, and long-lived (5 feet, living to 3 years), whereas newer varieties tend to be short and compact, a bit tender, and essentially annuals in South Florida. Old-time tall red-flowered forms are best for hummingbirds. Egyptian starclusters will reseed themselves.

Largeflower Mexican Clover (*Richardia grandiflora*)—Nn, Ln, In, AS

A naturalized lawn weed in South Florida, this is a low-growing, 3–4-inch perennial plant with ½-inch purplish-white flowers that attract bees, including honey bees, and many species of butterflies. It is common in diverse lawns.

Left: Superb butterfly plants, Egyptian starclusters, better known as pentas, have flowers that also attract hummingbirds and a notable selection of other nectar-seeking insects.

Right: Largeflower Mexican clover contributes many insect pollinators to a diverse lawn.

Lamiales

Black Mangrove (*Avicennia germinans*)—Na, Tr, Aq, Wt, Ns, Pr, St, In, AS

This is the mangrove of salty pans, located naturally inland of red mangroves along the South Florida coast. Fragrant, ⅛-inch, clustered flowers occur in spring and throughout the summer, attracting bees, flies, and butterflies, including spectacularly the great southern white butterfly, and producing a well-appreciated honey crop. Insects also occur in the tight foliage and fissured bark, including caterpillars of mangrove buckeye and statira sulphur butterflies, all of which attract insect-eating birds. Although black mangroves can be large trees, to 60 feet, they seldom achieve that height in South Florida garden settings, where they are mostly 20 feet or less. Their strong branches and closed canopy provide shelter and structure for bird nesting. They can be grown on land anywhere in South Florida, as long as the soil is relatively moist, providing beautiful and well-used specimen trees.

Sanchezia (*Sanchezia speciosa*)—Nn, Ss/Sh, Bt, St, Nc, AW

Also called shrubby whitevein, this is usually planted for its attractive white-veined leaves; however, it is also a bird plant owing to spring through fall production of tubular 2-inch flowers, usually yellow with red bracts (although cultivars may be red-orange, gold, or yellow). All varieties attract Ruby-throated Hummingbirds in fall, as well as butterflies and other nectarivorous insects. They can grow 4–8 feet tall, spreading widely and tolerating dappled light. Sanchezia is best used as borders of shrub or tree areas, where its beautiful foot-long leaves provide cover for birds.

Firespike (*Odontonema cuspidatum*)—Nn, Ss/Sh, Bt, Wf, Nc, AW

Also known as *Odontonema strictum*, firespike features amazing displays of red flowers. It has stiff, upright branches that readily grow to 8 feet with seemingly overabundant 12-inch panicles of brilliant red 1-inch tubular flowers. Originally from Central America, it is quite at home in South Florida, blooming erratically in late summer through winter, coinciding with the hummingbird season. This is one of the best flowers for attracting Ruby-throated Hummingbirds and Spot-breasted Orioles and can be used as specimen shrubs or hedged, adding colorful edges to garden plantings. Once established, they are hardy in southern South Florida, although dying back in winter farther north. Purple firespike (*Odontonema callistachyum*) also has tall blooms up to 6 feet, attracting hummingbirds and large butterflies. This is a nice complement to red firespike since their blooming is offset, red firespike lasting into spring.

Bush Clockvine (*Thunbergia erecta*)—Nn, Sh, Bt, St, Nc, AS

This African species, more usually called king's mantle, unlike others of its genus, is a sprawling shrub rather than a vine. It has 2-inch blue and yellow, trumpet-shaped flowers that attract butterflies and occasionally hummingbirds and orioles. It blooms nearly year-round in South Florida, peaking in summer and fall. Generally about 5 feet tall, it is best used in mixed-shrub or low hedge areas. It tolerates being pruned; however, its naturally dense, sprawling growth form with multiple small branches makes it an excellent sheltering plant for small birds. For birds, the larger and more viny the clump, the better.

Shrimp Plants—Nn, Ss/Sh, Bt, St, Nc, AW/AS

In South Florida gardening, this name applies to several species: shrimpplant (*Justicia brandegeeana*), with salmon-colored bracts; Mexican fringe plant (*Justicia fulvicoma*), with fuzzy red-orange flowers; golden shrimpplant (*Pachystachys lutea*), with yellow bracts; and cardinal's guard (*Pachystachys coccinea*), with red spikes. These plants are among South Florida's old-time landscaping elements and remain excellent nectar plants today. Year-round flowers have high nectar content used by butterflies and, in winter, by Ruby-throated Hummingbirds, orioles, and buntings. They are shade tolerant and drought resistant, reaching 3–6 feet.

Browne's Blechum (*Ruellia blechum*)—Nn, Ln, Bt, Wf, AS

Also called green shrimp plant, *Blechum pyramidatum*, or *Blechum brownei*, this plant has ¼-inch violet flowers on small, upright spikes. Flowers attract insects, especially butterflies. Despite being non-native, the plant is a larval host for an array of butterflies, including malachites (including the non-native *Spiroeta stelenes* from Cuba), white peacocks, Cuban crescents, painted ladies, and buckeyes. It can grow upright to about 2 feet so it can be part of a wildflower garden, but its stems can also run along the ground, making them also suitable for diverse lawns.

Thickleaf Wild Petunia (*Ruellia succulenta*)—Na, Ss, Bt, Wf, In, AS

Small, ground-hugging plants, their purple, morning-opening, trumpet-shaped flowers attract morning-flying butterflies. Endemic to extreme southern pine rocklands in South Florida, they are 4–18 inches high and tend to spread laterally. Also native, Carolina wild petunia (*Ruellia caroliniensis*) grows to 15 inches with pink to blue flowers. Both species are host plants for common buckeye, white peacock, and non-native malachite butterflies. Both attract birds to their insect supplies. In gardens, they are ideal as ground cover, short edge plantings, or in rock gardens.

Left: Several South Florida plants are called shrimp plants. This one is a Mexican fringe plant. Shrimp plants are part of South Florida's old-time landscaping that persist today as excellent butterfly and hummingbird plants.

Right: Thickleaf wild petunia is a low-lying plant with showy flowers that attract butterflies and other insects, like the tiny black flies in this picture.

Trumpet Creeper (*Campsis radicans*)—Nn, Vn, Ns, St, In, Nc, AW

Also called trumpet vine, trumpet flower, or, in North America, hummingbird vine, this begonia relative was one of the earliest American plants to be taken to Europe for cultivation, resulting in numerous cultivars and flower colors. It is native to forests and river bottoms of southeastern North America at least as far as Central Florida, and its natural range more or less coincides with the nesting range of the Ruby-throated Hummingbird, which feeds on its nectar and pollinates its orange, trumpet-shaped flowers. In South Florida bird gardens, in the hummingbird's winter range, trumpet vine's flowering season does not overlap the winter residency of the hummingbird; nonetheless, its flowers attract butterflies, moths, honey bees, bumble bees, and ants, as well as birds to eat them. The fruit is a tapered pod 4 inches long containing flat seeds that are eaten by sparrows, goldfinches, squirrels, and other seed eaters. The vines can be large, woody, vigorous, wide spreading, and easily out of control, growing 30 feet or more but providing good cover for birds.

Trumpet Trees (*Tabebuia*)—Nn, Tr, St, In, Nc, AW

Staples of South Florida's old-time tropical plantings, their trumpet-shaped flowers attract hummingbirds and nectar-seeking insects, including honey bees. One species, Bahama tabebuia (*Tabebuia bahamensis*) or beef shrub, is nearly a native, being from the nearby Bahamas. More widely planted are the white cedar (*Tabebuia heterophylla*) and Caribbean trumpet-tree (*Tabebuia aurea*). Given their size, the latter are best used as specimen trees. All are drought resistant and deciduous in the dry season, bursting into spectacular color when they flower before leafing out.

Cape Honeysuckle (*Tecoma capensis*)—Nn, Sh/Vn, Ns, St, In, Nc, AW

These sprawling vinelike shrubs, originally from southern Africa, have clusters of orange to scarlet, tubular 2-inch flowers that bloom year-round, peaking summer to fall. In fall and early winter, the flowers attract Ruby-throated Hummingbirds, orioles, and catbirds. Depending on pruning, they can be used as massing shrubs, screens, or wall and embankment cover. They re-root where stems touch the ground, creating a tangled growth that provides excellent cover for birds.

Tropical Sage (*Salvia coccinea*)—Nn, Ss, Bt, Wf, In, Sd, Nc, AW

Also called blood sage, tropical red sage, and scarlet sage, this magnificent red-flowering plant is native to Florida, although its range stops just short of South Florida. It does grow well here. Its tubular, fiery-red flowers, blooming nearly year-round, attract Ruby-throated Hummingbirds in winter and honey bees, bumble bees, and butterflies at any time. The tiny seeds are eaten by Painted Buntings, cardinals, and sparrows. As perennials 2–3 feet tall in South Florida, they are best planted in flower beds and butterfly gardens. Numerous cultivars and related species are also available, offering many flower color options. Forsythia sage (*Salvia madrensis*) is a tall (10 feet), thick, yellow-flowered Mexican plant that hummingbirds visit. Blue anise sage (*Salvia guaranitica*) is also attractive to hummingbirds and highly recommended for its flower color. Commonly planted in winter as an annual in South Florida, another scarlet sage (*Salvia splendens*) is a less hardy perennial from Brazil whose impressive cultivars are considered less attractive to hummingbirds and butterflies than is tropical sage.

Chinese Hat (*Holmskioldia sanguinea*)—Nn, Sh/Vn, Bt, St, Nc, AW

The orange-red trumpet flowers of Chinese hat are important attractors for Ruby-throated Hummingbirds and large butterflies. They are sprawling plants that can be trimmed to vinelike shrubs to 8 feet tall or trained to trellises. Their sprawling form provides excellent shelter for small birds. Native to low elevations in the Himalayas, they nonetheless do well in South Florida, although they may lose leaves in the dry season.

Florida Swampprivet (*Forestiera segregata*)—Na, Sh/Tr, St, In, Fr, AS

Left: Chinese hat plants attract hummingbirds and butterflies, also providing shelter to these and other birds if grown as a shrub.

Right: The fragrant flowers of Florida swampprivet attract numerous insects and insect predators, like this Blue-gray Gnatcatcher.

Also called wild olive or even more commonly Florida privet, this small-leaved, thickly branched plant forms excellent garden borders and hedges, especially on limestone soils. It has attractive clusters of fragrant, ⅛-inch yellow-green, sometimes purplish flowers blooming profusely along stems, peaking in spring but extending to fall, attracting bees, flies, ants, and small butterflies. These insects attract a notable number of birds, especially migrating warblers and vireos. The ¼ × ¼–inch dark purplish, olive-like fruits are available from late spring through winter; despite small size, they are very attractive to catbirds, mockingbirds, jays, cardinals, Red-bellied Woodpeckers, warblers, vireos, and about any other frugivorous bird in the neighborhood. The leaves support a large supply of insects as well as spiders that entwine terminal leaves with their webs. Two forms of the plant occur naturally in South Florida, a tall tree form in coastal hammocks (subspecies *segregata*) and a compact, smaller-leaved, smaller-statured shrub (subspecies *pinetorum*) in pinelands. The shrub form provides excellent cover in gardens and can be tightly hedged. Both male and female plants are needed for fruiting, so they are best planted in clusters.

Florida Fiddlewood (*Citharexylum spinosum*)—Na, Sh/Tr, Ns, St, In, Nc, AS

These striking plants with glossy dark green leaves, beautiful fragrant flowers, and admirable small fruits readily attract birds, insects, and people's attention. Highly fragrant, summer-blooming, white flowers on drooping spikes attract obvious hordes of bees, wasps, butterflies, and evening moths. Nectar supplies are prodigious enough for fiddlewoods to be considered honey plants. On female plants, fleshy, sweet ⅓-inch fruits, orange turning red-brown as they ripen in summer and fall, never fail to attract fruit-eating birds. The dense leaves, deciduous in winter, and stems support beetles, weevils, leaf-footed bugs, thorn bugs, stink bugs, ants, termites, whiteflies, spiders, and moths (*Epicorsia oedipodalis*). As flowers, fruit, and insects tend to coincide, birds are all over these plants from summer through fall. Usually in South Florida, fiddlewoods are shrubs or small trees to 12 feet (although 30 feet is possible) having multiple, thin, upright stems, providing excellent cover. Fiddlewood's natural North American range is restricted to hammocks and pinelands in extreme southern South Florida and the Keys. Although cold sensitive, it can be planted north of this range along the coast. For birds, it is best used on the edges of mixed-shrub plantings or as a screen, though it also does well in commercial, parking lot, and roadside plantings.

Golden Dewdrops (*Duranta erecta*)—Na?, Sh/Tr, Bt, St, In, Nc, AS

Also called pigeon berry and sky flower, these plants have attractive flowers and fruit, usually simultaneously. Small blue, purple, and white flowers attract insects summer to fall, including butterflies and bees, as well as Ruby-throated Hummingbirds in fall. Their ½-inch golden fruits are attractively clustered on drooping branches. Although the fruit is considered poisonous to humans, it certainly is not to birds, attracting

Red-bellied Woodpeckers, mockingbirds, cardinals, thrushes, thrashers, catbirds, and grackles. Golden dewdrops is native to the Bahamas and arguably native to South Florida; it has been planted in the tropics throughout the world, in some places becoming a pest. The species is well behaved in South Florida, where it is a shrub or small tree to 20 feet tall. Its spreading growth on spiny, multistemmed, droopy trunks provides excellent cover for birds. Golden dewdrops plantings provide a good backdrop to butterfly gardens. A variety of cultivars exist with variegated leaves or larger flowers.

Waterhyssop (*Bacopa*)—Na/Nn, Ss, Aq, Wt, In, AS

These are small, creeping aquatic and semiaquatic plants, also called bacopa or water purslane. Lemon bacopa or blue waterhyssop (*Bacopa caroliniana*), named for its lemon-scented leaves, has blue flowers. Herb-of-grace or smooth waterhyssop (*Bacopa monnieri*), tropical waterhyssop (*Bacopa innominata*), and creeping waterhyssop (*Bacopa repens*) have pale pink to white flowers. Creeping waterhyssop, a non-native, is found throughout the Neotropics and has naturalized in South Florida. Grasshoppers and butterflies occur on waterhyssops, and smooth waterhyssop is a larval host

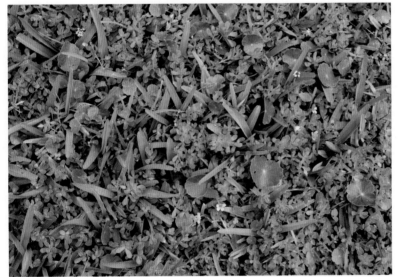

of white peacock butterflies. These plants are ideal for landscaping pools, where they grow submerged, providing cover for fish and invertebrates, or rooted at the very edges, providing transitional cover as they creep onto adjacent land. Bacopa is hardy enough to become weedy in some situations.

Herb-of-grace (with rounded yellow-green leaves and white flowers in this photograph) makes an excellent transitional ground cover between natural water feature edges and diverse lawns.

Firecracker Plant (*Russelia equisetiformis*)—Nn, Ss/Sh, Bt, St, In, Nc, AW

Also called coral plant and fountainbush, this Mexican species has long been naturalized in South Florida. It has year-round, 1-inch, tubular bright red flowers positioned in downward-weeping terminal clusters that are perfect for hummingbirds. Additionally, it attracts large butterflies and other nectarivorous insects. It grows about 3 feet high, with stems falling over and drooping downward, the mass providing excellent shelter for small birds. It can be used as a shrub, hedge, border, foundation plant, accent, or in a hanging basket. Related red firecracker or red rocket (*Russelia sarmentosa*) is more upright, to 6 feet tall, also attracting hummingbirds with clusters of deep red tubular flowers.

Butterflybush (*Buddleja*)—Nn, Sh, Bt, St, In, Fr, AW

The butterflybush of America, *Buddleja davidii*, is available in nearly any nursery, but unfortunately, these wonderful butterfly plants and staples of the northern butterfly garden do not do well long-term in South Florida. Madagascar butterflybush (*Buddleja madagascariensis*) is the better South Florida substitute. Also known as smokebush for its silvery leaves, it is a hardy plant, producing clusters of small, orange to yellow fragrant flowers that attract bees, wasps, flies, and butterflies. Flowers are followed by 1-inch dark blue to purple fruit, also in terminal clusters, attracting birds. It is a viny shrub with dense, sprawling habits, growing to 10 feet tall and providing substantial cover.

Above: Although the popular butterflybush of the north does not grow particularly well in South Florida, the Madagascar butterfly bush grows splendidly and successfully attracts butterflies, including monarchs as shown here.

American Beautyberry (*Callicarpa americana*)—Na, Sh, St, In, Fr, AS

Despite its tropical feel, beautyberry is native throughout southeastern North America and is among the more typical native shrubs in South Florida gardening and one of the most flexible. It blooms in spring, the white to pink flowers attracting many butterflies, bees, and other insects. Even more visually appealing are the clusters of ¼-inch purple (sometimes white) fruit that line the stems and stay on the branches for many months from fall through winter. Many birds eat the ripe berries, especially mockingbirds, which guard plants within their territories, but also cardinals, Black-throated Blue Warblers, Red-bellied Woodpeckers, catbirds, thrashers, thrushes, waxwings, robins, bluebirds, Common Grackles, jays, Blue-headed and other vireos, also bobwhites, deer, raccoons, and green iguanas. Given this take by wildlife, it is interesting that the seemingly ripe fruit can stay for so long, into late winter, adding to both its visual appeal and the length of time for bird service. Beautyberry has thin arching branches growing 5–10 feet tall. It is best planted at the edge of the canopy, where it will insinuate its tall branches into the neighboring shrubs and trees. It is less leggy if planted in the sun. For birds, it is best planted in masses so there are berries over a long enough time to interest them.

Below: Aptly named, American beautyberry's brilliant purple berries attract many fruit-seeking birds, such as Gray Catbirds.

Lantana (*Lantana*)—Na/Nn, Sh, Bt, Wf, In, Fr, Nc, AW

These are prolific shrubs with flowers that are exceptionally attractive to butterflies and fruit that is eaten and dispersed by birds. Buttonsage (*Lantana involucrata*), also known as butterfly sage, wild sage, and wild lantana, has year-round clusters of white and yellow flowers that attract butterflies, ants, and bees, which in turn attract spiders, gnatcatchers, warblers, vireos, bulbuls, Eastern Phoebes, and other flycatchers. The flowers, even though small, are visited by Ruby-throated Hummingbirds. When ripe, the ¼-inch dark blue to purple fruits are eaten by many birds, including cardinals, thrashers, Hermit Thrushes, jays, doves, bobwhites, and mockingbirds. They are small, rounded shrubs, 3–6 feet tall, native to pinelands and edges of hammocks, but also naturalized along roadbeds and cleared lots. Tough, adaptable, and drought tolerant, they should be in any South Florida bird or butterfly garden. Rockland shrubverbena or pineland lantana (*Lantana depressa*) is a native species attractive to birds for its yellow flowers and fruit. This is usually a short, sprawling plant to 1 foot but can become shrubby to 2–4 feet. This native plant is endemic to pinelands in Miami-Dade. Shrubverbena (*Lantana camara*, also *Lantana strigocamara*) is an aggressive non-native shrub readily available in nurseries but should not be planted in situations where it might hybridize with the native species. Trailing shrubverbena (*Lantana montevidensis*) is an increasingly popular South American species that is a viny shrub or ground cover. It flowers year-round in frost-free areas having clusters of purple (sometimes yellow) blooms.

Long-tailed skipper is one of the myriad insects that regularly seek out buttonsage.

Moujean Tea (*Nashia inaguensis*)—Nn, Sh, St, In, Fr, AS

Known also as Bahama berry and pineapple verbena, this shrub is native to the Inagua islands of the Bahamas. The fragrant, clustered, tiny white flowers attract bees, flies, and especially butterflies. The ¼-inch red-orange berries are eaten by birds. Natively they occur on sunny, rocky outcroppings, where their creeping habit protects them from sea breezes. In cultivation, however, they are loose, spreading, multibranched shrubs up to 6 feet tall, providing cover for small birds within the thin stem structure.

Famous for butterflies, moujean tea lures many other insects such as this scoliid wasp.

Turkey Tangle Fogfruit (*Phyla nodiflora*)—Na, Ln, In, AR

These endearing little plants go by many names, such as creeping charlie, matchweed, capeweed, or just fogfruit. The ¼-inch flowers, white with dark centers, attract more than their size's share of insects, especially small bees, a primary pollinator, but also honey bees, bumble bees, flies, beetles, and more than a dozen butterfly species. Fogfruit also serves as a larval host for caterpillars of many species of butterflies. Ground-feeding birds commonly forage on this treasure trove of insects, especially mockingbirds, cardinals, grackles, Palm and other warblers, and phoebes. It is a small, creeping, herbaceous plant, no more than 1–3 inches high, with flowering spikes perhaps reaching 6 inches. It is among the most desirable species for diverse lawns in South Florida.

Fogfruit are coveted diverse lawn plants because of their ability to attract insects, particularly butterflies, disproportionate to their tiny flower size.

Coastal Mock Vervain (*Glandularia maritima*)—Na, Ln, In, AS

Also known as beach verbena, coastal vervain, and *Verbena maritima*, this small, hardy plant attracts insects, including butterflies, with pink to rose to purple ½-inch flowers clustered on short stalks. A Florida endemic and state endangered species, it is a native beach dune and pineland plant. At 2–12 inches tall with a creeping growth form, it can be part of a diverse lawn.

Blue Porterweed (*Stachytarpheta jamaicensis*)—Na, Ss, Bt, Wf, In, Nc, AS

This attractive, low-growing plant has ¼-inch blue flowers on spikes that lure a continual procession of potential pollinators such as ants, honey bees, bumble bees, wasps, and butterflies, including such garden favorites as zebra longwing, gulf fritillary, Julia, swallowtails, sulphurs, and buckeyes. As this native species reaches only about 1 foot tall, the flowers tend to be too low to the ground to habitually attract hummingbirds. Very locally, it is a larval host plant for tropical buckeye butterflies. Many species of small birds are drawn by these insects, including gnatcatchers, warblers, vireos, and flycatchers. A short-lived (2–5 years) perennial, the native blue porterweed occurs natively in pinelands, beaches, and shell mounds and has colonized disturbed sites such as roadsides. It is self-seeding and can be weedy. Native blue porterweeds are best planted as ground cover borders between lawn and shrubs or as part of butterfly gardens but can also be used in containers or even hanging baskets.

A very similar non-native species, Jamaica porterweed or nettleleaf velvetberry (*Stachytarpheta cayennensis*) (Nn, Ss/Sh, Bt, Wf, In, Nc, AW) is widely sold, usually labeled as blue porterweed. It is more upright, woody, and tall, reaching 5 feet with

Perfect for butterfly gardens, porterweed draws in mangrove skippers, other butterflies, and numerous insects, all of which attract small insectivorous birds.

somewhat more purplish flowers. Compared with the native blue porterweed, it is equally attractive to insects and more appealing to hummingbirds because it is taller; however, it is aggressive and invasive. Pink porterweed (*Stachytarpheta mutabilis*) (Nn, Ss/Sh, Bt, Wf, In, Nc, AS) is a less threatening non-native whose ½-inch salmon-colored flowers are even more attractive to Ruby-throated Hummingbirds than are the blue species. If choosing a porterweed for a hummingbird garden, this one may be best.

Pepper Relatives

Bird Pepper (*Capsicum annuum*)—Na, Ss/Sh, Vg, Wf, Fr, AW

Ancestor of commercial hot peppers, bird pepper is native to Florida (or at least has been here for hundreds of years), and its common name indicates its main role in a South Florida bird garden. The ¼-inch exceptionally hot fruits are available from spring to fall and adapted to be attractive to birds but not mammals. They are relished by mockingbirds and cardinals and eaten as well by other birds such as thrashers, catbirds, jays, grackles, blackbirds, and parakeets. Natively, it is a short-lived (3–4 year) perennial shrub in coastal hammocks and so is best planted with other small-statured plants at the edge of shrub zones but can also be grown in vegetable gardens. Many hot peppers of commerce are also readily available for the vegetable garden and, depending on size, can also be attractive to birds.

As the name suggests, the bird pepper, ancestor of commercial hot peppers and native to South Florida, is well loved by birds. It is hard to out-compete birds for peppers on the shrub.

Garden Tomato (*Solanum lycopersicum*)—Nn, Ss, Vg, St, In, Fr, AW

Vegetable gardens should not be overlooked as part of a complete bird garden, and tomatoes are kings of most vegetable gardens. Originally from South America highlands, tomatoes are a winter crop in South Florida. Their ½-inch flowers attract bees, with bumble bees their primary natural pollinating agent. The many varieties produce various-sized fruit; the smaller ones are eaten by birds. Tomatoes host an array of insects that also attract birds, including tobacco hornworms (*Manduca sexta*), tomato fruitworms (*Helicoverpa zea*), stink bugs (*Euschistus servus, Acrosternum hilare*), leaf-footed bugs (*Leptoglossus phyllopus*), potato aphids (*Macrosiphum euphorbiae*), and whiteflies (*Bemisia*) to name a few. Of course, the bird gardener has to refrain from using pesticides to provide this food supply for birds.

Garden tomato plants can be a great source of caterpillars and other insects for birds, like this Common Yellow-throat.

Skyblue Clustervine (*Jacquemontia pentanthos*)—Na, Vn, St, In, Fr, AS

Also known as blue jacquemontia, this rare native of Keys hammocks and beach dunes has exceptionally showy, ¾-inch, blue trumpet flowers. Produced year-round but peaking in fall, the morning-blooming flowers attract bees, flies, and butterflies. A federally listed endangered species but available in cultivation, this vine can provide good cover for birds, growing over shrubs, trellises, or fences.

The endangered skyblue clustervine attracts a variety of insects, and its vining habit provides cover for birds.

Hollies

Dahoon (*Ilex cassine*)—Na, Sh/Tr, St, In, Fr, AS

This is an excellent native holly for bird gardeners. The ¼-inch, yellow to white flowers attract bees for their pollen. In late fall and winter, this holly provides an abundance of bright red ¼-inch fruit for Red-bellied Woodpeckers, mockingbirds, cardinals, and jays, as well as for wintering phoebes, robins, catbirds, thrushes, and waxwings. Multiple stems provide excellent shrubby cover for small birds. The foliage hosts an array of insects, including caterpillars of striped hairstreak and Henry's elfin butterflies, and also spiders that form small webs among its leaves. In South Florida, this holly ranges from shrub-sized to an erect, small tree, up to 25 feet tall. Dahoon occurs naturally in damp, low-lying hammocks and wetland tree islands but has adapted well to drier conditions in gardens and commercial and roadside plantings. It can be used as a specimen tree or as part of a shrub or small tree zone, or trained into hedges. A hybrid between the dahoon and the common northern American holly (*Ilex opaca*) is a vigorous, adaptable, fast-growing shrub to small tree, 15–20 feet high, that bears large quantities of exceptionally showy fruit. The similar yaupon (*Ilex vomitoria*), an excellent bird plant, does not occur naturally in South Florida.

Dahoon, a native holly, is covered in red fruit in the winter, attracting a range of wintering birds.

Krug's Holly (*Ilex krugiana*)—Na, Sh/Tr, St, In, Fr, AS

Also known as tawnyberry holly, this holly is covered with clusters of ¼-inch white flowers in spring that attract numerous insects, followed in summer by large clusters of ¼-inch yellow-red (i.e., tawny) fruit ripening to black. These are eaten by resident birds, especially mockingbirds and cardinals. Krug's holly is a shrub to small tree, 10–20 feet high, occasionally reaching 30 feet. Its small, 1-inch, deep green, pointy leaves droop on flexible stalks, providing excellent cover for birds and other wildlife. Natively it is a shrub to small tree in the understory of rocky hammocks of southeastern Florida and so does best in mixed-shrub and mixed-tree plantings. Unlike the other hollies, this is a tropical species and so does better in southern than in northern portions of South Florida.

Inkberry (*Scaevola plumieri*)—Na, Sh, St, In, Fr, AS

This beach shrub, also called fanflower and beachberry, is native to Florida and the Caribbean but has been transported by the ocean and by humans to other parts of the world. White to pink 1-inch summer flowers attract bees and butterflies. The small 1–3-inch purple fruits, persisting on the plant nearly year-round, are eaten by pigeons, mockingbirds, raccoons, and iguanas but do not seem overly attractive to them. Seeds are dispersed primarily by water. For birds, inkberry's primary feature is the cover it provides—dense leaves on multiple stems reaching about 5 feet to create a thick bushy clump. It is an excellent plant for beachside or otherwise dry sandy gardens, parking lots, and other poorly tended sites. A similar plant from the Pacific, the beach naupaka (*Scaevola taccada*), is to be avoided as it is incredibly invasive on beaches in Florida and especially in the nearby Bahamas. It is larger, growing to 10 feet, and has white fruit.

Composites

Composites are flowering, short-statured, usually herbaceous plants that play an important role in bird gardens, providing nectar, foliage insects, and seeds. Many composites available in seed packets are non-native and do not do well in South Florida, but native species are increasingly available from nurseries. Flowers attract hordes of pollinating insects: bee flies (Bombyliidae), diurnal moths, carpenter bees, miner bees, honey bees, bumble bees, leaf-cutting bees, wasps, scarab beetles, and butterflies, especially skippers but also monarchs, swallowtails, sulphurs, painted ladies, and whites. Flowers produce thin, dry seeds that are consumed by seed-eating birds, especially buntings, warblers, towhees, native sparrows, and House Sparrows. Their foliage supports an array of insects, including caterpillars of painted lady, sulphurs, and pearl crescent butterflies. Various birds habitually scour these plants for food, including Mourning Doves and Common Ground-Doves, Red-bellied Woodpeckers, phoebes, mockingbirds, catbirds, grackles, jays, cardinals, Painted Buntings, Indigo Buntings, towhees, sparrows, vireos, and migrating and wintering warblers, especially Palm Warblers. Most native South Florida wildflowers are 1–4 feet tall and can be used as borders between lawn and shrub areas, in clustered wildflower gardens, rock gardens, and butterfly gardens. Some when mowed can be part of diverse lawns. In South Florida, success at gardening with composites is not guaranteed. Sometimes various species have to be tried in multiple places before the correct location and conditions are found. Bringing asters into bird gardens is rather important for seed-eating birds because South Florida has relatively few other natural seed plants.

Tickseed (*Coreopsis*)—Na/Nn, Ss, Bt, Wf, In, Sd, AW/AS

Tickseeds are among South Florida's well-used and best wildflowers for bird and butterfly gardens. They attract insects, especially honey bees. They natively occur in damp areas in pinelands and edges of hammocks but have taken to roadsides, ditches, and waste areas. Their yellow 1–2-inch flowers may bloom all year but concentrate in spring and summer. They are almost always annuals in South Florida but will often self-seed. The plants themselves are slight in appearance and 2–3 feet tall, so they are best clustered in beds or in clumps.

Leavenworth's tickseed (*Coreopsis leavenworthii*) is a delicate-looking, fast-growing, multibranched plant about 2 feet tall with thin leaves. One-inch yellow flowers with brown disks are produced year-round. Coastalplain tickseed (*Coreopsis gladiata*) is native to low pinelands and swamps, growing to 3 feet tall and doing best in damp or irrigated situations. Florida tickseed (*Coreopsis floridana*) grows 2–3 feet tall, with 1-inch flowers blooming primarily in spring and summer. A Florida endemic, it is natively a plant of wet pinelands. Lance-leaf tickseed (*Coreopsis lanceolata*) is perhaps the most readily available coreopsis. Native only as far south as north Florida, it is short-lived in South Florida and best planted as an annual.

Beggarticks (*Bidens alba*)—Na, Ss, Ln, Bt, Wf, In, Sd, Nc, AR

Almost always called Spanish needles in South Florida, it is 1–3 feet tall with 1-inch flowers, white with yellow cores. In South Florida, this is one of the very best insect-producing weeds. Dozens of insect species have been recorded using it for nectar or pollen, and it is especially attractive to honey bees. It is also the host plant for caterpillars. These insects attract ground- and low-foraging birds such as mockingbirds, cardinals, Palm Warblers, phoebes, vireos, and goldfinches. The plants are best known for their dry seeds that annoyingly grab any passersby but are eaten by all seed eaters such as Indigo and Painted Buntings, House Sparrows, and native sparrows. Beggarticks are not usually recommended for gardens, but they should be in every bird-friendly garden. They can be used at edges, in borders, and within diverse lawns.

Seldom viewed as more than a nuisance weed in South Florida, beggarticks, more commonly known as Spanish needles, is a vital component of a bird garden. It supports a large number of insects, including butterflies like this cassius blue.

Bushy Seaside Oxeye (*Borrichia frutescens*)—Na, Ss/Sh, Wf, St, In, Sd, AW

Also called silver seaside oxeye or bushy seaside tansy, this is a moderately sized perennial, about 2–3 feet tall with thick, silvery foliage and yellow 1-inch flowers that bloom all year, attracting nectar-seeking butterflies. The seeds attract seed-eating birds. It spreads by rhizomes, forming multistemmed clumps that function more as shrubs than ground cover and provide considerable shelter for small birds. Native to sea beaches, salt marshes, and swamps, this is a hardy plant and among the most versatile composites for dry, sunny sites.

Tree Seaside Oxeye (*Borrichia arborescens*)—Na, Ss/Sh, Wf, St, In, Sd, AW

Also called green sea oxeye daisy or tree seaside tansy, this is a medium-sized shrub, 3–4 feet tall, with succulent green leaves. The 1-inch yellow flowers peak in summer, providing nectar to various insects, especially butterflies. Sparrows and other seed eaters are attracted when it is in seed. Common in coastal areas, it does best in well-drained gardens in full sun. This composite can be used in borders, in flower beds, or even as accent plants, given that it can become woody and shrublike. It spreads by rhizomes into thick beds that provide good cover for ground birds.

Straggler Daisy (*Calyptocarpus vialis*)—Nn, Ln, Wf, In, Sd, AR

A small plant with ¼-inch yellow flowers, the straggler daisy attracts lawn butterflies such as skippers. The seeds are similarly small and consumed by the seed-eating birds. Native from eastern Mexico through southern Texas, it now occurs on disturbed sites throughout much of southern North America. It has sprawling, ground-hugging stems that form mats by rooting at periodic nodes and so can be part of diverse lawns.

Sunflowers (*Helianthus*)—Na, Ss, Wf, Sd, AW/AS

Sunflowers are well known, and commercial varieties serve as the primary food in bird feeders. Commercial sunflower plants do not do well in South Florida, but there are native alternatives that produce seeds that attract birds. All of them also attract insects, especially butterflies and honey bees, to their flowers. Southeastern sunflower (*Helianthus agrestis*), also known as swamp sunflower, prefers wet areas, damp pinelands, especially following fire, and marshes. It grows to 6 feet tall. Stiff sunflower (*Helianthus radula*) is a perennial plant of sandy pinelands. Growing 3 feet tall, from summer to fall it produces tiny flowers comprising yellow to straw-colored petals on large purple disks. East coast dune sunflower (*Helianthus debilis*) is an annual, 1–2 feet tall with 2–3-inch yellow flowers that bloom year-round. A native spreading plant of beach dunes, it is capable of forming large patches and is best as a border planting.

East coast dune sunflowers make an attractive, seed-producing ground cover.

Firewheel (*Gaillardia pulchella*)—Na, Ss, Bt, Wf, In, Sd, AW

Also known as Indian blanket, this plant is excellent for providing not only insects but also color accents in any garden. The inch-wide red to purple flowers with yellow tips appear singly on longish stems. They are likened to pinwheels, explaining the plant's name. It occurs naturally in South Florida as coastal sand dune plants and on disturbed sites. In South Florida gardens, it is generally used as an annual, reaching 1–2 feet tall and mounding to 12 inches across. It can flower anytime during the year and is useful in borders or as parts of wildflower or butterfly gardens. Drought resistance makes it a good short-term wildflower for commercial and roadside use. Related species and the many cultivars do not do as well in South Florida as the wild plants, but those are what are offered in most seed packages. The more common species of trade is blanketflower (*Gaillardia aristata*), from Canada and the western United States. Another common wildflower is the hybrid *Gaillardia* × *grandiflora*, which often has double to multiple flowers that cannot be used by butterflies.

Firewheel flowers provide pollinating insects and seeds for birds.

Narrowleaf Yellowtops (*Flaveria linearis*)—Na, Ss, Bt, Wf, In, Sd, AS

Among the more common native wildflowers, yellowtops occurs naturally in damp pinelands, coastal areas, and salt marshes, from which it has colonized roadsides and other disturbed sites. The ⅛-inch yellow flowers are produced on branched clumps that cover the top of the plant and are followed by numerous ⅛-inch seeds. The summer flowering can be spectacular, attracting numerous insects, especially butterflies. It is a perennial and once established may self-seed. Reaching only about 3 feet tall with a sprawling habit, it is a good edge plant.

Blackeyed Susan (*Rudbeckia hirta*)—Na, Ss, Bt, Wf, In, Sd, AW/AS

The native Florida representative of the well-known blackeyed Susan, this plant gets 1–3 feet tall and has 2-inch yellow flowers with purple to brownish disks from summer through fall. Native to pinelands and now waste areas, it is a hardy plant useful in borders or a wildflower garden. In South Florida, it tends to be an annual. It is a great attractor of honey bees to the garden. This species and many cultivated varieties are marketed under various names, such as gloriosa daisy. Not all will grow in South Florida. Local plants do better, although they are far less available.

Eastern Purple Coneflower (*Echinacea purpurea*)—Nn, Ss, Bt, Wf, In, Sd, AW

Native to the southern United States, this tough perennial grows 2–3 feet tall, displaying purple flowers with purple-brown disks. In South Florida, it flowers from summer through fall. Although plants may die back in winter (temporarily or permanently), seeds remain on the plants that may self-seed. Coneflowers are widely cultivated, so many varieties are available. Experimentation is needed to determine which will grow in a South Florida garden.

Goldenrod (*Solidago*)—Na, Ss, Bt, Wf, In, Sd, AW

Goldenrods, known for their brilliant yellow flowers, attract myriad insects, especially beetles, but also butterflies and bees including honey bees. Both the insects and seeds attract small birds, especially warblers and sparrows. Several species are native to South Florida. Pinebarren goldenrod (*Solidago fistulosa*) is a perennial growing 3–4, even 6 feet tall. It spreads by rhizomes to form clusters. Wand goldenrod (*Solidago stricta*), growing to about 6 feet tall, produces tightly spaced yellow florets spiraling around a tall single stem. Sweet goldenrod (*Solidago odora*) is up to 2–3 feet tall with an open array of yellow flowers in fall. Seaside goldenrod (*Solidago sempervirens*)

One of the native wildflowers suitable for edges, goldenrods are beautiful and appealing to insects such as this wasp.

Attracting Birds to South Florida Gardens

occurs in open coastal areas. It can be 4 feet tall with dense flowering stalks appearing nearly all year, peaking summer to fall.

Coastalplain Goldenaster (*Chrysopsis scabrella*)—Na, Ss, Wf, In, Sd, AS

A native of sand scrub habitat, this wildflower does well in dry, sunny conditions. Its 1-inch yellow flowers bloom in late fall from 2–3-foot stalks. They are best planted clumped in wildflower gardens. Very similar mariana or Maryland goldenaster (*Chrysopsis mariana*) is also native, though rare, in South Florida, where it blooms in the fall.

Narrowleaf Silkgrass (*Pityopsis graminifolia*)—Na, Ss, Wf, St, AS

For part of the year this wildflower appears as bundles of silvery grasses, but from summer to winter, peaking in late fall in South Florida, its 2–3-foot flowering stalks boast showy ¾-inch yellow flowers. Natives of pinelands and prairies, it is drought tolerant and does best in full sun. It is best planted in wildflower gardens where it can sucker and spread, providing good cover for small ground birds.

Climbing Aster (*Symphyotrichum carolinianum*)—Na, Vn, Bt, Wf, St, In, Sd, AS

A vinelike aster capable of climbing upward of 12 feet, the climbing aster is a woody perennial with distinctive furled leaves and a sprawling habit. It produces purple to pink 1–2-inch ray flowers over much of the year, especially from late summer through winter. These attract bees and butterflies, including monarchs. Native to wetlands throughout southeastern North America, it is adaptable if placed in moist soils or is well watered. It is best planted to twine among other plants.

Rice Button Aster (*Symphyotrichum dumosum*)—Na, Ss, Bt, Wf, In, Sd, AS

Native to both dry pinelands and damp prairies, this variable composite species has readily taken to disturbed areas. Narrow stems 1–2 feet tall have ⅜-inch, bluish ray flowers with yellow centers. It blooms year-round, attracting various butterflies to the nectar, especially hairstreaks, crescents, and blues. It also serves as host plant to pearl crescent caterpillars.

Pineland Purple (*Carphephorus odoratissimus* var. *subtropicanus*)—Na, Ss, Bt, Wf, In, Sd, AS

This plant is also called false vanillaleaf because, unlike the more northern variety (var. *odoratissimus*) whose vanilla-scented leaves were once mixed with tobacco for fragrance, the leaves of this subspecies lack odor. The plant has a basal rosette, 1–3 inches high, until summer and fall, when flowering stalks bearing terminal clusters of small purple flowers grow to 3 feet. Endemic to sandy flatwoods from central to southern Florida, it is a plant for sandy soils, not limestone. Other natives are the coastalplain chaffhead or Florida paintbrush (*Carphephorus corymbosus*) and hairy chaffhead (*Carphephorus paniculatus*). All share the characteristic of attracting insects, particularly butterflies.

Florida Shrub Thoroughwort (*Koanophyllon villosum*)—Na, Ss, Wf, Sd, AS

More commonly called shrub eupatorium, these plants have year-round aster flowers that individually measure ⅛-inch and are white to pink but occur in multiple showy heads. They can be tallish shrubs, to 6 feet. This otherwise West Indian species natively occurs only in rockland hammocks of Miami-Dade but can be planted much more widely. It is listed as endangered in Florida.

White Crownbeard (*Verbesina virginica*)—Na, Ss, Wf, In, AS

This fall-blooming composite has showy white-petaled flowers bunched into clusters 3–6 inches across that attract numerous insects, especially bees—honey bees, bumble bees, carpenter bees—as well as wasps, flies, and butterflies, including monarchs and sulphurs. The flower head produces tiny seeds that hold on the plant during winter and are available for buntings. It is also known as iceflower or frostweed, from the thin icy sculptures it produces when it freezes, which is not an event to expect in a South Florida garden. It grows to 3–4 feet and forms clumps, spreading by rhizomes.

Blue Mistflower (*Conoclinium coelestinum*)—Na, Ss, Wt, Bt, Wf, In, Sd, AS

This composite has multiple small, fuzzy florets, blue to purple, although ranging to pinkish white. Blooming in summer, flowers attract bees and butterflies, especially numerous skippers, including obscure skipper, salt marsh skipper, southern broken-dash, and three-spotted skipper. Widespread in the eastern United States, in South Florida it occurs natively in interior wetlands, low pinelands, and solution holes, as well as in ditches. Growing 1–2 feet tall, it is a perennial that spreads by rhizomes and will cover any allotted space.

Queen butterflies are one of the many insect visitors to the summer blossoms of blue mistflower.

Attracting Birds to South Florida Gardens

Creeping Oxeye (*Sphagneticola trilobata*)—Nn, X?, Ss, Ln, In, Sd, AW

Native to Central America, it has been naturalized around the world, including in South Florida, where it is commonly known as wedelia, *Wedelia trilobata*, creeping daisy, water zinnia, and trailing oxeye. It is generally a prostrate herb, 1–2 inches high, with year-round, yellow, 1-inch daisylike flowers. It provides exceptional ground cover and is attractive to both insects and birds. It is considered invasive and is discouraged near native plant communities. If not a threat to nearby natural areas, there are few better plants for diverse lawns or other low herbaceous stands in a bird garden.

Gayfeather (*Liatris*)—Na, Ss, Bt, Wf, In, AS

These attractive, small herbs, also called blazing star, are generally 2–3 inches tall and boast spectacular displays of ¼–½-inch purple-rose flowers clustered along tall spikes several feet tall. They are excellent at attracting insects, including honey bees, to their flowers, seeds, and leaves. Some species prefer moist soils; others do well in drier conditions, and most are quite hardy. Blazing stars can be used in wildflower or butterfly gardens, where they should be placed behind smaller plants. They are heat tolerant, preferring full sun. Chapman's gayfeather (*Liatris chapmanii*) is a native pineland plant that tolerates poor soils and dry conditions. It has purple, sometimes white, flower spikes, 2–3 feet tall. Shortleaf gayfeather (*Liatris tenuifolia*) is a perennial native of South Florida's pinelands and wet prairies, with varieties differing in leaf hairiness and size. Its flower spikes grow to 3 feet, supporting multiple ¼-inch rose-purple, fall-blooming flowers. Slender gayfeather (*Liatris gracilis*) is similar to *tenuifolia*, reaching 3 feet and with purple flowers blooming summer and fall. Dense gayfeather (*Liatris spicata*) can have amazingly tall spikes, 3–6 feet, bearing rose-purple flowers from summer to winter. It occurs natively in pinelands, blooming especially after natural fires.

Dense gayfeathers, like all the blazing stars, are appropriate for butterfly or wildflower gardens, where they will attract bees, butterflies, and many other insects.

Purple Thistle (*Cirsium horridulum*)—Na, Ss, Bt, Wf, In, AS

This biennial has spiny basal rosettes of leaves, producing 2–3-foot flowering stalks with 2–3-inch yellow, cream, pink to purple flowers. The year-round flowers peak spring to fall and are amazing insect attractors. It is a larval host plant for little metalmark and painted lady butterflies. The oil-rich seeds attract small seed-eating birds. In South Florida, purple thistle occurs natively in pinelands and prairies, but it is a hardy plant that thrives in full sun in any well-drained, nutrient-poor soil.

Honeysuckles

Elderberry (*Sambucus nigra*)—Na, Sh/Tr, St, In, Fr, AW

Also known as American elder, South Florida plants used to be classified as their own species, *Sambucus simpsonii*. Large clusters of ¼-inch white flowers occur year-round, but peak in summer, attracting numerous flies, bees, wasps, beetles, and butterflies. These in turn attract processions of insectivorous birds, including phoebes, Great Crested Flycatchers, warblers, orioles, vireos, Ruby-crowned Kinglets, tanagers, thrushes, and mockingbirds. Clusters of numerous ¼-inch purple fruit are eaten by nearly any frugivorous bird, including Downy Woodpeckers, Red-bellied Woodpeckers, jays, phoebes, Great Crested Flycatchers, Eastern Kingbirds, Carolina Wrens, thrushes, mockingbirds, towhees, cardinals, catbirds, orioles, robins, waxwings, bluebirds, Painted and Indigo Buntings, and sparrows. Because of the long flowering season, flowers and fruit are often available together for much of the year, increasing the plant's use. Planting trees from different stocks can increase the temporal extent of flowering. Elderberry in South Florida is a fast-growing shrub to short tree, 8–15 feet, with multiple suckering stems that form a colony, providing substantial cover for midlevel birds. In South Florida, it is natively a plant of swamps and marshes but does

Elderberry provides thick cover, insect-attracting flowers, and tasty fruits that benefit birds and humans alike.

especially well on disturbed soils. It is best for birds as parts of mixed large shrub or tree plantings, allowing the suckering to produce cover.

Viburnum (*Viburnum*)—Na/Nn, Sh/Tr, St, In, Fr, AS

Beautifully flowered plants that are quite diverse over temperate North America, viburnums are well-known bird garden plants in the north. Their flowers and fruit attract birds, and their dense, dark green, small-leaved foliage and suckering tendency make them useful landscape elements as part of mixed-shrub areas, close-clipped hedges, barriers, and even buffers in commercial and highway applications. Walter's viburnum (*Viburnum obovatum*) is South Florida's only native viburnum. Also known as small-leaf viburnum, it is natively a rare plant in hammocks of Broward and Miami-Dade. A shrub to small tree, it grows to 10–20 feet. In spring, fragrant showy white flower clusters cover the plant, attracting not only its primary pollinator wasps but also butterflies and other insects. Red turning black ½-inch fruits available in summer and fall are eaten by resident cardinals, thrashers, mockingbirds, and Red-bellied Woodpeckers, as well as by migrants. Sandankwa viburnum (*Viburnum suspensum*) is a popular non-native shrub in South Florida having 1½-inch white tubular flowers in clusters that yield red berries. These attract birds in fall. Plants are usually 6 feet tall, but up to 12 feet and about as wide, creating excellent bird shelter. Also non-native, sweet viburnum (*Viburnum odoratissimum*) is potentially a larger shrub, reaching 15 feet high and wide, but can be trimmed. Its showy 1-inch white tubular flowers create sweet-smelling clusters up to 6 inches across for insects, and ½-inch red ripening to black fruits attract birds.

Coral Honeysuckle (*Lonicera sempervirens*)—Nn, Vn, Bt, Ns, St, In, Fr, AW

Also called trumpet honeysuckle, this is a beautiful vine well worth trying in a South Florida bird garden. The flowers are fragrant, trumpet shaped, red-orange to pink on the outside and yellow within, clustered into drooping whorls of two to six flowers. The flowers appear designed for Ruby-throated Hummingbirds, whose summer range it overlaps farther north, but in South Florida, it blooms in spring and summer and so misses the hummingbird season, though it does attract butterflies. Its red ¼-inch fall fruits are eaten by mockingbirds, cardinals, thrashers, catbirds, robins, bluebirds, orioles, thrushes, and many other birds. This is an entwining vine 15 feet or more long, natively climbing forest edges, affording cover and nesting sites for birds. The related Japanese honeysuckle (*Lonicera japonica*) is invasive and should not be used in gardens.

Blooming of coral honeysuckle in South Florida tends to miss the winter hummingbird season, but plenty of insects and butterflies visit, and the berries are loved by many birds.

Sweet Fennel (*Foeniculum vulgare*)—Nn, Ss, Bt, Vg, In, AW

A non-native plant from the Mediterranean, this garden plant is a larval host for desirable butterflies, famously black swallowtails as well as other swallowtails. It can be tall, up to 6 feet, and planted as part of a vegetable, herb, or butterfly garden. Other garden herbs that provide swallowtail caterpillars for birds include parsley (*Petroselinum crispum*), coriander (*Coriandrum sativum*), and dill (*Anethum graveolens*).

7

References and Further Study

Many books have been written on gardening, many on birds, and some on gardening for birds; and increasing numbers of Web sites and other electronic media are available on these topics as well. There is much to be learned from this treasure trove of information; unfortunately, a lot of it is also confusing to a South Florida bird gardener, who is best-off focusing on a few sources pertinent to the region so as to minimize the need to ignore irrelevant and misleading information derived from northern gardens. Sources that discuss overarching rationales and provide deeper understanding of bird gardening tend to be less geographically challenged.

Many sources also provide information on horticulture, planting, and garden care. This too must be approached with caution because, as we have said repeatedly in this book, "South Florida is different."

The present book is not about birding, but any bird gardener will likely want to be a fair enough bird identifier to appreciate what is happening in the garden. Many very good sources are available to help improve this skill, including field guides, checklists, and Web sites. Learning to identify birds soon leads to wanting to know more about them, perhaps their behavior, ecology, plumage variation, or seasonal migrations. Several sources are available for information on the biology and distribution of birds found in South Florida; none focus solely on South Florida, but some do cover Florida as a whole; others cover a wider geographic scale but include species found in South Florida.

Information on plants growing in South Florida can be found in books and online. Common tropical non-native plants are relatively easy to identify, but the same cannot be said for native plants. There are many of them and many look similar. It usually takes multiple sources and sometimes advice from experts to be sure, but both are readily available to a South Florida bird gardener.

This book has taken an ecological approach, looking at gardening in bird-friendly ways starting from basic ecological principles and the specific on-the-ground environmental conditions found in South Florida. Knowing more about the South Florida environment is invaluable in providing a basis of bird garden design, establishment, and maintenance, especially for creating a garden that helps restore South Florida's native landscape.

Observing plants and birds and their interactions in the garden provides opportunities for the gardener to engage in citizen science programs that allow information from one garden to aid in conservation across the continent.

Below are listed books and online sources that we recommend, and also a bit about why we recommend them.

Gardening for Birds

Barker, M. A., and J. Griggs. 2000. *The Feederwatcher's Guide to Bird Feeding*. Harper-Collins, New York, N.Y.

Based on Project Feederwatch, this book recounts success stories of backyard bird watching.

Condon, M. A. 2006. *Nature-friendly Gardening*. Stackpole Books, Mechanicsburg, Penn.

Although not oriented to South Florida, this is a book of well-reasoned argument and advice on gardening in an environmentally sensitive way. Much of the advice echoes and further explains guidance in the present book.

Florida Extension Service. Florida Backyard Landscapes for Wildlife Program. University of Florida, Gainesville, Fla. www.wec.ufl.edu/extension/landscaping/fblw/

This Web site provides information on plants that enhance habitat for wildlife in general.

Kress, S. W. 2006. *The Audubon Society Guide for Attracting Birds*, second edition. Cornell University Press, Ithaca, N.Y.

Perhaps the best book on fundamentals of bird gardening and good for an excellent overview of the topic. Having to cover the continent, it has only bits of information particularly pertinent to South Florida.

Martin, D. L. 2011. *Secrets of Backyard Bird-feeding Success*. Rodale, New York, N.Y.

A relatively complete guide to artificial bird feeding; like most such books, it is mostly from a northern perspective.

Minetor, R. 2011. *Backyard Birding: A Guide to Attracting and Identifying Birds*. Lyons Press, Guilford, Conn.

This book provides advice on birding, artificial feeding, and planting in one's yard, but from a continental, rather than Florida, perspective. It is best used as an overall guide to the bird-friendly yard but not for information on what to do specifically in South Florida.

Tallamy, D. W. 2009. *Bringing Nature Home*. Timber Press, Portland, Ore. www.bringingnaturehome.net

A definitive scientific and philosophical argument for the importance of using native plants in gardening to further conservation. This is the best book to explain the "why" of bird gardening.

Bird Conservation

American Bird Conservancy. www.abcbirds.org

Programs cover most critical bird conservation issues.

American Bird Conservancy Cats Indoors Program. www.abcbirds.org/cats/

> Describes how to combat the critical problem of outdoor cats, the single most important killer of birds, especially of birds using gardens.

Big O Birding Festival. www.bigobirdingfestival.com

> Annual multiday bird festival along the southwest shores of Lake Okeechobee.

BirdLife International. www.birdlife.org

> The most important international bird conservation organization, with national affiliates around the world, including in the United States, the National Audubon Society.

BirdLife International. Important Bird Areas. www.birdlife.org/action/science/sites/

> BirdLife International identifies critical locations for bird conservation, called Important Bird Areas.

Cornell Laboratory of Ornithology. Great Backyard Bird Count. www.birdsource.org/gbbc

> Annual event devoted to identifying and counting birds in backyard gardens.

Cornell Laboratory of Ornithology. NestWatch. www.NestWatch.org

> Program for observing and sharing data on bird nesting, based on standardized procedures.

Cornell Laboratory of Ornithology. Project FeederWatch. www.birds.cornell.edu/pfw

> National program and database of counts of birds using feeders. Every bird gardener should consider participating.

Cornell Laboratory of Ornithology. YardMap. www.yardmap.org

> A citizen science project providing guidance and tools to understand backyard bird habitat.

Cornell Laboratory of Ornithology and Audubon eBird. www.ebird.org

> Online system for archiving bird observations and counts, including from individual bird gardens. Data for each garden location can be managed individually online and also become part of a national database for use in science and conservation. We highly recommend participation by all bird gardeners.

Environment for the Americas. International Migratory Bird Day. www.birdday.org/birdday

> An annual program celebrating migratory birds in North America.

Everglades Foundation. www.evergladesfoundation.org

> Organization focused on restoration of the Everglades, the crucial South Florida environment for water birds.

Fairchild Tropical Botanic Garden. Fairchild Bird Conservation Program. www.fairchildgarden.org/livingcollections/jamesakushlanbirdconservationprogram/

> Miami's premiere institutionalized bird conservation and gardening program, including a bird trail in the Garden and gardening for bird conservation.

Fairchild Tropical Botanic Garden. South Florida Bird Festival at Fairchild. www.fairchildgarden.org/events/bird-festival/

The bird festival is an annual multiday event held in October in Coral Gables. Field trips, seminars, presentations, and displays provide information and experiences in birding, gardening, photography, and bird conservation.

Florida Keys Birding and Wildlife Festival. www.keysbirdingfest.org/

This bird festival is held annually in the Florida Keys.

Friends of the Everglades. www.everglades.org

Membership organization focused on Everglades conservation.

Florida Ornithological Society, Official Florida State Bird List. www.fosbirds.org/official-florida-state-bird-list

The official state list of the birds documented as occurring in Florida. FOS is the statewide organization for birders and professional ornithologists.

International Union for Conservation of Nature (IUCN). www.iucn.org

One of the primary conservation organizations worldwide, with numerous member organizations.

International Union for Conservation of Nature. The IUCN Red List of Threatened Species. www.iucnredlist.org

The official international listing of imperiled species, derived from application of standardized criteria.

Loss, S. R., T. Will, and P. R. Marra. 2013. The impact of free-ranging domestic cats on wildlife of the United States. *Nature Communications* 4, article 1396, doi:10.1038/ncomms2380. www.nature.com/ncomms/journal/v4/n1/abs/ncomms2380.html

A must-read, definitive scientific analysis of the devastation to wild birds caused by cats in the United States.

National Audubon Society. www.audubon.org

One of the oldest and largest national conservation organizations. The Florida chapter, Florida Audubon, is even older and concentrates on environmental issues in Florida.

National Audubon Society. Christmas Bird Count. www.birds.audubon.org/Christmas-bird-count

Annual nationwide census of wintering birds within specified count areas.

North American Bird Conservation Initiative. www.nabci-us.org

National and also a tri-national partnership of government and private institutions for planning and facilitating bird conservation.

North American Migration Count. community.gorge.net/birding/namcstasz.htm

Annual count of birds during the migration period.

Partners in Flight. www.partnersinflight.org

Partnership of government and private bird conservation organizations focusing on the conservation of Neotropical migrant birds.

Roebling, A. D., D. Johnson, J. D. Blanton, M. Levin, D. Slate, G. Fenwick, and C. E. Rupprecht. 2013. Rabies prevention and management of cats in the context of trap–neuter–vaccinate–release programmes. *Zoonoses and Public Health*. doi: 10.1111/zph.12070

Study demonstrating a clear public health concern with feral cats as carriers of rabies. It also shows that trap, neuter, release programs are ineffective in the control and management of feral cat populations and in reducing the number of birds they kill.

Tropical Audubon Society. TAS Miami Bird Board. www.tropicalaudubon.org/tas board/index.html

South Florida's preeminent discussion site for local birding news.

Waterbird Conservation for the Americas. www.waterbirdconservation.org

Hemispheric partnership focusing on the conservation of water birds.

World Migratory Bird Day (WMBD). www.worldmigratorybirdday.org

Worldwide program to highlight migratory birds and their conservation.

Gardening and South Florida Plants

APG (Angiosperm Phylogeny Group). APG III system. Wikipedia, October 21, 2012; based on Haston, E., J. E. Richardson, P. F. Stevens, M. W. Chase, and D. J. Harris. 2009. The Linear Angiosperm Phylogeny Group (LAPG) III: a linear sequence of the families in APG III. *Botanical Journal of the Linnean Society* 161, 128–131.

This is the latest definitive classification and nomenclature of families of plants. The order of presentation of plants in the present book generally follows this classification.

Appelhof, M. 2003. *Worms Eat My Garbage: How to Set Up and Maintain a Worm Composting System*. Flower Press, Kalamazoo, Mich.

Considered the definitive guide to worm composting, this is an excellent resource for apartment residents who would like to compost.

Bell, C. R., and B. J. Taylor. 1982. *Florida Wild Flowers*. Laurel Hill Press, Chapel Hill, N.C.

Photographs and descriptions of Florida plants.

Beriault, J. G. 2000. *Planning and Planting a Native Yard. Florida Native Plant Society*, Vero Beach, Fla.

A timeless pamphlet on planting native plants in Florida.

Better Homes and Gardens. Container Gardening. www.bhg.com/gardening/con tainer/plans-ideas

Information on gardening in small spaces.

Brown, P. M. 2005. *Wild Orchids of Florida*. University Press of Florida, Gainesville, Fla.

Identification and biology of native orchids in Florida.

Druse, K. 1989. *The Natural Garden*. Clarkson N. Potter, New York, N.Y.

> Of little specific pertinence to South Florida, this book is nonetheless quite good for putting environmentally sensitive gardening in perspective.

Fairchild Tropical Garden. www.fairchildgarden.org

> Miami's premier public garden. Its Web site provides excellent information on tropical plants for use in South Florida gardens and its plant and bird conservation programs.

Florida Exotic Pest Plant Council. Invasive Plant List. www.fleppc.org/list/list.htm

> Lists of plants to be wary of planting or that may need to be removed from South Florida gardens.

Florida Extension Service. Florida Backyard Landscapes for Wildlife Program. University of Florida, Gainesville, Fla. www.wec.ufl.edu/extension/landscaping/fblw

> Information on gardening for wildlife in Florida.

Florida Native Plant Society. www.fnps.org

> Organization devoted to the promotion of native plants.

Gann, G. D., M. E. Abdo, J. W. Gann, G. D. Gann Sr., S. W. Woodmansee, K. A. Bradley, E. Grahl, and K. N. Hines. 2005–2014. *Natives for Your Neighborhood*. The Institute for Regional Conservation, Miami, Fla. www.regionalconservation.org/beta/nfyn/default.asp

> Excellent online source of information on native landscape plants for South Florida.

Haehle, R. G., and J. Brookwell. 2004. *Native Florida Plants: Low-maintenance Landscaping and Gardening*. Taylor Trade Publishing, Lanham, Md.

> Excellent accounts of Florida plants, including South Florida plants, useful for gardens.

Hammer, R. L. 2002. *Everglades Wildflowers*. Falcon Guide, Helena, Mont.

> Photographs of South Florida flowers, an identification guide.

Hammer, R. L. 2004. *Florida Keys Wildflowers*. Falcon Guide, Helena, Mont.

> Photographs of South Florida flowers, an identification guide.

Harrison, M. 2005. *Southern Gardening: An Environmentally Sensitive Approach*. Pineapple Press, Sarasota, Fla.

> A discussion of natural gardening.

Haynes, J., J. McLaughlin, and L. Vasquez. 2006. *Native Landscape Plants for South Florida*. IFAS Extension. Miami-Dade.ifas.ufl.edu/lawn_and_garden/fyn_pub_native_plantslist.shtml

> List and information on 135 native plants for South Florida gardens.

Huegel, C. N. 2010. *Native Plant Landscaping for Florida*. University Press of Florida, Gainesville, Fla.

> An excellent and revealing book on use of native plants in Florida landscaping. It provides good basics and explanations on gardening for wildlife, including birds. Its focus is statewide, but it has good accounts of some of South Florida's plants as well.

Jarrett, A. 2002. *Ornamental Tropical Shrubs*. Pineapple Press, Sarasota, Fla.

> Guide with descriptions and photographs of native and non-native shrubs.

Key West Botanical Garden. www.keywestbotanicalgarden.org

A great resource for studying native species of the Florida Keys.

Kramer, J. 2006. *100 Orchids for Florida*. Pineapple Press, Sarasota, Fla.

Identification and tips on growing orchids in Florida.

Kramer, J. 2011. *Bromeliads for Home and Garden*. University Press of Florida, Gainesville, Fla.

An indispensable introduction to growing bromeliads in Florida.

Kushlan, J. A., and K. Hines. 2014. *Birds of Fairchild*. Acclaim Press, Morely, Mo.

An account of the birds of a premier South Florida garden.

Long, R. W., and O. Lakela. 1978. *A Flora of Tropical Florida*. Banyan Press, Miami, Fla.

The complete flora of South Florida.

MacCubbin, T., and G. B. Tasker. 2002. *Florida Gardener's Guide*. Cool Springs Press, Nashville, Tenn.

A guide to gardening and garden plants throughout Florida, including material from South Florida.

Miami-Dade County. Landscaping Tips. www.miamidade.gov/environment/tips-landscaping.asp

Local government's advice on trees and plantings.

Naples Botanical Garden. www.naplesgarden.org

Based in Naples, it includes a Florida garden and a sanctuary highlighting native habitats.

Nellis, D. W. 1994. *Seashore Plants of South Florida and the Caribbean*. Pineapple Press, Sarasota, Fla.

Thorough information about plants found on West Indian shores, in addition to excellent background on their use in ornamental settings.

Nelson, G. 2000. *The Ferns of Florida: A Reference and Field Guide*. Pineapple Press, Sarasota, Fla.

Reference for the ferns found in Florida.

Nelson, G. 2003. *Florida's Best Native Landscape Plants*. University Press of Florida, Gainesville, Fla.

Reference for the native plants that can be used in landscaping in Florida, including some in South Florida.

Nelson, G. 2011. *Trees of Florida: A Reference and Field Guide*, Second Edition. Pineapple Press, Sarasota, Fla.

Reference for the trees found in Florida.

Osorio, R. A. 2001. *Gardener's Guide to Florida's Native Plants*. University Press of Florida, Gainesville, Fla.

Reference on native plants for use in landscaping in Florida

Rogers, G. 2012. *Landscape Plants for South Florida. A Manual for Gardeners, Landscapers & Homeowners*. www.plantbook.org/index.html

Online and hardcopy book on plant species for landscaping in South Florida.

Schaefer, J., and G. Tanner. 1997. *Landscaping for Florida's Wildlife*. University Press of Florida, Gainesville, Fla.

Backyard gardening for wildlife, primarily for northern Florida.

South Florida Cactus and Succulent Society. www.sfloridacactus.org

Organization for the horticulture and conservation of cacti and other succulents in South Florida.

South Florida Water Management District. Florida-Friendly Landscaping: Tips for the home gardener. www.sfwmd.gov/portal/page/portal/xweb%20-%20release%20 3%20water%20conservation/florida%20friendly%20landscaping

Eco-conscious landscaping tips for South Florida including links to lists of preferred garden plants.

Stebbins, M. K. 1999. *Flowering Trees of Florida*. Pineapple Press, Sarasota, Fla.

Reference for the trees that can be used in landscaping in Florida.

Tasker, G. 2001. *Enchanted Ground. Gardening with Nature in the Subtropics*. Fairchild Tropical Garden, Coral Gables, Fla.

Book focused on gardening in South Florida.

Taylor, W. K. 1992. *The Guide to Florida Wildflowers*. Taylor Trade Publishing, Lanham, Md.

Reference for the flowering plants in Florida.

TREEmendous Miami. www.treemendousmiami.org

Organization focused on promoting trees in Miami-Dade County.

University of Florida Institute of Food and Agricultural Sciences, Miami-Dade County Extension Office. miami-dade.ifas.ufl.edu/lawn_and_garden/home_gardening .shtml

A primary source for local South Florida information on horticulture.

Walton, D., and L. Schiller. 2007. *Natural Florida Landscaping*. Pineapple Press, Sarasota, Fla.

Reference for the native plants that can be used in landscaping in Florida.

Watkins, J. W., T. J. Sheehan, and R. J. Black. 2005. *Florida Landscape Plants*. University Press of Florida, Gainesville, Fla.

A revision of the longtime standard book on Florida plants that can be used in landscaping, first edition published 45 years ago. Thoughtfully updated to the present-day horticultural scene, the book provides informative one-page accounts for more than 400 plants. Other books should be used for identification, but this one provides the background.

Wasowski, S. 2004. *Requiem for a Lawnmower*. Taylor Trade Publishing, Lanham, Md.

An argument for using xeriscaping and other ground cover in place of monocultural sod. An example of how widespread nontraditional lawns have become.

Wunderlin, R. P., and B. F. Hansen. 2011. *Guide to the Vascular Plants of Florida*, third edition. University Press of Florida, Gainesville, Fla.

The definitive guide to the plants of Florida, providing an annotated checklist with identification keys.

Wunderlin, R. P., and B. F. Hansen. 2008. *Atlas of Florida Vascular Plants* (www.plant atlas.usf.edu/), [S. M. Landry and K. N. Campbell (application development), Florida Center for Community Design and Research.] Institute for Systematic Botany, University of South Florida, Tampa, Fla.

The online source for the names and distribution of Florida plants. This site has superior search capabilities and is considered to be the current authority on the use of names of plants found in Florida.

Birding and South Florida Birds

American Ornithologists' Union. 1998. *Checklist of North American Birds.* AOU, Washington, D.C. http://checklist.aou.org/

The definitive scientific list with scientific and English names of the birds found in North America.

BirdLife International. Species. www.birdlife.org/datazone/species/search

Accounts of the biology of the world's bird species, particularly those listed as threatened.

Bluebirds Forever. www.bluebirdsforever.com

An online store providing information and selling birdhouses and other materials for bluebirds.

Cornell Laboratory of Ornithology. All About Birds. www.allaboutbirds.org

Short accounts of the biology of bird species of North America.

Cornell Laboratory of Ornithology and the American Ornithologists' Union. Birds of North America Online. www.bna.birds.cornell.edu/bna

The definitive accounts of each of the species of birds in North America.

Cox, J. 2006. *The Breeding Birds of Florida Part II: Trends in Breeding Distribution based on Florida's Breeding Bird Atlas Project.* Special Publication No 7, Florida Ornithological Society, Gainesville, Fla.

Analysis of the change in species richness down the peninsula of Florida.

Dunn, J. L., and J. Alderfer. 2011. *National Geographic Field Guide to the Birds of North America*, sixth edition. National Geographic, Washington, D.C.

An easy to use guide with drawings of multiple species per page, making comparisons easy. Provides a good representation of age and seasonal differences within species and good coverage of South Florida's established non-native species. Considered by many to be the best guide to use in the field.

Epps, A. A. 2007. *Parrots of South Florida*. Pineapple Press, Sarasota, Fla.

A guide to many of the parrots to be found in the wild in South Florida.

Florida Fish and Wildlife Conservation Commission. 2003. Florida's Breeding Bird Atlas: A collaborative study of Florida's birdlife. www.myfwc.com/bba

Accounts of the breeding distribution of the birds of Florida based on a survey conducted throughout Florida from 1986 to 1991.

Florida Rare Bird Alert. listserv.admin.usf.edu/archives/flarba.html

Listserv that compiles bird reports for South Florida.

Great Florida Birding Trail. www.floridabirdingtrail.com

Established by the Florida Fish and Wildlife Conservation Commission to connect important bird conservation areas, designates good birding spots.

International Hummingbird Society. www.hummingbirdsociety.org

Information on hummingbirds and their conservation.

International Osprey Foundation. www.ospreys.com

Web site providing information on osprey conservation and recovery.

Kaufman, K. 2000. *Birds of North America*. Houghton Mifflin, New York, N.Y.

Similar in design to the Golden and Peterson guides, with several related species per page, but uses cutout photographs instead of drawings.

Maehr, D. S., and H. W. Kale II. 2005. *Florida's Birds*, second edition. Pineapple Press, Sarasota, Fla.

An illustrated list of the birds of Florida, including short but pertinent species accounts.

Martin, D. L. 2008. *Best-ever Backyard Birding Tips*. Rodale, New York, N.Y.

Solid general advice on watching birds in the garden, but not aimed at the situation in South Florida.

North American Bluebird Society. www.nabluebirdsociety.org

Conservation and research on bluebirds.

Peregrine Fund. Plans for building osprey nest platforms. www.peregrinefund.org/nest-structures-osprey

Information on Osprey nest platforms.

Peterson, R. T. 2008. *Peterson Field Guide to Birds of North America*. Houghton Mifflin, Boston, Mass.

Based on the early and influential fully illustrated birding guide, with large pictures and identification cues. Maps provide information on seasonality.

Pranty, B., K. A. Radamaker, and G. Kennedy. 2006. *Birds of Florida*. Lone Pine Publishing International, Auburn, Wash.

Accounts and images of the birds expected in Florida.

Rapoza, B. 2007. *Birding Florida*. Falcon Guides, Helena, Mont.

Definitive guide to where to find birds in Florida, should be consulted for where and when to go for birds.

Robbins, C. S., B. Brunn, and H. S. Zim, revised by J. P. Latimer, K. S. Nolting, and J. Coe. 2001. *A Guide to Field Identification, Birds of North America*. St. Martin's Press, New York, N.Y.

For many years, Chan Robbins and this "Golden Guide" provided the best field guide, bringing similar birds, their ranges, seasonality, and vocalizations onto a single page for comparison. This remains, perhaps, the easiest guide for a beginner to use.

Robertson, W. B., Jr., and J. A. Kushlan. 1974. The southern Florida avifauna. In: P. J. Gleason, Editor. *Environments of South Florida, Present and Past*. Miami Geological Society, Miami, Fla.

On the character and origin of the South Florida avifauna.

Robertson, W. B., Jr., and G. E. Woolfenden. 1992. *Florida Bird Species: An Annotated List*. Special Publication 6, Florida Ornithological Society, Gainesville, Fla.

Definitive analysis of the biogeography of the birds of Florida.

Sialis. www.sialis.org

Information on bluebirds, their biology, nesting, and conservation.

Sibley, D. A. 2000. *The Sibley Guide to Birds*. Alfred A. Knopf, New York, N.Y.

In our opinion, the best single guide to identification of North American birds, with brief but definitive descriptions of species and of variation within a species; the layout of one or two species per page allows good detail to be presented on appearance and behavior useful in identification. Although it may be a bit bulky for some to take in the field, it is the best tool for learning the birds either in the field or in the home garden.

Sibley, D. A. 2002. *Sibley's Birding Basics*. Alfred A. Knopf, New York, N.Y.

Erudite, detailed, and helpful guide to birding.

Stevenson, H. M., and B. H. Anderson. 1994. *The Birdlife of Florida*. University Press of Florida, Gainesville, Fla.

The definitive modern technical monograph on the distribution and status of the birds of Florida.

Stokes, D., and L. Stokes. 2010. *The Stokes Field Guide to the Birds of North America*. Little, Brown, New York, N.Y.

Multiple photographic images helpfully show variability within a species.

Woolfenden, G. E., and W. B. Robertson Jr. 2006. *The Breeding Birds of Florida. Part 1: Sources and Post-settlement Changes*. Special Publication 7, Florida Ornithological Society, Gainesville, Fla.

Analysis of the changes of bird populations in Florida over the historic period.

Other Garden Wildlife

Ashton, R. E., and P. S. Ashton. 1991. *Handbook of Reptiles and Amphibians of Florida*. Windward, Miami, Fla.

Descriptions of the reptiles and amphibians in a multibook series.

Baker, R. J., L. C. Bradley, R. D. Bradley, J. W. Dragoo, M. D. Engstrom, R. S. Hoffmann, C. A. Jones, F. Reid, D. W. Rice, and C. Jones. 2003. *Revised Checklist of North American Mammals North of Mexico, 2003*. Occasional Papers Number 229, Museum of Texas Tech University, Lubbock, Tex.

A naming authority for North American mammals.

Brown, L. N. 1997. *Mammals of Florida*. Windward, Miami, Fla.

Natural history of Florida's mammals.

Crother, B. I. (ed.). 2012. Scientific and Standard English Names of Amphibians and Reptiles of North America North of Mexico, with comments regarding confidence in our understanding. SSAR Herpetological Circular 39:1-92.

Naming authority for amphibians and reptiles.

Daniels, J. D. 2000. *Florida Guide to Butterfly Gardening.* University Press of Florida, Gainesville, Fla.

Butterfly gardens for Florida.

Florida Bat Conservancy. www.floridabats.org

Information on identification and conservation of bats found in Florida.

Minno, M. C., and M. Minno. 1999. *Florida Butterfly Gardening: A Complete Guide to Attracting, Identifying, and Enjoying Butterflies.* University Press of Florida, Gainesville, Fla.

A guide to creating butterfly gardens in Florida.

North American Butterfly Association. *Checklist of North American Butterflies Occupying North of Mexico.* www.NABA.org

Organization focused on butterfly identification and conservation. The standard for names of butterflies.

Tasker, G. 2010. *Butterfly Gardening in South Florida.* Fairchild Tropical Botanic Garden, Coral Gables, Fla.

Butterflies and their plants in South Florida.

South Florida Environment

Florida Natural Areas Inventory. www.fnai.org and www.dep.state.fl.us/parks/planning/forms/FNAIDescriptions.pdf

Information on the native plant communities.

Grunwald, M. 2006. *The Swamp.* Simon & Schuster, New York, N.Y.

Definitive story of the politics involved in the destruction of the South Florida environment.

Lodge, T. E. 2010. *The Everglades Handbook,* third edition. CRC Press, Boca Raton, Fla.

Readable, complete, semipopular account of the plants, animals, communities, and ecology of the Everglades and nearby South Florida.

Meyers, R. L., and J. J. Ewel. 1990. *Ecosystems of South Florida.* University Presses of Florida, Gainesville, Fla.

Excellent technical descriptions of the environments of Florida, from geology to native plant communities.

Ransazzo, A. F., and D. S. Jones. 1997. *The Geology of Florida.* University Press of Florida, Gainesville, Fla.

A technical account of Florida geology.

Acknowledgments

We thank Stephen Davis, Carl Lewis, Steve Pearson, Brian Rapoza, and another UPF reviewer for their reviews of an earlier draft of the book. Steve Pearson, particularly, provided many editorial suggestions. We thank Mike Poller of Poller & Jordan Advertising Agency for drafting the maps and charts. We also thank our editors Meredith Morris-Babb, Catherine-Nevil Parker, and Lucinda Treadwell. We thank the many individuals who have provided their advice and guidance over the years. We wish to acknowledge the ornithological guidance of the late Herbert W. Kale, Oscar T. Owre, and William B. Robertson Jr., as well as the advice of Joe Barros, Paul Bithorn, Robin Diaz, and Brian Rapoza. We similarly acknowledge our mentors in the study of South Florida's plants: George Gann and the late Taylor R. Alexander, Frank C. Craighead, and William T. Gillis. We also thank Keith Bradley, Mary Collins, Jimi Sadle, Georgia Tasker, and Steven Woodmansee for sharing their knowledge of South Florida's plants.

Index

Page numbers in italics indicate illustrations.

Parks, 2

Parrots: African Gray Parrot, 113; Amazons, *119*, 119–20; Black-hooded Parakeet, 115; Budgerigar, 113; Cockatiel, 113; Conures, *116*, 116–17, *117*; Macaws, 118, *118*; Mitred Parakeet, 116, *116*; Monk Parakeet, 114, *114*; Red-masked Parakeet, 116, *117*; Rose-ringed Parakeet, 117; Rosy-faced Lovebird, 113; White-eyed Parakeet, 117, *117*; White-winged Parakeet, 7, *7*, 114–15, *115*; Yellow-chevroned Parakeet, 115

Parthenocissus quinquefolia. See Virginia creeper

Passerculus sandwichensis. See Savannah Sparrow

Passer domesticus. See House Sparrow

Passerina ciris. See Painted Bunting

Passerina cyanea. See Indigo Bunting

Passiflora edulis. See Passionfruit

Passiflora incarnata. See Purple passionflower

Passiflora pallens. See Pineland passionflower

Passiflora suberosa. See Corkystem passionflower

Passionflowers, 65, 87, 207, 207–8. *See also specific passionflowers*

Passionfruit (*Passiflora edulis*), 208, *208*

Patagioenas leucocephala. See White-crowned Pigeon

Patio gardening, 82, 82–83

Pavo cristatus. See Indian Peafowl

Pavonia, *124*

Pavonia bahamensis. See Bahama swampbush

Pavonia paludicola. See Swampbrush

Peacocks, 97, *97*

Peanut butter, 58

Peanuts, 54, 56–57

Pegoscapus mexicanus. See Fig wasps

Pegoscapus tonduzi. See Fig wasps

Pentas lanceolata. See Egyptian starcluster

Pepper relatives: bird pepper, 271, *271*; garden tomato, 271, *272*; skyblue clustervine, 272, *272*

Peppers and lizard tails: cinnamon bark, 172–73, *173*; lizard's tail, 172, *173*

Peregrine Falcon (*Falco peregrinus*), 105, *105*

Perfumed spiderlily (*Hymenocallis latifolia*), 177

Persea americana. See Avocado

Persea borbonia. See Red bay

Pesticides, 87, 91, 159

Petrochelidon fulva. See Cave Swallow

Pheucticus ludovicianus. See Rose-breasted Grosbeak

Phlebodium aureum. See Golden polypody

Phocides pigmalion. See Mangrove skipper

Phoenix canariensis. See Canary Island date palm

Phyla nodiflora. See Turkey tangle fogfruit

Phyllanthrus amarus. See Gale-of-wind

Phyllanthus tenellus. See Mascarene Island leafflower

Physiographic regions, *10*, *11*

Phytolacca americana. See American pokeweed

Pickerelweed (*Pontederia cordata*), 188, *188*

Picoides pubescens. See Downy Woodpecker

Picramnia pentandra. See Florida bitterbush

Pied-billed Grebe (*Podilymbus podiceps*), 98, *98*

Pigeon plum (*Coccoloba diversifolia*), *198*, 198–99

Pigeons: Common Ground-Dove, 112, *112*; Eurasian Collared-Dove, 47, *104*, 110–11, *111*; Mourning Dove, 38, 112, *112*, 170; Rock Pigeon, 110; White-crowned Pigeon, 110, *110*; White-winged Dove, 111, *111*

Pileated Woodpecker (*Dryocopus pileatus*), 128, *128*

Pineapple guava (*Acca sellowiana*), 227

Pineapple verbena. *See* Moujean tea

Pineland acacia (*Vachella farnesiana var. pinetorum*), 212, *212*

Pineland croton (*Croton linearis*), 204, *204*

Pineland passionflower (*Passiflora pallens*), 87, 207, *207*

Pineland purple (*Carphephorus odoratissimus var. subtropicanus*), 279

Pinelands, *11*, 106. *See also specific species*

Pine Warbler (*Setophaga pinus*), 146, *147*

Pink muhly. *See* Hairawn muhly grass

Pink porterweed (*Stachytarpheta mutabilis*), 270

Pinks and cacti, 194–95, *195*; American pokeweed, 196, *197*; blolly, 196; bougainvillea, 34, 195–96, *196*; Cape leadwort, 197; common chickweed, 195; pigeon plum, *198*, 198–99; pricklypear, 194, *195*; rougeplant, 197, *197*; seagrape, *129*, 198, *198*

Pinus clausa. See Sand pine

Pinus elliottii. See Slash pine

Pipilo erythrophthalmus. See Eastern Towhee

Seed eaters: Indigo Bunting, *8, 89,* 157; Painted Bunting, 56, *56, 157,* 157–58, *217*

Seed feeders, 4, *55,* 55–60, *56, 57, 59, 60, 111, 137, 164. See also* Tube feeders

Seeds, 52–53; bald- and pond-cypress, 171; black oil sunflower, 55, *55*–56, 59, 74, *74;* blue porterweed, 270, *270;* bushy seaside oxeye, 275; commercially available, 55; coralbean, 217, *217;* fakahatcheegrass, 191; Florida Keys blackbead, 213; gumbo limbo, 240; live oak, 218; mixes, 57; nutgrass, 190; portion management, 60; sand pine, 170; sensitive plants, 210; slash pine, 169; sweet acacia, 212; sweetbay, 175–76; tamarind, 215; tropical sage, 263. *See also specific plants*

Seiurus aurocapilla. See Ovenbird

Selasphorus rufus. See Rufous Hummingbird

Senna mexicana. See Chapman's wild sensitive plant

Senna pendula. See Valamuerto

Sennas, 210–11

Sensitive plants, 210–11

Serenoa repens. See Saw palmetto

Serinus canaria. See Island Canary

Serinus mozambicus. See Yellow-fronted Canary

Setophaga americana. See Northern Parula

Setophaga caerulescens. See Black-throated Blue Warbler

Setophaga coronata. See Yellow-rumped Warbler

Setophaga discolor. See Prairie Warbler

Setophaga dominica. See Yellow-throated Warbler

Setophaga palmarum. See Palm Warbler

Setophaga petechia. See Yellow Warbler

Setophaga pinus. See Pine Warbler

Setophaga ruticilla. See American Redstart

Setophaga striata. See Blackpoll Warbler

Setophaga tigrina. See Cape May Warbler

Sevenyear apple (*Genipa clusiifolia*), 259, *259*

Sharp-shinned Hawk (*Accipiter striatus*), 103

Shiny Cowbird (*Molothrus bonariensis*), 160

Shiny oysterwood. *See* Crabwood

Shorebirds, Killdeer, 108

Short-leaf fig. *See* Wild banyan tree

Short-statured plants, *36,* 36–37; in landscape design, 81; recommended options, 37. *See also specific plants*

Short-tailed Hawk (*Buteo brachyurus*), 104

Shrike, Loggerhead, 131, *131*

Shrimp plants, 262, *262*

Shrubby whitevein. *See* Sanchezia

Shrubs, 31, 32; in landscape design, 80–81; pruning, 32; recommended options, 33; trees and, 27, 32–33. *See also specific shrubs*

Sialis sialis. See Eastern Bluebird

Sida ulmifolia. See Common wireweed

Sideroxylon celastrinum. See Saffron plum

Sideroxylon foetidissimum. See False mastic

Sideroxylon salicifolium. See Willow bustic

Sideroxylon tenax. See Tough bully

Silica, 13

Silver seaside oxeye. *See* Bushy seaside oxeye

Simarouba glauca. See Paradisetree

Simpson's stopper (*Myrcianthes fragrans*), 231, *231*

Skyblue clustervine (*Jacquemontia pentanthos*), 272, *272*

Slash pine (*Pinus elliottii*), *147,* 169, *170;* dead, 170

Slugs, 71

Smilax. See Greenbriers

Smooth strongbark (*Bourreria cassinifolia*), 249–50, *250*

Snails, 71

Snakebark. *See* Soldierwood

Snakes, 72, *72*

Snowberry (*Chiococca alba*), 252

Soapberry (*Sapindus saponaria*), 244

Sod grasses, 39–40, *40,* 41, 192, *192*

Soil, 13–16, 83; compost, 85, *86,* 86–87; in Miami-Dade, *15. See also specific types of soil*

Solanum lycopersicum. See Garden tomato

Soldierwood (*Colubrina elliptica*), 221

Solidago. See Goldenrod

Sophora tomentosa. See Yellow necklacepod

Sorghastrum secundum. See Lopsided Indiangrass

Sorghum bicolor. See Milo

Sour oranges (*Citrus × aurantium*), 242

Southern cattail (*Typha domingensis*), 193

Southern coast and islands, *10, 12*

Southern hackberry. *See* Sugarberry

South Florida: biogeography of, 20–22; climate and weather of, 16–20; geographic location of, 9–12; geology and soil of, 13–16. *See also specific counties*

Southwest coast, *10, 12*

Spanish bayonet (*Yucca aloifolia*), 179

Spanish clover. *See* Zarzabacoa comun

Spanish moss (*Tillandsia usneoides*), 133, 189, *189*

Spanish needles. *See* Beggarticks

Spanish stopper (*Eugenia foetida*), 229, *229*

Sparrows, 6; Chipping Sparrow, 154; Eastern Towhee, 154; Grasshopper Sparrow, 154, *154*; Lark Sparrow, 154; Savannah Sparrow, 154; Swamp Sparrow, 154; White-crowned Sparrow, 154, *155*

Spartina bakeri. *See* Sand cordgrass

Sphagneticola trilobata. *See* Creeping oxeye

Sphinx moths, 178

Sphyrapicus varius. *See* Yellow-bellied Sapsucker

Spice Finches. *See* Nutmeg Mannikin

Spicewood (*Calyptranthes pallens*), 227–28

Spiders, 70, *70–71*, *143*, *150*

Spiderworts: dayflowers, 188, *188*; pickerel-weed, 188, *188*

Spindalis zena. *See* Western Spindalis

Spineless acacia. *See* Cinnecord

Spinus tristis. *See* American Goldfinch

Spiny black olive (*Terminalia molinetii*), 225–26

Spizella passerina. *See* Chipping Sparrow

Spot-breasted Oriole (*Icterus pectoralis*), 162

Squirrels, 60, 73, 74, *238*

St. Augustinegrass (*Stenotaphrum secundatum*), *40*, 41, 192

Stachytarpheta cayennensis. *See* Jamaica porterweed

Stachytarpheta jamaicensis. *See* Blue porterweed

Stachytarpheta mutabilis. *See* Pink porterweed

Staghorn Fern (*Platycerium bifurcatum*), 167, *167*

Standard gardening, 4

Standingcypress (*Ipomopsis rubra*), 245

Starlings, 51; Common Myna, 144, *145*; European Starling, 143–44, *144*; Hill Myna, 144

Stelgidopteryx serripennis. *See* Northern Rough-winged Swallow

Stellaria media. *See* Common chickweed

Stenotaphrum secundatum. *See* St. Augustinegrass

Sternula antillarum. *See* Least Tern

Stickpea (*Calliandra*), 212

Stopper (*Eugenia*), 229

Straggler daisy (*Calyptocarpus vialis*), 276

Strangler fig (*Ficus aurea*), 22, *110*, 223, *223*

Strawberrytree (*Muntingia calabura*), 237

Strelitzia. *See* Bird of paradise

Streptopelia decaocto. *See* Eurasian Collared-Dove

String-lily (*Crinum americanum*), 178

Strix varia. *See* Barred Owl

Structure. *See specific trees and shrubs*

Sturnus vulgaris. *See* European Starling

Stylosanthes hamata. *See* Cheesytoes

Suet, 57, *57–58*

Sugarberry (*Celtis laevigata*), 220–21

Sumac, citrus, and relatives: citrus, *241*, 241–42; Eastern poison ivy, 238; faux persil, 243; gumbo limbo, 25–26, 52, *52*, *155*, 239, *239*–40; inkwood, 243; Key lime, 241–42; lychee, 243; mango, 237, *237*–38; orange jessamine, 242; paradisetree, 244; poisonwood, 238, *238*; sea torchwood, 242; soapberry, 244; sour oranges, 242; West Indian mahogany, 240, *240*; white ironwood, 243; wild lime, *242*, 242–43; winged sumac, 239

Summer grape (*Vitis aestivalis*), 199–200

Summer Tanager (*Piranga rubra*), 155

Sunflowers (*Helianthus*), 276, *276*. *See also* Black oil sunflower

Sunshine mimosa. *See* Powderpuff

Suriana maritima. *See* Bay cedar

Surinam cherry (*Eugenia uniflora*), 230

Surinam pink powderpuff (*Calliandra surinamensis*), 212

Swainson's Thrush (*Catharus ustulatus*), 140, *140*

Swallows: Cave Swallow, 136, *136*; Northern Rough-winged Swallow, 135; Purple Martin, *49*, 135, *135*; Tree Swallow, 136, 219

Swallowtail caterpillars, 284

Swallow-tailed Kite (*Elanoides forficatus*), 103

Swampbrush (*Pavonia paludicola*), 236, *236*

Swamp fern (*Blechnum serrulatum*), 166

Swamp rosemallow (*Hibiscus grandiflorus*), 234

Swamp Sparrow (*Melospiza georgiana*), 154

Sweet acacia (*Vachella farnesiana*), 212

Sweetbay (*Magnolia virginiana*), 175–76

Sweet fennel (*Foeniculum vulgare*), 284

Swietenia mahagoni. *See* West Indian mahogany

Swifts, Chimney, 124

James A. Kushlan is a biologist, conservationist, writer, and former wildlife biologist at Everglades National Park, director of Patuxent Wildlife Research Center, and president of the American Ornithologists' Union. Specializing in the biology and conservation of water birds and wetlands, he has published more than 200 professional papers on these and related topics as well as several books, including *Storks, Ibises and Spoonbills of the World* (1993), *Heron Conservation* (2000), and *The Herons* (2005). He was the founding chair of Waterbird Conservation for the Americas and of the Bird Conservation Alliance, and has served on boards of the American Bird Conservancy and North American Bird Conservation Initiative. He serves on the boards of Fairchild Tropical Botanic Garden, Zoological Society of Florida, and the Everglades Foundation.

Kirsten Hines is a writer, nature photographer, environmental educator, conservation biologist, and operator of Kirsten Nature Travel (www.KirstenNatureTravel.com). She has studied plants, reptiles, and mammals in South Florida and the Bahamas. She is an environmental educator at Biscayne Nature Center, has published in scientific journals and popular publications, won awards for her photography, and served on the board of the Tropical Audubon Society. She is coauthor of *Natives for Your Neighborhood*, a guide to the landscape use of native plants in South Florida.